My So-Called Disorder

Autism, Exploding Trucks, and the Big Daddy of Rock and Roll

Peter O'Neil

ISBN 9798218156985

Published by Peter O'Neil

Seattle, Washington

Jacket design Jenna Anderson O'Neil

Photographs Kirk Hostetter

Contents

Introduction

There is a saying that if you've met one autistic person, you've met one autistic person. This book is about just one of us. I can't and don't speak for other autistic people—only for myself, with what little understanding I've gained after being identified as autistic at the age of sixty-five. My hope is that some of it resonates, perhaps with you, or that perhaps bits of my story will help you understand someone you know, or love, or work alongside.

Being identified as autistic at an advanced age is a revelation—an "aha!" moment of the first order. It's like being told, at sixty-five, "But *mon ami*, you are French! You did not know?" Suddenly, and for the very first time, the accent, the beret, the funny car, and your weirdly intense interest in Jerry Lewis all make sense.

I say after being "identified." I could say after being "diagnosed," but though I use the word a few times in this book I don't like it in the context of discerning that a person is autistic. Diagnosis suggests an illness or disorder, and I say "no thank you" to both terms. My autistic brain works quite well, and is only disordered in certain contexts of the "neurotypical" world. In a world made up mostly of autistic people, we would not have a disorder. *We* would be typical.

So I don't like the word diagnosis, or pejorative medical terms like disability or disorder when talking about autistic people. If we need a word that starts with "D," let's choose "different." I am different and always have been. Different is good. Differences, as in variety, are the spice of life. Differences bring us diversity, and diversity makes us stronger, wiser, more beautiful, and more interesting as a people.

But this is not a book about neurology, psychology, disability, or medicine—it's the story of one autistic boy, turned teenager, turned man, turned lawyer, turned older man, who has done well for himself despite, or perhaps *because of,* his so-called disorder.

My so-called disorder.

In practical, monetary terms, my "disorder' has made lots of money for lots of people. In my work as a lawyer my "disorder" has found and organized thousands of important documents and connected a small galaxy of important dots. It has uncovered secrets large corporations and negligent municipalities hoped would remain buried. It has done this with a sense of humor, a sense of wonder, a sense of discovery, and mostly for the sheer fun of doing it.

On the more personal side my "disorder" has intensified my interest in dozens of subjects, some personal, some work-related. For a time I might teach myself about birds. For a time I might focus on learning Italian. For a period of years I might only have eyes for the exploding trucks that brought unimaginable suffering to clients I loved. I grab onto something that interests me and don't let go until I'm satisfied. Satisfaction varies. I satisfied my itch for bird names by learning to identify the dozen or so species that frequent my neighborhood—bushtit, house finch, scrub jay, song sparrow, house sparrow, wren, etc. I'll be satisfied with Italian when I can stumble with coarse fluency through conversations about god, life, politics, family, memories, and work—so still a ways off.

In many aspects of life I did well, albeit oddly, from the get go. I learned to read early. I invented various quirky childhood pastimes. Baseball and team sports were not for me, but I entertained myself beautifully. I repaired rosaries for profit and published newspapers and books, two or three copies at a time, but with all the trimmings, including copyrights and advertisements. I taught myself to know the stars and to use a telescope to find the fuzzy hidden things in space like nebulae and galaxies. I taught myself music and wrote songs—good ones. In fact, I taught myself practically everything I know, or know how to do, including how to live in this neurotypical world.

But other parts of life came later and with more difficulty. Though I have always grabbed and held on to subjects that interest me, it wasn't always so with people. For years I let go of people too easily—even those who tried to connect with me.

That was the one hard part about being autistic for me—finding love in a social world I didn't understand. I understood the life I found in novels, or saw in films, but I couldn't figure out the world of people who surrounded me. How did they find friends? How did they find love? As the star of my own movie I was lost, even on the rare occasions when the love interest came right to me and introduced herself.

My first kisses came a bit late, in part because I waited for the girls who brought them to come to *me*—I had no idea how to find them on my own. Moreover, I was surprised each time a first kiss arrived. Whatever a girl might have said with her eyes, her smile, her touch, or her words, flew past like a foreign language, with little or no comprehension on my part. At best I'd wonder why she said or did such a thing. Then bang, if I was lucky, she'd make it clear.

I will tell you more than I want to about my early, failed romances because they are an important part of my story. For decades they were the biggest mysteries in my life, and the most painful things in my life that didn't involve the death of a family member.

Over the course of nearly seven decades I learned to negotiate the neurotypical world well enough to survive and even thrive. I learned to make eye contact, even when it hurt. I learned to recognize and understand the complex language of the neurotypical world—the meaning of a wink, or a smile, or a touch. I learned the importance, in that world, of sometimes talking about nothing. After my first marriage crumbled, I found my wonderful wife Rebecca—or, rather, she found me. But when she did, I understood the small touches, her smile, and I understood how important it was not to let her slip away.

Autistic people have done this for centuries. We learn. We adapt.

Sometimes it takes the form of "masking," a kind of play acting that is necessary to get by in the larger world. We pretend we are someone we are not, that eye contact and small talk are easy, or that we are not quite so fantastically interested in Chuck Berry as we really are. We do it to survive. Most of us wouldn't be here if we didn't. We might look so odd to that world that we would be shunned (which many of us are). Alternatively (and this, I think, was my case) we might be mostly invisible to the larger world. So we conform to expectations. We mask. We fake typicality as best we can.

But we are most decidedly here. We're here because, like immigrants, we learn to survive, and sometimes to thrive, in a world that isn't completely our own. We are here because, like immigrants, we bring value to the larger world, and because we find a way forward.

Unaware I was autistic I often described myself as a "late bloomer," or as a person who had to "learn to operate" my own personality.

I became a lawyer at forty-three, after a fifteen year, stunningly successful career as a paralegal. As a new lawyer I immediately tried a case against Ford Motor Company involving a thirty year-old, badly maintained dump truck that had burst into flames after a crash. We won. It wasn't a big win—I have often said we "fought to a bloody draw"—but it was a win. Over the ensuing decades I built a solid and successful legal career on my own somewhat quirky terms.

At fifty-one, I became a marathoner, running my first 26.2 mile race in a drizzle of sleet and ice-cold rain. I was slow, but I finished. I finished because I had prepared so thoroughly over a sixteen week period, including runs of twenty, twenty-two, twenty-four and twenty-seven miles in the final six weeks of training. That sort of ultra preparation seems thoroughly autistic to me now, and matches the one hundred or so practice bar exams that I gave myself in the weeks prior to the real bar exam. It's how I prepare for new and frightening challenges.

At fifty-four, I completed a book manuscript—my first since I was a child publisher of six page pamphlets. It was an odd manuscript and didn't get published, but I now see it as a wonderful bit of autistic literature and remain proud of it. Maybe some day its name will be in lights.

At fifty-five, I climbed on stage with an electric guitar for the very first time after spending a lifetime aimlessly noodling at home, mostly for the comfort that musical noodling provided me. It was a small stage and a short climb, but a big accomplishment for me. I had spent my life looking at musicians on stage and wondering if I could do that. Turns out, I can. One small step for autistic man, one great leap towards self-realization.

And ten years later, at sixty-five, I learned I am autistic.

These late life accomplishments seem all the more important after my late identification as autistic, because they point to the perseverance, preparation, and willingness to take risks that were necessary to whatever successes I've had in life. It took courage to make an opening statement against Ford Motor Company in a case I had begun as a paralegal, but I did it. It took courage to run a 26.2 mile race I had been told I could never finish. It took courage to step on stage with a loud guitar I felt uncertain about playing. It takes courage to lay huge parts of my life bare in these pages, an act I have second and third thoughts about every day. But I did all of these things, and did them with full knowledge that I might fall on my face or fail. Preparation, courage, perseverance, and a willingness to take risks (something that did not come naturally or easily to me) were huge and necessary parts of my development as a fully functional human being.

This book is to some extent the story of my legal work, an accidental career where I managed to succeed almost entirely on my own terms, in my own way, concentrating on just a few cases at a time so that I could give each one my full focus and attention. I began my career with energy, hard work, good instincts, and unstoppable curiosity. I knew, even at the start, that I was oddly good at a job I'd never imagined myself doing.

I now approach the end of that career with a hard earned confidence—the knowledge that I'm no longer *oddly* good at what I do, I'm *remarkably* good, and that what I do, and how I do it, are unique. There are millions of lawyers in this world but I've never met one quite like me. If you're out there, we should talk.

This seems as good a place as any to provide a warning: I repeat myself at times in this book, and in many things I write. I've sometimes been criticized for that, and try to eliminate repetition in legal briefing, but I've decided it reflects my different way of learning. I do not learn systematically. I learn by almost random and repetitive sampling. I return again and again, grazing here and there, until I finally understand the whole, sometimes missing names or numbers the first time through because my mind is still pondering some important detail. Since I hope that many or most of my readers will be neurodivergent people, I have decided to honor my own learning style and not edit out every repetition. If you see it twice, it's likely because I think it's doubly important.

I have limited the "war stories" in this book to a few important cases, focusing especially on a string of lawsuits that involved people who were badly burned in the "exploding trucks" of the sub-title. For about five years, as an underpaid legal assistant, my work caught the full attention of one of the world's biggest corporations. I didn't capture that attention in a flashy, Mercedes Benz, Italian suit sort of way, with big verdicts and press coverage. I did it the way a mosquito or flea catches your full attention. I was a pesky irritant, but definitely noticed, and drew blood.

When I was first identified as autistic it became my newest special interest. I read, watched, and listened to everything I could find about being autistic. I write about my work because I learned early in my research that a disheartening percentage of autistic people are either unemployed or underemployed. That bothered me because

I knew how valuable my own work has been to clients and to the firms I worked with. I felt an immediate obligation to try to show employers how valuable an autistic mind can be to any organization.

I don't try to tell the whole story of my cases. I leave out the work of many heroes to the litigation I describe. I have worked with a small army of spectacular paralegals, clerks, word processing experts, engineers, doctors, artists, attorneys, and so on, each of whom performed his or her own magic. And though each case is a matter of public record, I have decided to use only the first names of my former clients and some coworkers, and have changed or omitted the names of various other individuals for the sake of their privacy.

But ultimately, this is *my* story—the story of how my autistic brain made me uniquely capable of ferreting out the secrets of large corporations and organizations.

As I learn more about autistic people, I have begun to understand that although autistic people want to be respected, and though, like everyone, we appreciate a discrete compliment for something we've done well, we rarely seek full credit for our accomplishments. Our focus and joy is the work itself, and we usually shy away from self-promotion or publicity.

But after remaining in the back and off to the side for most of my life, I don't mind walking center stage, (even if it is a small one,) removing my beret, and taking a small bow for my autistic contributions. Perhaps other autistic and neurodivergent people will recognize themselves in my stories. Perhaps neurotypical people will recognize one of their coworkers. And perhaps, by the end, you'll know you've met one autistic person, and that he is different, but all the more valuable for exactly that reason.

1

Exploding Trucks

In the early to mid-1990s, I thought about exploding trucks all the time. They were everywhere in those days. I remember driving my daughters Jade and Gemma to the zoo and playing a game we called "count the exploding pickups." The girls knew how to spot them. "There's one!" they'd shriek. We counted some outrageous number—twenty-seven, or thirty-four—on the short drive from our house to the zoo.

To be accurate, the trucks don't explode. Exploding vehicles mostly happen in the movies. In real life there's a crash. A vehicle smashes into the side of the truck, dives under the sheet metal, and crushes the truck's gas tank while simultaneously ripping the tank open to release a spray of gasoline. Sparks from steel scraping asphalt ignite gasoline vapor as ten or twenty gallons of gasoline pour from the ruptured tank. Then the whole thing goes up in a giant "whoomp" and burns people alive.

But "exploding truck" is short, bitter, and to the point.

Luckily, by 2023, these trucks have largely disappeared from the highways. I hardly see them anymore, and the few I see are often either beautifully restored showpieces or jalopies loaded with gas cans and lawn mowers. It's good they are disappearing because the trucks are dangerous.

Most pickup truck fuel tanks are located in a relatively safe and protected location beneath the truck bed and inside the truck's heavy steel frame. On the exploding trucks, the gas tanks—usually two—are mounted *outside* the frame rails, one under the driver and a second under the passenger, where they are vulnerable to an impact from the side. If you learn to look, you can see the unprotected tank bottoms hanging below the sheet metal of the cab and bed, waiting to be torn asunder in a crash. It is a profoundly stupid location with little real protection for the tank.

Our first exploding truck case involved a man named Doug, who was in a crash on election day 1992. I worked on Doug's case with my mentor, Paul Whelan, a Washington State product liability attorney who had become famous trying cases involving lead poisoning and asbestos. Doug was driving an exploding truck when an old sedan crossed the centerline, sideswiped the pickup, and tore a foot long hole in the gas tank just beneath Doug.

Doug wasn't injured in the crash, so he was alert and conscious as he sat at the steering wheel and watched flames grow around his pickup. He knew he only had a few seconds to make an impossible decision and act on it. He could stay in the driver's seat and die horribly, or he could open the door and jump into the fire.

He jumped into the fire.

Burning gasoline stuck to his shoes and fire splashed onto his pants. His clothing and hair caught fire. 911 callers gave us horrifying verbal imagery. One caller described flames as high as roadside evergreens, Douglas firs that climbed 100 feet or more into the night. Another described a man on fire running from the truck and then diving to the highway to smother the flames that burned his skin and clothing. He probably used his hands, too, which explains the fried chicken look of his fingers for a time.

A year later at his deposition, Doug described his second impossible decision. I was there. For reasons I'll never understand, I volunteered to videotape the proceeding. I was a legal assistant then. Our office had a camera, a soundboard, and microphones. I had no experience operating them, but I managed to put them together.

"It had better work," the opposing attorney snarled at me.

This attorney was a man I would later, jokingly describe as "the evilest man alive." His words terrified me, but within the year I would frighten him more than he frightened me. I would figure out more than how to operate a recording setup. I would uncover much of the hidden story of Doug's truck.

Luckily the videotape worked, and so did my sound system, so there was a visual record of Doug, still wearing pressure garments to help reshape his badly scarred skin, quietly describing the crash and its aftermath.

"And then what?" asked the evilest man alive.

Doug paused.

"I had to decide whether to leave the comfort of the fire" he said, slowly and quietly, his voice high and raspy, with a bit of Puyallup, Washington twang.

"Did you say 'the comfort of the fire?'"

It was the only time in the next ten years I would see this particular lawyer taken aback by something. He was a man I once heard chuckle as he described a truckload of immigrants who burned in a pickup fire. The suffering of mortals had little effect on him.

Doug answered affirmatively but made no effort to explain himself.

I have always believed Doug's words reflected an immediate, instinctive understanding of his predicament—an understanding that if he survived the fire, he would suffer months of painful hospitalization, surgeries, and debridement procedures, and that his face, hands, arms, legs, and skin would be forever changed.

Doug's pickup truck was one of nearly ten million similar Chevrolet and GMC pickups sold in the United States and Canada between 1973 and 1987 that resulted in hundreds of fiery crashes and hundreds of burned people, many of whom were horribly maimed, and many of whom burned to death in post crash fires. It was no doubt in most respects a fine truck, but with a singularly defective and dangerous fuel tank design—an example of corporate negligence that dwarfed any mayhem caused by the better-known Ford Pinto fiasco.

Like its competition from Ford and Dodge, the GM pickup truck was usually sold with two gas tanks. But while Ford and Dodge put the fuel tanks between the trucks' heavy steel frame rails for protection, GM chose to put the fuel tanks of its 1973-1987 model year pickups *outside* the frame rails to squeeze an additional four gallons into their design, and hence, the advertising. It was a disastrous, last-minute decision, after months of effort to put the tanks where they belonged.

The gas tanks failed and leaked in three of the first four pre-market side-impact tests run by Chevrolet. The fourth test didn't leak because it included a heavy-duty steel shield that protected the fuel tank from impact. GM draftsmen and engineers would later design and test a variety of shields, reinforcements, and fuel tank liners that were never offered to customers, and ultimately a flimsy plastic one that was sold with the truck in its final years.

But we didn't know this yet.

In the next several years, working as a legal assistant, I would put my full focus on this issue. I spent days and ultimately weeks in the grim suite of Detroit rooms called the "General Motors Document Repository," and later received shipments of dozens of bankers boxes of old, photocopied documents. I collected hundreds-of-thousands of pages of documents and returned to them again and again until (in the words of an artist I admire) they "gave up their secrets" to me. I worked nights, organizing the documents and absorbing their contents. I ducked under trucks on the streets near my home, studying details and spotting changes that General Motors made over the course of fifteen years in a deranged and hopeless effort to stanch the bloodshed, burns, and lawsuits caused by a terrible and flawed design. I haunted libraries. I spent hours on the phone with counterparts across the nation, sharing tidbits of information. I read dozens of depositions and scripted dozens more. I stared for hours at fragmented, over-photocopied black and white images from ancient crash tests until the ghostly images of long forgotten shields and reinforcements suddenly presented themselves. I connected a few pages of random drawings and overhead projector slides to words scribbled on a napkin. I found new evidence that GM's top brass were given a secret and forceful education in a defect they had denied knowing anything about. I tracked down retired draftsmen, engineers, and executives, including former General Motors Chairman Roger Smith, who called me after I left a carefully crafted message with the woman who first answered the phone. I carried on a brief and comical faxed flirtation with former Chevrolet General Manager John DeLorean—in my view the chief culprit in the truck's fuel system design. I posted want ads for witnesses and arranged for the construction of colorful full-scale mockups of parts meant to protect the fuel tank that Chevrolet engineers designed but that GM executives never allowed to be put into production. I visited a mentally troubled former engineer at his home and followed him fearfully into his basement where he wanted to show me some secret thing. (When he pulled aside a flimsy curtain, I half expected to see the drying bones of the last paralegal who had followed him down to this trap.)

Over the course of a few years and several more exploding truck cases I wove together a detailed and formerly secret history of corporate stupidity, negligence, and greed that resulted in thousands of fuel fed fires that burned thousands of people, both in the pickups themselves, and in the cars and trucks that had the misfortune to strike them.

Then I studied law without going to law school, became a lawyer, and put my knowledge to work in a two-day long deposition of the pickup's chief engineer that forced him to confront and admit to parts of a story he had forgotten or didn't even know.

I did what I did with hard work. But it turns out I had an assist from an undiagnosed neurological difference—autism—that affected every aspect of the first sixty-five years of my life without my knowledge. My autistic brain gave me persistence and eye for important details that I needed to get the job done. It helped me absorb and master a huge number of facts and see the important connections between them. It allowed me to invent innovative ways to pry loose corporate secrets.

It also caused its share of pain and bewilderment as I tried to navigate the "neurotypical" world—something that, for me, was much more difficult than learning about trucks, or product liability law, or figuring out how to operate a camera and soundboard.

But all of that in due time. For now, let us begin where it all begins for me—with he who is, who was and who always shall be:

Ladies and gentlemen, the big, big daddy of them all—Mr. Chuck Berry!

2

My Imaginary Friend

It's 2010. I'm riding along in my automobile. My hero is still very much alive, and I am newly consumed with him because I have started a website where I post several times a day to a small but dedicated audience. I am trying to make sense of my lifelong love for the man and his music, and this means that for a period of years I cannot stop thinking about two subjects—Chuck Berry, and my own, odd life.

I'm with Gemma. At seventeen, she is a beauty, a poet, and a budding piano player. She's telling me something important about her own life—something to do with friends. I begin to respond. I tell her I never had many friends as a kid or as a grownup—that I've always been satisfied with a few really good ones. I'm already appalled by my own conversation, which so often comes back to me, me, me. But I continue. Undiagnosed, and not yet aware of the quirks and isolation so often associated with autism, I tell her a new theory of mine: that life happened this way for me because of the outlandishly alcoholic home I grew up in—that I wasn't comfortable inviting people into it. It gets quiet. Gemma is losing patience. She has heard this before. As we drive in momentary silence my mind clicks and rolls like a slot machine and all of a sudden a new idea tumbles out like a small fortune in heavy coins.

"Chuck Berry is my *imaginary friend*!" I say, as if I've discovered something important. Gemma rolls her eyes violently and our conversation crashes to a halt.

But I'm on to something—right? My mind is abuzz as we drive on in irritated silence.

In bed that night, *a propos* of nothing, I tell Rebecca. She laughs, hard.

I explain to her that I'm not confused or delusional. I know I don't *know* the man. I know he's not my friend. I don't talk to him in the sandbox. And I *know* I don't know that I've made the proper *clinical* diagnosis.

But isn't that the explanation?

Because almost all my life this public person I don't know has been an important part of my world. The people around me have had to live with him, too. Gemma and her sister Jade grew up to stories about the man. As a small child their bewildered brother Rafferty thought Chuck Berry was the answer to almost any question I asked. Who's singing, Rafferty? Do you know who wrote that song, Rafferty? Who plays that sort of guitar, Rafferty? Do you know the name of the President of the United States, Rafferty?

The hesitant response was always the same: "Chuck Berry?"

Rebecca comes home to stories about people in England, France, Delaware, or Sweden, whom I've never met.

"Jan sent me a CD today!" I tell her. She has to work to find context.

"The guy in Iowa?"

"Germany."

I edit myself constantly—even with family—so that I might appear less mentally suspect. One day Peter K. from Sweden posts an old magazine spread on Facebook showing the young Chuck Berry and his family posing in front of a 1950s style hi-fi. Berry's son, Charles, comments, "They still have that Silvertone!" I am thrilled by this bit of trivia. It is to me as potent as haiku. I react like an old CIA analyst to some tidbit from the Kremlin. "They" means that in 2010 "they"—Chuck Berry and his wife of nearly 70 years—are still a couple who jointly own furniture and appliances. Their child perceives them as "they." I like that. I am happy because—forgive me—in some more theoretical and perhaps less strictly factual sense, I, too, am his child, right? Glad to know dad and mom are together! And I am equally moved by the fact that "they" still have that Silvertone! I still have my camera and drums from 1971, the guitar I bought in 1975, and a scrap of metal I picked up on Greenback Lane when I was 15. I keep important things, and so, I learn, does Chuck! I've learned online that in addition to the 1950s hi-fi, he still has his 1980 Caddy, his 1960s psychedelic sport coat, various guitars, the dates of all his concert appearances! I know from the movies that his old tour bus sits disintegrating on his property, that he retains charred scraps of personal history rescued from a fire, and that as late as 1986 he still had at least three well-preserved, tarpaulin covered 1970s Cadillacs in storage. I want to tell Rebecca about the hi-fi, but I don't. Later I want to tell her again, but I don't again.

My self-control is the product of fear. Once diagnosed, and once I have begun my research into autism, I will understand that by hiding my intense interest in Chuck Berry I am "masking," trying to make myself appear less quirky and weird in a neurotypical world. But I don't know that yet. I imagine calling Rebecca, explaining the magazine spread, and telling her that my Facebook friend Charles, whom I don't really know, has said thus and such about an old hi-fi. She would feign interest through glazed eyes. She would think to herself, "Who is this man that I married and who fathered my child?" I remain silent, but look again the next day, and smile.

A day or two after my "eureka" moment I do some internet research on imaginary friendship and discover a professor of psychology in my own city, Seattle, who studies the subject in a serious way. "I'm beginning to think it never goes away," she tells the Seattle Post Intelligencer. "It morphs into a different form." She and her colleagues interviewed 50 novelists about their characters and found that the characters took "a life of their own."

That's not exactly how it is with me. After all, in 2010 my imaginary friend actually *had* a life of his own. But it's close. The professor tells the reporter that "many of these authors developed *personal relationships* with the characters in their novels and had imagined conversations with them."

I don't have very many imagined conversations with Chuck Berry. It's difficult to manage in a convincing way. To make it work I have to invent situations that would put me in a position to actually talk to the man, which is harder than it sounds. To up the level of difficulty I have to imagine why Chuck Berry might want to talk back, once I have put myself in a position to utter inanities. And to be honest, I'm not sure I *want* to get to know him in real life. There's a YouTube video showing former Rolling Stones bassist Bill Wyman saying that he loved Chuck Berry until he met him. (I *know* I don't want to meet or know Bill Wyman.) Really getting to know the man might spoil a good thing. But there's no doubt that I constructed an ongoing, evolving "personal" relationship with a person I never really knew in real life.

Indeed, everyone who really knows me has had to live with Chuck Berry to some degree, the way others who know an autistic person might have to live with the Antarctic, trains, or Harry Potter. They do draw lines. "I'm tired of your stupid Chuck Berry!" Gemma has told me more than once. Rebecca refused for years to watch "the Chuck Berry movie." Others, like Jade, just nod and wait for me to stop. But they can't avoid him entirely. My stories keep coming.

Of course, those not like family simply don't know. Masking, again, I don't tell them. At best, cornered by circumstance, I might admit "I'm a big Chuck Berry fan," as if that explained it.

But it doesn't. Being a "big Chuck Berry fan" doesn't explain the dreams.

I dream about him regularly. In one dream I drove him around in my car. He was old, quiet, and a little sad, and wore his captain's hat. He looked straight ahead through dark glasses. We parked, and I told two women in a ticket booth that Chuck Berry was in my car. They were reasonably excited. He got out of the car to sit by himself on a bench near dark water. He returned to my car and was just about to answer my question about his version of the blues "turnaround" when five year old Rafferty jumped into our bed and woke me. I narrowly avoided scolding my young son and telling him that he'd interrupted an important conversation with Chuck Berry.

In another dream I watched from a balcony as members of my extended family came off the golf course with Chuck. I remember Liz, Paul, Ann and Maggie, all happy. Chuck must have had a bad round. He was scowling from under one of those stupid golfer caps with a tuft of yarn on top as he pushed open the door to the men's locker room and disappeared. This was not my only revery about Chuck Berry as athlete. In 1977 or 1978, soon after I moved to Seattle and my brother Paul introduced me to the NBA, which quickly became a new obsession, I dreamed that, like television "Rifleman" Chuck Conners, Chuck Berry had once been a professional basketball player. In my dream I watched grainy, black and white dream footage of the journeyman Berry executing a layup. "I never knew that about him!" I dreamt.

After looking at some of her research I look up the psychology professor's university e-mail address and send her a detailed outline of my psychosis. I ask if I am on the right track with the diagnosis of "imaginary friend." She doesn't immediately respond, but later I find a description of a talk she gave where the reporter wrote that she was "exploring whether there is a similar kind of imaginary companionship at work in teenagers who idolize a movie or music star and imagine conversations with that person."

I take that as a yes.

It will be many years before I am identified by a psychologist as autistic. Then I will learn that fixated special interests are a common feature of autistic life. For some kids it might be Harry Potter, or Star Wars, or ponies. For me it was—and remains—the father of rock and roll. I think I chose well.

But I don't know about autism yet. When I finally have a diagnosis and learn something about autism my odd life will begin to make sense to me for the first time, including that part of life when most people are cavorting wildly with one another and I found myself almost completely alone—which is where we go next, for a brief visit.

3

Approaching the Void

It's 1979. There's no Gemma, no Jade, no Rebecca, no Rafferty, no Leila. Because I have become absorbed in 1950s jazz, even Chuck is mostly out of the picture for now. I'm not a lawyer. I'm not a paralegal. I am an English major working two part time jobs and finishing up college at the University of Washington, my fifth and final university. I have led a starkly solitary existence since I went away to college in January, 1973, at the age of 16, but Seattle, from 1977 to 1980, is the nadir. I am as alone as I have ever been, or ever will be for the next four decades. Aside from minor interactions with teachers and coworkers I don't know or interact with anyone in this town other than my brother Paul, his wife, Gina, and my landlord. I have begun to feel frightened—to believe I might be one of the untouchable people, and that what I have always seen as limbo, and impermanent, will become a lifelong hell.

It's my second apartment in Seattle—a basement apartment with a view. My windows look north across a small lawn and through a short cyclone fence to the freeway and beyond. I see Lake Union in the distance, and further west, the Space Needle, and even further west, the sparklingly bright Olympic Mountains covered with a dusting of snow. Everything looks frigid. In 1979 the watery parts of Seattle still have a bit of Alaskan frontier feel, with seaplanes, fishing boats, cannery companies, and now and then a raft of logs pushed or pulled through the lakes and canals by tugboats. But that rough and ready quality is starting to fade. Soon my view will be erased by sleekly drab new buildings.

In my building I speak only to the owner and his son, who is the manager. I mainly see them to drop off rent. The owner is elderly, and for a time is disabled by an outbreak of shingles that covers his entire face and shuts one of his eyes. His face is one giant red scab and it hurts even to look at him. I deal with his son more often. The son, middle-aged and a bit overweight, is part of the chorus at the Seattle opera, which impresses me. I imagine him on stage with a Viking spear, or colorful tights, leaning this way or that while singing well enough to be in the opera. But like I say, they are the only two people in the building I talk to. Otherwise, I check the gold painted mailbox (I only get one bill, for the telephone, but occasionally receive letters) and slip wordlessly downstairs, past a boiler room, and down a dark, funky smelling corridor to my apartment.

My studio apartment comes with a functional Murphy bed, a table, a chair, and a scratchy brown couch from the 1920s that smells faintly of cigarettes, cigars, aging hemp, and some past resident's urinary incontinence. I like the thick basement walls that mean I don't hear the neighbors on either side except when they are in the corridor.

I have few possessions. I have a tiny black and white tv, a turntable, two speakers, and an old tube powered stereo amplifier. The amplifier is missing its housing but sounds good, and the exposed tubes look cool when glowing hot. I have several dozen records, mostly jazz and blues, and two guitars, one electric, one acoustic. I also have art supplies and will create half a dozen pieces in this room that I will keep and remain proud of. One is a view of the Duomo and the Palazzo Vecchio in Florence, Italy, where I once lived, seen through the gothic window of some imaginary building that is much too tall to be in Florence. Still, it's a beautiful painting, set in the dark of night, with torches burning on the Palazzo Vecchio's tower. Another, in a gothic frame cut from cardboard and gilded with model paint, shows me in an electric chair. A third is a poem illustrated in the style of William Blake that I did for my Geology 101 class. Its four pages depict the births and deaths of the Cascade volcanoes in heroic language and imagery. More than forty years later I still like each of these pieces.

But back to 1979. Every now and then I hear my neighbors to the west, a group of deaf people, probably Filipino, who make speech-like sounds as they pass my door. The sounds aren't English, so I can't tell if they are language or simply noises made while signing, but the sound is always cheerfully social. When I happen to meet them in the hallway silence falls. The young women in the group avert their eyes and the man, who is a bit older, nods politely but gravely. I can tell he feels sorry for me—they all do. I never learn how many people live in that apartment, but whatever number, they are together and have community, and they know I am alone and do not.

In the eighteen months I live in this apartment I have only five visitors—Paul and Gina come once, and my friend Greg once visits from California. My sister Ann and her then husband, Gianni, also come once. When Gianni, who is Italian, enters the ornate front doors of the building, he spreads his hands and exclaims operatically, "The stairway to paradise!" but then watches me take the less exalted stairs to my underworld.

I am twenty-three-years-old, in the prime of youth, thin, tall enough, good looking enough, though poorly dressed and not well enough groomed. I have not yet learned to cut my own hair, so I suffer through occasional chop jobs by a talkative barber who smells like a dozen pungent lotions and colognes. He has no talent beyond getting my four dollars.

I work just enough hours to support myself. Early mornings I work on campus at the undergraduate library. Later in the day I work at a fancy restaurant up the hill from my apartment. Sometimes I work a split shift there.

At the library I am the manager's favorite. Her name is Pam. She is a small, nervous but happy middle-aged woman with short, curly hair. I am her utility player. I do pretty much everything. I process new books, help at the front desk, gather piles of books that are scattered around the library and take them to the sorting shelf. I sort books. I shelve books. I rinse and repeat. The Seattle Sonics have been really good for a few years, so Pam and I share Sonics news from time to time. It's a sign of their current popularity and success that Pam can speak fluently about "Downtown" Freddy Brown, Dennis Johnson, Gus Williams, and Jack Sikma.

I like the library. It's full of information and art. I don't spend much free time at the undergraduate library, but I love to hang out in the other, bigger, or more specialized branches. I would consider becoming a librarian, but I have learned from the assistant manager, who is seeking a graduate degree in library sciences, that any decent library job, except Pam's, requires an advanced degree. That seems crazy to me. How much can you study about libraries in 1979? There are books, there are periodicals, and there are audiovisual materials. I don't want or need a master's degree in library science to understand a 1970s library.

I work with five other people besides the manager and her assistant. One is an Iranian athlete. I forget if he plays soccer, or lacrosse, or some sort of handball, but someone tells me he is an Olympic athlete, which I find even more impressive than being in the chorus of the opera. This is during the Iranian revolution when Americans are being held hostage in Iran, and lots of the students at the University of Washington are young, Republican, and enraged, so I worry about him to a degree, but he is wealthy, handsome, and athletic, and seems to be doing fine. I once see him shooting past in a black Trans Am.

Another of my coworkers is a cheerful young woman with short black hair. I find her attractive in every way, and she and I often talk. She seems to enjoy our conversations, but she is nice to everyone, so it's hard for me to know what to make of that. I will eventually screw up the courage to ask her to a basketball game and she will sweetly decline, then I will see her leaning over the front desk in whispered conversation with our basketball team's only legitimate star, a future NBA player and coach, who whispers back with a confident grin.

There is a quiet girl from Japan who is equally pretty, seems equally sweet, and is clearly as shy as I am. I'm sure she speaks English well, but she doesn't provide much evidence. I think that with our equally quiet ways we might be a good match, but I will not find courage twice this year so my interactions with this girl will be limited to greetings.

I work with two other people. There is a young man I sometimes describe as "incompetently blind." I feel wrong describing him that way—we often fail to appreciate the obstacles people are faced with, and I know that if I were suddenly blinded, I would be far less competent than he is—but he hasn't mastered skills that many blind people have and often asks me for help. Several times I find him lost in different parts of the library. Once I find him tapping his cane at a brick wall, seemingly stuck there, returning again and again to tap at the same spot as if the wall might suddenly open and let him pass. I escort him where he wants to go. Decades from now I will see him again, asking for money outside of an urban Taco Bell. I will walk past without a whisper or sound. What could I say? "Do you remember the guy who found you tapping the wall?" There was nothing about me for him to remember.

Finally, there is the guy who puts magnetic security strips into new books. That is all he does. He is my age but seems elderly. He works slowly and quietly, always seated in the same spot. He responds politely and efficiently without eye contact and with few words. If someone is talking, I know he listens because if something funny is said he smiles vaguely but appropriately while looking down at his work. I wonder about him. He has a student job so I know he is a university student and smart, but he provides no other evidence. He never once initiates a conversation or even joins one. I learn, however, that he is the manager's other favorite. "He is so dependable," she tells me with affection and pleasure. "He's just like you!"

I will see him, too, decades hence, when we are both in our sixties. He will be walking slowly downtown in his expensive trench coat, unmistakable with his Mona Lisa smile, carrying a briefcase, still dependably employed, and judging by his clothing, somewhat lucratively.

Once while working at the front desk, I'm approached by a young woman with dark hair and a heart shaped face who surprises me with a smile and a question and more smiles. As I help her I wonder if she is Donna, a girl with whom I fell into mostly unrequited love in San Jose four years earlier. Donna would not recognize me now. My hair is eighteen or twenty inches shorter, and whatever shimmer of hope she might have seen in my eyes four years ago is fading and covered with clear plastic glasses. I can't tell if it's Donna or not, and I don't ask or make any small talk whatsoever. She walks away giving me a backward glance and another smile, which is what Donna would have done.

At the restaurant, which is called Henry's Off Broadway, I am called an "assistant waiter," which means I am a busboy. I wear tight, polyester bell bottom slacks retained after a brief stint making change at a Lake Tahoe casino, and a frilly salmon colored tuxedo shirt that Jimi Hendrix pulled off, but that makes me look like an underpaid underling. I don't care. All of us are men and all of us wear the same shirt. I pour water for women who say, "Goodness! I'm going to float away!" I serve dark roast coffee long before it's a thing in the United States, and if one of the many Nancy Reagan clones who dine at Henry's tells me, "This coffee is delicious! What is it?" I am trained to respond, "It's called Starbucks, ma'am. It's local." In 1979 this is inside information.

I am not a good assistant waiter. My polyester pants, influenced by a year in Italy, are so tight that when I pull the Bic lighter from my back pocket, friction spins the little flame adjustment wheel, and when I lean in to light another skinny rich woman's cigarette, fire shoots out like a blow torch and threatens to cremate her nose job.

The real waiters are Type A wannabe men who are universally nasty towards me, barking orders, criticizing, and never sharing tips. I suppose the waiters have their reasons for hating me. I have learned the table numbers and can carry three plates of food through the kitchen doors but I cannot follow the numbering system for place settings or the absorb the brusk verbal instructions— "Salmon at table twenty-seven, position two, Steak position three, and Pollo *Pretenzioso* at position five!" Forty-three years hence, I will learn that this difficulty taking verbal direction is hardwired into my neurology, but for now it is just another fact of life to deal with. The guests never mind if I ask who has the salmon or who has the steak—in fact they like to help me; it gives them a brief purpose—but my incompetence enrages the waiters. I honestly don't care. After one berates me in the kitchen, I threaten retaliation by visibly and dangerously sticking my foot in front of him as he exits the kitchen holding an order of steaming pretentiousness high above his head. I give him an evil look for emphasis. He recognizes the threat, sees the evil in my eyes, and backs off.

The only interaction I have with kitchen staff (aside from accepting the staff meal) is with the Mexican dishwasher. When I clear a bottle of wine that isn't empty, he and I share it, tipping it back, drinking from the bottle, and laughing. It's good wine and would cost me a day of work, so why not enjoy? Eventually the wine steward catches wind of our parties and insists we give all unfinished bottles to him. "I must know the wines," he tells us. He probably sips and spits it out, which strikes me as a waste of solace. Years later he will have a newspaper column on wine.

The restaurant job pays well in the evening, but at lunchtime I work one hour for minimum wage plus a dollar. It's only worth my while because they give me lunch, which is invariably a piece of meat, a vegetable, and a potato, and because it's required. Theoretically busboys and the kitchen staff get a percentage of of the gross sales as a tip or bonus. The night manager always gives me a used envelope, stapled closed, with a tip that reflects how busy the night was. If a lot of people come and I work hard, I get more money, a mix of bills and coins. The lunchtime manager, a coldly pretty woman not much older than myself but far more elegantly dressed, gives me an envelope with exactly one dollar, every day, no matter how busy it is or how hard I work serving and clearing *Croque-Monsieurs*. She hands it to me with a defiant glare. We both know she's cheating me, probably to her own benefit.

My life is simple and uncluttered. I ride my bike or take the early bus to the university. I work a couple of hours at the library. I go to classes. Between classes I wander the libraries looking for interesting things—a recording of Dizzy Gillespie and Charlie Parker or the manuscripts of William Blake. One day I find a contemporary 1850s review trashing an incompetently written new novel called *Moby Dick*. Some days I work the lunch shift at the restaurant. I go home and read piles of assigned English literature or the Bible (I'm taking a class in the Bible as literature) then go back to work the night shift at the restaurant. I go home. I write long letters, often adopting a comically biblical tone that I have absorbed from my reading. I make art with a comically gothic religious tone.

If I am not working a night shift at the restaurant I might go back to the university to watch a basketball game. I never cared about sports growing up, but since moving to Seattle basketball has become a huge new interest of mine. I learn all about it. The Sonics are close to becoming world champions and are a fun team to watch. Games are cheap and also televised. I have learned to recognize just about every player in the NBA and know their particular skills. I like going to the Pac Ten college games because I can sit in the front row and see future NBA players. Our college team is not very good but has its good moments and good players, and there are legitimate stars on the other teams that pass through town. Student tickets are $19 for the season—less than two bucks a game. My two dollars get me a court side bench seat where I sit alone. Other students sit together above me.

Once I see a game that was videotaped and shown on television later, and there I am, a small black and white blur, decidedly alone. It seems like a public invasion of my too private life.

In fact, I am alone all the time. I visit used bookstores alone. I go to bars to hear music alone. For a brief time, the blues legend J. B. Hutto is a resident of Seattle. He reminds me of one of my blues heroes, Elmore James, and I go to hear and see him as often as possible. Once, inspired by his music, I venture away from aloneness by asking a woman to dance. She looks at my boots and asks if they are my dancing shoes. This sort of question is a puzzle to me. I have no idea what I am expected to say. I shrug or say "yeah," or perhaps say nothing, and at the end of the song we go our separate ways.

I see punk rock bands. I go to museums and libraries. I go to plays. I paint pictures. I write stories. I use paper mache to create things and paint them. When I get depressed, I walk eight or ten blocks by myself for my 1970s version of Prozac, which is a greasy double-cheeseburger called the "Dick's Deluxe."

The only times I am not alone I am with my brother Paul and his wife Gina who are obviously worried about me. They take me to see Alvin Ailey and Baryshnikov, Itzhak Perlman, Earl "Fatha" Hines, Bob Dylan, Miles Davis during his electric period, and a nearly endless opera called *Le roi de Lahore*. I take them to see zydeco legend Clifton Chenier and a new guy named Elvis Costello. We sometimes hike at Mount Rainier or visit the ocean.

One night Gina and Paul invite me to their house for dinner and I find they have also invited a young woman from Paul's office. I'm not expecting anyone else to be at the dinner and I can only guess now what I look like or how I act. Badly cut brown hair. A gray cotton military or work shirt approved by the Chinese Communist Party. (I wasn't going to make it with anyone anyhow.) Big aviator shaped glasses with clear plastic frames. (Were they broken yet? Had I taped them?) The young woman is clearly appalled. She's a working woman with a career. I'm an assistant waiter, a student, and awkward. Who knows if I even spoke other than to respond to questions.

After dinner Gina says enthusiastically that I can drive the young woman home, that I'm going her way. The girl panics and actually begs Gina to drive her, which would be a ten mile round trip, but Gina holds cheerfully firm and hope drains from the young woman's eyes. I drive her home. As we cross town in my Fiat, I try to make conversation, and she treats me like I am a bomb set to explode at any moment. At her old brick apartment, she jumps from the car and I never see her again.

A few years before this I presented differently. Out of high school I wore a leather jacket and hair that fell nearly to my waist. I was 16, but when I finally shaved off the hint of a mustache that gave away my youth, I attracted a certain number of young women confused by my rock star plumage. I didn't keep them. They blew past me like dry leaves on a windy day.

After that I went to Italy for a year. I was in it to win it. I got Italian jeans, an Italian shirt, and Italian boots. I cut my hair to my shoulders. My leather jacket was joined by a black knitted scarf. Decades later my teenaged daughters would shriek with surprise how good their dad once looked. I remember two Italian girls at the university cafeteria in Perugia who spoke under their breath in words I could understand. "He must be German," one told the other. I was just like the guy in the library. I listened and said nothing.

But that is ancient history. The young lady escapes from my car with visible relief. I drive another few blocks home and park.

When I started college at San Jose State University, Ronald Reagan was still governor of California. Today lots of people see him as a jolly old man and statesman, but that was an act, like the chimp movies he was known for before becoming President. As governor in the 1960s he defunded California's mental health system and put thousands of disabled people on the streets. When he became President he would repeal most provisions of the Mental Health Services Act that Jimmy Carter signed into law that same year. I started college before Apple and the whole Silicon Valley thing, and in those days San Jose was a tough, poor, ethnically rich city undergoing hard times, and it often seemed like all of the mental patients Reagan had thrown out of hospitals found themselves wandering the streets of mid-town San Jose in a Thorazine daze. Once I saw a woman who used an old zipper as a strap to hold her glasses to her head. I was with my one friend, Stan, and his girlfriend, and we laughed at her oddball inventiveness.

In San Jose I learned to walk the nighttime streets alone, primarily to give my dormitory neighbors the impression that I had things to do and places to be. I remember seeing people on campus in twos and threes and I remember my own conscious understanding that I had no idea how to make myself like them or find friends of my own. Despite that, and despite my aloneness, I had hope. If there was a problem, it was their problem, not mine. They were dullards, and stupid, or so I told myself. I wrote long letters to my sister Rooney describing the stupidity of everyone around me, all those happy people that I didn't know, and I satisfied myself with constant exploration of what was around me—movies, music, the city, the surrounding cities and countryside.

On my eighteenth birthday, my sister Ann visited from Santa Cruz and brought me the reggae masterpiece *The Harder They Come,* which included the Jimmy Cliff song "Sitting in Limbo." That was me. I was in limbo, but confident that a better day was coming. In the words of the song, this little boy was moving on.

But now in Seattle I see a man on the sidewalk wrapped in a dirty blanket and mumbling incoherently. I am noticing these people more and more. The woman with the inventive optical repair had made me smile, but now I begin to feel a terrible kinship with the unwashed, muttering person on the bus and the drunk man sleeping in some tall grass near my apartment.

I am a fabulously interesting person, an artist if I want to be, a musician if I want to be, a world traveler, a potential writer. I paint and draw pictures. I love blues, jazz, and early rock and roll, art, movies, and theater. I write brilliant letters and beginner short stories. I write songs.

But I have begun to understand that I am just breaths away from the place where a similarly brilliant person shivers and mumbles, and it scares me.

How and why does it scare me?

When I was a child Paul took me to Lake Berryessa in California. Berryessa is manmade, and near the dam there is a unique feature—a perfectly round hole, perhaps 20 feet in diameter where excess water drains from the lake. In drought-stricken years the hole usually looks like a massive pipe that rises from the water, but when Paul took me, water flowed smoothly and inexorably over edge of the hole. It was terrifying. I imagined myself in that water, caught by the current and pulled helplessly towards that horrible and deadly void.

Which is how I feel now as I walk past this huddled and mumbling person and try not to look at him. Limbo is no more. I feel the ice-cold brutality of a life with no human contact, without companionship, without human touch—a hellish void that's already waiting for me, pulling me closer and closer.

But instead of falling into that void, I do exactly the right thing: I join the Peace Corps and move to Africa, where the locals see me as being just as weird as every other foreigner, but no weirder, and where, after learning a few social rules, I begin to feel connected, whole, and fully human for the first time in a decade. I will tell you about that—one of many people, places, and things I credit with saving my life, including my family, Peach Tree High School, Paul Whelan, and Rebecca.

But first let's tell a therapist.

4

My First Attempt at Therapy

The first time I seek the help of a mental health therapist is in the fall of 2019, right before the Covid pandemic, back when it's still easy to find such a person. I choose someone almost randomly—a young woman, more or less in the neighborhood, who looks kind. She returns my email with a suggestion we talk on the phone for a few minutes to see if we are a good fit.

A few days later, on the phone, I tell her the most immediate reason I am seeking help. For a month or so I've been experiencing a nagging, low grade blueness or depression. It isn't serious or disabling. It doesn't keep me in bed, or affect my appetite, or spoil life. I am in the middle of one of the biggest cases of my career and I'm able to work without a problem. I go on occasional dates with Rebecca, watch television and laugh with Rafferty, and speak appropriately to neighbors when I see them. In short, I'm living my life, but I don't feel right. The sensation is almost physical—a heavy wet blanket of sadness on my head and forehead, and I can't shake it.

That last part is unusual for me. Usually, if I feel bad, I walk outside, look at nature, some trees or the sky, and the bad mood evaporates. At least that's how it has always been. This time it won't go away.

But although the depression is real, and bothersome, it isn't the only reason I am seeking help, and maybe not even the real reason. There is another, bigger issue I carry in my back pocket. It's something I thought I had escaped decades ago, but that bothers me now more than when I was actively living it—my bizarrely solitary life as a young man. At the time it was simply life as I knew it. Now, as an older man with grown and growing kids, it bothers me more. I see it as youth wasted. I see my own mistakes and failures. I want to go back in time and help the kid I used to be, to give him advice. But the older me needs advice, too. I want help getting my older self past the pain of it—pain that only really announced itself when Rebecca, slightly tipsy, asked a wholly innocent question.

After a short phone chat the therapist and I agree to meet, and I spend the next week or two taking long walks and carefully scripting the words I will use during my first visit. There is nothing unusual about this behavior, at least for me. That's what I do. It's what I've done my entire life. I walk and talk to myself, sorting things out, or preparing myself for future conversations with real people. I will eventually learn this is a very autistic thing to do, but for now it's just me. As I walk I talk to myself, or I talk to friends, or family, or enemies, or a therapist, none of whom are actually there. It's my way of organizing my thoughts and preparing to share them.

And to hear those thoughts, I must enunciate them to some small degree. So I walk and move my lips and appear somewhat crazy. I suppose I could buy ear buds and pretend I'm talking to some unseen person on the phone, but I think the people who do that—who walk down the street loudly and self-importantly shouting at the unseen recipient of their call—look even crazier than someone like me who is just a bit odd and mumbles humbly to himself or to imaginary companions. So, I walk, talk, and mumble, and sometimes I get caught. I turn a corner and boom—a person who is clipping her hedge hears me writing my script.

The day of my first appointment, I drive. It's a bit far, and it's Seattle and raining, and besides, I have to be there on time. So I drive, and on the way I think of two new things I want to tell my new therapist—things that aren't already in my prepared script. I want to tell her I felt loved as a child, and I want to tell her that the crazy and horrible nuns who taught me in primary school did me one real favor: in first, second, and third grades, they made me feel smart, and rightly or wrongly, that confidence in my own intelligence never left me. It's interesting that these two thoughts tack themselves to my script so late in my preparations, and that I know I must say them first. In retrospect they are awesomely important. I was loved and hence knew I was lovable, even in the worst of times; and because I was convinced of it early, I never lost my own belief that I was smart—smart enough to take on General Motors and the evilest man alive. These are gifts not everyone receives, and certainly not every autistic person. Some autistic people I've encountered since my diagnosis got messages from their early childhoods that were just the opposite of what I received. I was lucky and remain so.

My therapist's office is in a pale gray building packed with a lot of other therapists. There is a small waiting room where I help myself to fruity flower bud tea. I would prefer something caffeinated, but it's a prop I can carry into the session, something to hold and fiddle with.

At the appointed hour she appears to greet me. She is small and quiet. She lets me choose a place to sit inside her little room. She asks me what has brought me. I make a very determined effort to hold eye contact with her.

"Like I told you, I've been blue lately. Usually if I feel blue, I can shake it almost immediately. But this time it's clinging."

She listens and nods. I like right away that she is a good listener and sympathetic. I feel comfortable speaking. The script is strong.

"The other thing is something I've wanted to talk about for a while."

I tell her how much I am bothered by those "college years," and how alone I was.

"So how would you like to begin?" she asks me.

I tell her my plan—that I'd like to use most of this session telling her what I can about my life. And she allows me to perform the entire soliloquy.

I tell her the stuff about being loved and feeling smart. I tell her about the good stuff in my current life: Rebecca, my kids Jade, Gemma and Rafferty, my granddaughter Leila. I tell her about my work and my pride in doing it my way. I tell her that I am the most solitary person I know. I tell her that I work from home, that I spend many of my days walking, reading, researching, largely alone. I tell her about my childhood, the youngest of seven, packed into a small house; about our ascent into the upper middle class; about my ninth birthday, when we moved into a new house and I figured out, in a flash, that alcohol was at the root of our family misery; I tell her about the nightmarish but nonetheless amusing days that followed, about the shouting, and singing, and drunkenness. I tell her about having to change my dad's wet underwear as a ten-year-old, and trying, as a group, to lift his 250 pounds of dead-drunk weight off the floor; I tell her about the arrival of ambulances and priests; about the hospitalizations; about the miraculous recoveries. I tell her about my one sleepover, shut in my room with a friend while Daddy hollered; I told her about leaving him after an especially crazy day, when he and my brother Stevo joined forces, threw pee at each other, and Stevo hit my mother over the head with a fiberglass table top. I tell her how we moved out the next day, at my request, and about our new life in the country, my new and wonderful high school, my myriad interests in things like pigeons, astronomy, telescopes, horseshoeing, gold panning, photography, movie-making, and music. I tell her about going off to college too early and too young and finding myself suddenly and utterly alone. I tell her about the girls I couldn't hold onto. I tell her about Italy. I tell her about Stevo's violent death. I tell her about finding myself more and more alone. I tell her about Africa, and the beginnings of a normal life. I tell her about my first marriage, and my divorce, and then, more happily, about my second marriage.

When I finish, with ten or so minutes to go, she rubs her hands and smiles. She tells me my life is a "candy store" for someone in her profession—that she hardly knows where to begin.

(My life is like a box of bittersweet chocolates. With nuts.)

One of the words she mentions during that first session is trauma. This surprises and interests me. I am so far removed from the trauma that I no longer think of my childhood that way. When talking about it with my sister Ann we laugh. We describe it to our children as a grand and gaudy spectacle of alcohol, ambulances, priests, hollers, and laughter, or a rollicking novel filled with crazy, smart, and talented people. My preteen and teenaged friends were all profoundly interested and perhaps a bit jealous of how interesting and handsome my family was. But I seize on that word "trauma," or at least notice it, and the next day, as if by magic, my morning routine of coffee and online newspapers serves me an article in The Guardian that I would never have looked at until this day: an article about how childhood trauma can affect our ability to form adult relationships. The article calls this "attachment theory," and describes an "avoidant" attachment style that sounds a bit like me. This idea, new to me, becomes the focus of our talks for the next several weeks.

The problem is that it doesn't quite fit. My childhood was sometimes crazy, and yes, often traumatic, but underlying any trauma was the simple truth that I used to open our sessions: my parents loved us—*me*—and we knew it. My dad disintegrated before our eyes as he slipped deeper and deeper into alcoholic illness. He became a comic figure. We snapped a picture of him in a sombrero and laughed. He bobbed in the stiflingly hot water of our backyard pool and we laughed. (Danny designed a "Turkish Bobber"—a sort of brick well where Daddy could bob up and down in steaming water and leave our pool at a normal temperature. We laughed at that, too.) Daddy hollered that we "brutalized him" (we were assisting him across a patch of pebbled concrete in our backyard) and we laughed at that and at what the neighbors must think. He pinned strange notes to his shirt and spoke what he called "In'ian talk." (He wasn't a racist but played one while out of his mind.) We laughed through the pain a lot of times, but none of us doubted his love.

For her part, my mother was a saint.

I use that word with the therapist and she questions it.

"You use a lot of religious imagery and vocabulary. You called the country home you moved to 'heaven.' You call your mother a 'saint.' Why is that?"

I still make the sign of the cross when I'm talking about some hoped-for result. I once genuflected in the aisle of a crowded movie theater. Did she have no spiritual training?

"I was raised Catholic in the 1950s and 1960s," I say. "Parts of it are with you for a lifetime. So yes, I speak that way. But she was an unbelievably good person, she loved us, she took care of us, and she was our 'mom' until the day she died. In my book, that is a saint."

My therapist doesn't buy it.

"Sometimes a person wants to love us but can't express it. We feel abandoned."

My mother was not the sort of person who gave us lots of hugs, but there was no doubt.

"She loved us, and we knew it. Really, I always felt loved by both of them, and by my whole family. I'm sure I never felt abandoned by her. I think my father sort of abandoned us, but not on purpose."

We continue having sessions every two weeks. One day, after a month or so, I am on a long walk rehearsing the next session, when I burst out laughing—or at least into a huge, autistic smile, with possible sound effects. (There's no such thing as an autistic smile, but I can imagine what I look like to passersby as I remember what I'd forgotten.)

I show up at the next session with an actual smile—an irrepressible one.

"I forgot the biggest thing. The thing that has dominated my entire life. I actually wrote a book about it."

And then I tell her about Chuck Berry. She has never heard of him. There is no accounting for young people, today. But she is delighted. This berry flavored treat is, definitively, the sweetest bit of candy in the store. I tell her everything, and later that day, at her request, I send a PDF copy of my entire 225 page manuscript—a memoir of my lifelong relationship with someone I didn't know and hardly met. The book mixes chapters about my own life with chapters about the musical and cultural contributions of Chuck Berry. I can say with expertise it has some of the best writing about Chuck and his music that anyone has ever done, and wonderful writing about me, too.

What I didn't understand when I wrote it, and what I don't understand when I give it to this woman, and what I'm afraid she never would have come to understand, is that my manuscript is also a detailed memoir of autism. It is all there—and whatever isn't in the book, I have told her during our sessions.

A few weeks after I tell her about Chuck, Covid rears its ugliness in Seattle and shuts things down for two straight years. I stop our sessions, and it's probably just as well. Looking back it's clear—she had all the information, but even if we continued talking, she would not have come up with the real answer about what made and makes me be me, and what was at the root of those disturbingly solitary college years.

That would require a bit of magic and right person.

5

The Exact Right Person

I learned "the exact right person" concept in the summer of 1982, and it has followed me through life. That summer I was in the United States for a visit after finishing my first two years as a Peace Corps volunteer in the West African nation of Togo. The normal Peace Corps tour is two years, but at very end of my second, and after it was officially too late to make such a decision, a stranger ordered me to do a third.

"You have to stay!" she told me, and I obeyed.

A benefit of signing up for a third year was a trip home to visit family. I spent most of it in Seattle, but I also went to California to see my brothers and sisters who lived there. When I visited my sister Rooney in Oakland, she took me to meet her friend, a famous painter who had spent time in West Africa. Rooney knew he would have something worthwhile to share with me.

He did. He began speaking, without hesitation, almost as soon as we arrived at his house, and continued nonstop for however long we were there. He shared a lot, but the part I remember forty years later was about "the exact right person."

"You've experienced this," he told me, leaning forward, more confident than I was that I had, as if he knew it had just happened.

"You're in Africa. You have a problem. You don't know how to solve it. You're thinking about it, wondering what to do. And at that *very moment* a person enters your life—maybe someone you've never met—and that person solves the problem for you! That's happened to you, right?"

I wanted to say yes but couldn't. I had that feeling like an impending sneeze, when a word or a memory or a thought is hovering just outside your grasp.

Later, after we left, my brain relaxed and freed the memory of a beautiful young woman from Memphis whose mysterious intervention was entirely responsible for my third year in Africa. Because of her my life changed completely. Because of her I have two beautiful daughters and a wonderful and talented granddaughter.

It happened just weeks before Rooney's friend would talk to me about "the exact right person."

I had gone to the capital city, Lomé, to do my close of service training. That should have been the end of the line for me in Togo. It wasn't.

It was early evening. I was in the Peace Corps office. The only other person around was the young woman from Memphis. She introduced herself and asked if I wanted to go to dinner with her. Of course, I did. So, we walked the sandy streets of Kodjoviakopé to a new little restaurant that had opened up nearby, sat outdoors in the breezy night under bougainvillea, got sandwiches and beer, and talked for hours, enthusiastically, like best friends.

Perhaps you've enjoyed this sort of experience hundreds of times. You meet someone and instantly feel like friends. For me it remains exceedingly rare.

I had been aware of this woman since she arrived in Togo a year or so after me. She was the sort of person you notice—beautiful, assertive, and somewhat regal. I am certain she had never noticed me before, though I was sometimes around, in part because I am the sort of person you don't notice—quiet, nondescript, off to the side a bit—and in part because she *told* me she had never seen me before. I had seen her several times, and knew her name, but I had been invisible to her until this particular evening, when she became my friend, admirer, confidant, and counselor. And at the end of our long evening, she gave me the order: she told me I could not go home, that I still had work to do in Africa, and that I had to sign up for a third year.

Which is exactly what I did, and it changed my life forever.

Africa is where I began to feel fully human again—where I found a circle of friends, a place in the community, a girlfriend who became my wife, all things that seemed unattainable just a few years earlier, some of it thanks to this stranger.

It took several weeks to get permission for a third year. When I finally succeeded I went back to the capital for some business at the Peace Corps office and saw the young woman again. I told her the news.

She looked at me like I was a crazy person. She had no idea who I was.

When I explained that I had re-upped, like she told me to, and that I would be doing another year, she furrowed her brow, shook her head, and walked away.

I was invisible to her again.

So that is the magic Rooney's friend had told me about— "the exact right person," sent by the gods or the ancestors, or simply by magic, to help with a problem. It would happen again before I left Togo. It would happen back in Seattle, too.

I think it happens all the time.

Which leads us to my second attempt at therapy.

6

My Second Attempt at Therapy

Once again I have chosen almost at random—or maybe this time magic has intervened. I have made several efforts to find a therapist, but with so many people distraught about Covid no one is taking new patients. I will eventually learn that this particular person had an opening because she had taken time off to be with her daughter and is rebuilding her practice.

I spend the days before our first session preparing: walking, talking to myself, relearning, revising, and rehearsing my life story. I figure I will do what I did last time—until I show up, and my plan falls apart.

It's my first visit. Icy roads add to my nervousness. She has sent an email telling me to "take a seat in the waiting room" when I arrive. I can do that. The waiting room is broken into two adjacent areas with a handful of chairs in each part, and I take a seat by the front doors.

At the appointed hour my new therapist walks into the other part of the room, pauses for part of a second to look at the empty chair in front of her, then turns and walks over to me. We are both wearing masks.

"Peter?" she asks.

"Yes," I say, and begin to stand up. She's a lot younger than I am, probably half my age.

"You weren't where I expected you to be!" She points to the empty chair. "I thought you would be over there."

I am never brilliant with small talk but now I'm flummoxed. I am the only person in the waiting area and 15 feet from "over there."

I follow as she walks silently to her office and points me to a small couch. Now my own expectations go unfulfilled. I've prepared myself for a certain amount of chit chat, maybe about the icy weather, maybe the earlier snow, or maybe a meaningless question about whether I had trouble finding the place, but there is none. We have evidently used up our stores of small talk on my seating choice.

Although I don't know it yet, this awkwardness on both sides bodes well. It is a sign that I have come to the right place, that I am with the right person.

I fall onto the very center of the little couch and lean towards an armrest that is too far away. I wind up at a forty-five-degree angle. I am making the first impression of a crazy person, which, given her profession, is perhaps not surprising. After all, I am here to talk about my crazy life—but it's not the first impression I planned.

I pull myself up to a more dignified vertical and we begin. I have come with the firm intent to repeat the well-rehearsed story of my life to this new person, as I did with the last. She even knows this plan, because in my initial email I foolishly shared the "candy store" comment of the previous therapist. I promised good stories. But my plan sputters immediately into chaos. I jabber out bits and pieces. I breathe oddly. I talk about my current clingy depression. I talk about my painfully alone college years. I try to say something about the crazily alcoholic but loving home I grew up in. My voice warbles. I blame my ragged breath and speech on the mask I am wearing. She smiles and says, "It's okay. It happens. Just talk."

And within minutes, she begins ushering me gently towards an entirely new understanding of who I am—a unified theory of me that explains almost everything.

She doesn't tell me during our first session, but she has seen something, and I know this because at one point she talks aloud to herself, laughing a bit and shaking her head, saying, "It's not even a firm diagnosis yet!"

I'm listening and wondering, "What? What's not a firm diagnosis?"

Ten or fifteen minutes into our first session she says, "Do you like to read?"

"I do."

"Do you like nonfiction?"

"Anything. Everything."

"Oh good!" she says. "I'm thinking of a book you might like. It focuses on women, but you'll be able to see past that."

This is exactly what I have been hoping for—a book that will help me understand who I am and why I am that way. Because I have known most of my life that I am different.

And then she asks the big question.

"Do you know the term 'neurodiversity?'"

I do not—so she reaches back to a word I had used to describe my relationship with Rebecca. "We like each other and love each other and support each other despite our quirks," I told her.

She smiled. She smiles again now.

"It means 'quirky.' Neurodivergent people are people whose brains are wired *differently* from most people. Not badly, just differently. We see the world differently from most people."

We? Have I heard this properly? At any rate, I like it. I've known all my life I am wired differently, that I see things differently, that I've lived differently, and even lawyered differently. I'm proud of it. I can't wait to learn how and why.

As I'm getting ready to go she loans me a copy of the book—a volume so new and fresh it makes me nervous. I hurt the books I read. I spindle, fold, and mutilate. I cart them on long walks to read in bits and pieces from any dry bench. They wind up with arched spines and ragged pages spotted with drops of coffee and wine. But

I take the book home, protecting it from the winter elements, and immediately sit down in my customary spot (I have two) to gingerly open it and read.

I am immediately and stunningly disappointed. She hasn't understood me at all.

The book is about accomplished, neurodivergent women with a variety of neurological types and conditions. One of them is autism, and I am relatively certain that is the condition my therapist has in mind for me. I am disappointed because I investigated autism myself six or seven years earlier as the possible cause of me being me, and I ruled it out. I have done my research.

In those days, six or seven years before this, I enjoyed watching a vaguely but not completely corny television show called *Parenthood*. One of the children on the show was an autistic boy who knew a lot about bugs. He was an interesting character, but except for his intelligence, his poor eye contact, his lack of friends, and his negligible baseball skills, he rang no bells for me.

If I had managed to see a link between this boy's encyclopedic knowledge of insects and my own lifelong expertise in a certain prehistoric rocker, perhaps I would have felt a more immediate connection. But late in the series a new character was introduced—an awkward middle-aged man played by actor Ray Romano. He understood the kid instinctively and immediately. The show didn't tell us the Romano character was autistic, but we in the audience, educated by years of viewing, were supposed to see it for ourselves, even before he did, and before his eventual late diagnosis. And though he was different from me in many ways, I recognized the kinship—I saw *me* in him and him in me.

I've learned this is a common road to diagnosis. We see someone on television or in a movie. We see ourselves. We do our research.

So that night, six or seven years before my diagnosis, I paused the show and pulled out my ever-present laptop to do some research on autism, thinking I might finally have found an explanation for my weird life. I am good at quick and dirty research. In the old days I would go to the library. Now I go online. I check a bunch of sources. I get the lay of the land of whatever subject I'm investigating.

Unfortunately, everything I found out about autism that night was clinical, dour, and slightly horrible. According to the authorities I happened to query, autism was a complete drag and so, by extension, were autistic people.

The authorities told me autistic people have no sense of humor. I have a brilliant sense of humor, even if few understand it. My sense of humor expresses itself in bizarrely unprofessional emails broadcast to a largely dumbfounded company workforce.

Autistic people, the experts droned, have no understanding of sarcasm. (Maybe they have a point. I can't think of a response sarcastic enough to put here.)

The authorities said autistic people have no empathy. I do. They said autistic people have sensory issues relating to sound, light or texture. I don't. And they said that autistic people are wedded to routine.

Hey, I like my morning coffee, my morning websites, (in order,) and a slow 10 am start to the workday from my regular spot on the red couch in the green room—but other than that, variety is the spice of my life.

In other words, I told myself, I'm not autistic.

I closed my computer that night confident that autism was not on my own spectrum.

But then this quirky young therapist sees something and gives me this book.

So I keep returning to it. I see it almost as a duty.

On a neighborhood walk I tell Rebecca about my new therapist. When I say she used the word "neurodiversity" Rebecca shoots me a look.

"I don't think I'm autistic," I tell her. I tell her about *Parenthood*, Ray Romano, and my 15 minutes of research.

But the question nags me. After a single visit I already trust the new therapist.

We had spoken briefly about my ex-wife and my eldest daughter and she made a surprisingly bold but astute and scathing remark. It wasn't the sort of thing people say, but it was searingly and startlingly true. It tells me she has instincts, the way I have instincts about my cases. She knows her stuff, and she saw something in me.

So I keep reading. And when I don't find exactly what I'm looking for in the book she has loaned me, I begin to check other sources. This time I get lucky. Instead of dour, medical bullshit about "deficits" and disorder, Google serves up the exact right website: an article about autistic strengths.

And in that article, I find myself.

I call it an article, but is really a series of bullet points, and all of them seem to apply to me: intense interests, intense focus, perseverance, attention to detail, honesty, ability to work alone, self-motivated. I search google for "positive autistic traits" and find article after article, site after site, all more or less describing me in my personal life and in my work as a paralegal and later as an attorney.

I had asked that our sessions be two weeks apart because I like time to process whatever I am learning. I spend those two weeks ordering books, reading, studying, watching videos, watching *Ted Talks*, watching movies and television shows about autism, fiction and non-fiction, and recognizing myself in much of what I read, hear, and see—not all of it so positive.

I slowly come to the understanding this autism business might, in fact, be me.

A few days before my next appointment my daughter Gemma texts that she wants to stop by and read an essay she has written. At the age of twenty-nine, Gemma is going back to university to study early childhood education. The essay speaks of her struggles and successes in education and in life, and part of it is about me. Gemma first describes me as her hero, someone who has stood by her through her own life challenges. But she also describes me as someone who had been incapable of offering the sort of affection that she and her sister Jade needed when they were small girls.

As she speaks a forgotten episode rises in my mind. I suddenly remember myself as a stressed out single dad, on my bed, the bedroom door locked, searching for calm as Gemma and her sister Jade call for me from behind the locked door. It is a scene I had completely forgotten. In fact, I'm sure it happened more than once.

While doing my research I read about autistic people having "meltdowns" when overwhelmed. I suddenly understand that I had experienced the quiet meltdown of a struggling father.

We talk a bit about her essay. I tell Gemma it is beautifully written and powerful.

Then I ask if I can tell her something that I am just learning about myself—something her essay might have touched on.

Gemma nods, fully attentive.

I tell her about the new therapist. I tell her about the lingering depressions I'd had the last several years. I start to talk about the part of her essay where she says I wan't affectionate enough.

I become overwhelmed and find it hard to speak. "I'll tell you some other time."

Gemma encourages me to go on. I am on the verge of tears, but Gemma begins to smile.

"I think I might be...".

I pause for breath.

Now Gemma is smiling brightly in a way she's especially good at. She knows exactly what I am about to say. And when I finally get out the words "on the spectrum," she speaks them with me, then shrieks with joy.

"I knew it dad! Jade and I talk about it all the time! And dad, the people I like best are on the spectrum! They're all so smart and creative!"

Later that day I tell my son, Rafferty, and when she returns from a trip I tell my oldest, Jade.

I get no arguments.

7

A Gift From Stevo

My brother Stevo is the one who first told me about Chuck Berry. It came in two conversations—lectures really, because there was no give and take. And I doubt that he was talking to me. We weren't close then. He was older. My guess is that he was talking to our brother Danny, who was closer to Stevo's age, and that I was sitting nearby, listening.

If I were to guess again, I would say we were in a car, Danny at the wheel of his 1958 Chevy sedan, Stevo riding shotgun, pontificating with lots of hand motion and no eye contact. I was likely in back. But that is only a feeling, because this first lecture is disembodied in my memory, just Stevo's words describing an old rocker who was "better than Elvis." This was no recommendation. The Elvis I knew made bad movies and sappy ballads.

Though I have no visual of Stevo talking—only that vague sense of a moving car—I recall exactly the visual I formed of this Chuck Berry fellow. For me "Chuck" meant blond, with freckles. Chuck was the catcher on my little league team. Chuck was the actor who played "The Rifleman" on TV. So the mental image I formed was a 1950s rocker, tall and a bit menacing, with Connors' high cheek bones—David Bowie with a blond pompadour. He wore a checkered shirt and played an acoustic guitar.

Then one day I was listening to the beginning of The Mike Douglas Show, a daytime talk show and after school favorite of mine. I liked Mike. He seemed genuinely nice, and took time to talk to the musicians who appeared on his show.

This time I have actual memories. It is before my parents separate. I am in the swanky, suburban rambler that we occupy from the time I am nine until I am fourteen. I am listening to the chatter of a small black and white television when the announcer says that Chuck Berry will be on today's show. That gets my attention.

It is October 22, 1970. Four decades later I learn the date from a reference book and, through the miracle of YouTube, I watch again.[1]

Mike Douglas sits with Cher and Sonny. He says: "In the rock era of the fifties he was an innovator, with tunes like 'Maybellene,' 'Rock and Roll Music,' and 'Johnny B. Goode.' Here is Mr. Chuck Berry!" Sonny and Cher applaud without enthusiasm.

Chuck is standing on a series of risers that look like giant building blocks about four feet tall and three feet square. He's crowded by the mic stand. One misstep and he's an innovator with a limp.

He's wearing yellow pegged slacks that tighten about three inches above his shoes and show skinny ankles. He's got the purple paisley shirt I will later see in hundreds of pictures and at a couple of performances over the next 20 years or so. His upturned pencil mustache is mimicking Salvador Dali or Chaplin's Monsieur Verdoux. He has giant sideburns and slicked back hair. He has the high cheek bones I envisioned, and he might have freckles, but the pompadour is not blond.

The guitar intro is flawless. When he starts to sing, he recoils from the volume, but someone adjusts it and he settles into a grim, nearly joyless performance of "Johnny B. Goode." No wonder I wasn't overly impressed. The band plays a lifeless arrangement with bass and drums that are too neat and horns that are dorky. (A comment posted on YouTube says: "Man, that band is really dragging Chuck down. That bass player flat sucks!") During the instrumental break Chuck has to climb down from the riser without tripping over his guitar cord and killing himself, all the while picking a complicated solo. You can see his relief when he finally gets to the stage where he can dance and do his trademark "scoot," in which he propels himself across the stage, squatting, one foot extended forward, all the while playing lead guitar. With his too short pants he looks a bit like what Michael Jackson will look like ten or eleven years later in the *Motown* 25th anniversary show, except these pants are not stylish.

I watch, interested, but unchanged.

Why I remember that show I'm not sure. I had no real stake in Chuck Berry then. The obsession didn't hit until four months later, in winter. It is a testament to what Stevo told me about the man that I filed away fragments of this event as a lifelong memory. It is as if Stevo's words were an injection of live virus for which I had no antibodies. My coming fascination, though not yet in full bloom, was now embedded.

A few months later, in December, on the other side of the same split-level rambler, I'm awakened by loud music and voices. This has to be just days or weeks before our life at that house will end—days or weeks before we will leave my father and move to the old Victorian farm house on the edge of town. It can't happen too soon. The house and our life in it have become disturbing. There's too much craziness. Even the dark paneling on this side of the house—the side where I sleep—is nightmarish. In my young mind the dark waves of wood grain are like shrieking ghosts, the incarnation of what scares me about our life in this place.

This night Stevo and Danny are in the sunken, paneled room where my father usually watches television. It's around midnight. Danny and Stevo are watching the Dick Cavett show at high volume. They are laughing and talking. I sleep in the next room, but as Chuck says, "no use of me complaining, my objection's overruled." I get up and walk to the den, bleary with interrupted sleep.

I remember colored stage lights and glinting chrome. "Who is this?" I ask. "Chuck Berry," says Stevo. He's not lecturing now; he's annoyed at my interruption.

It's a color television, and a more exciting performance than I saw on Mike Douglas. I've learned since that Chuck was playing the brand-new song "Tulane," which some consider the last great Chuck Berry song.[2] My granddaughter's middle name is Tulane. It is a thrilling tribute, and she lives up to the moniker. But this is 39 years before Leila Tulane will be born. I watch, but I am too groggy to be affected. I go back to bed and to sleep.

And then, (because all of this happens over a fall and a winter,) maybe a few months later, Stevo again holds forth on Chuck Berry. I know this is later because we have left the suburban rambler. We are living in changed and changing circumstances—released from a five year nightmare of alcohol and insanity in the suburbs. The drunken howling is no more. The scary paneling is behind me. My mother, my sister Ann, and I have moved, just weeks prior, to a dream world: the Victorian farmhouse in Orangevale, with a three story tower, a rock garden, small pastures, and barns.

Stevo must be visiting. He has his own apartment—one of the dozens he occupied in those years. We are in the living room. Stevo is by the door. He moves from the door to the piano, waving his hands, lecturing again.

Stevo is short, stocky, and Irish in a half Irish family where the men tended to be tall and (in our youth) lean. He's got a mustache and goatee. He wears his brown hair pushed back, a bit like the man he's talking about. Stevo is giving us a continuation of the same lecture he started months before: Chuck Berry 101. He's describing a show he attended at the Fillmore in San Francisco, a show that was mostly blues.

"He's not really a blues guy," says Stevo, "not like Muddy Waters, or B. B. King, or Bobby 'Blue' Bland." Stevo, at age 20 or 21, has been toughened by fights and car crashes and stints in jail. His face is scarred. There is a half circle punched into his cheek by the steel rim of a steering wheel hub.

"You can tell he came up playing in blues clubs," he tells us. "He knows that stuff. He's good at it, too."

Stevo probably knows nothing about Chuck Berry's actual and specific history—how he started in North St. Louis and East St. Louis, playing blues and bits of country music at places like The Crank Club and the Cosmopolitan—but he'd seen Chuck Berry play a bluesy set and had processed it through his tremendous stores of pop culture knowledge and is here to testify, to teach, to bear witness. He leans over my mother's old baby grand piano and picks out a bit of two or three fingered boogie-woogie.

"He ain't a bluesman, but he can play it! He's good at it!"

I'm 14 years old. I don't know what a bluesman is, or who Bobby "Blue" Bland is, or that the boogie-woogie music Stevo is playing is what formed the backbone to so many of Chuck Berry's early rock 'n' roll hits. But Stevo's words have altered me. He has planted the seed of the first great "special interest" to capture my autistic mind. A few months later, in downtown Sacramento, I will feel a raw, loud guitar pouring double blue notes through the doors of an old civic auditorium, and when I push those doors open, my life will change forever.

8

Positive Traits of Autism

It is what a former vice president might call a "big fucking deal" to learn, at age sixty-five, that you are autistic. It shakes you up. It creates a new world order, or at least a new personal one, which is the same thing. It shifts your every paradigm. You are the same person, but different. You suddenly understand yourself and your life. You suddenly understand your insanely intense interest in Chuck Berry. You suddenly understand why you are so good with facts and so good at your job. You suddenly understand why you were so bad with girls and so often surprised by them.

You start to forgive yourself.

And if you're autistic, you can't stop thinking about this new version of you. You can't stop studying, and learning, and purchasing books—because that is one of the things autistic people do. We do our research. We also sometimes talk about our research and our interests, so if you're autistic you can't help wanting to talk about it, too much, the way you used to talk about Chuck—because, as Joe told Barack, this is a "BIG FUCKING DEAL!"

But you are sixty-five years old, and you learned a long time ago that Gemma has heard enough about "your stupid Chuck Berry," and that Rebecca might disown you if you mention Chuck's old Silvertone. So even though you want to talk about it, a lot, you bite your tongue when you can.

But autistic! At sixty-five!

If, like me, you were born mid-century and turned sixty-five in the 2020s, it is likely your early introduction to autism, sometime in the late 1960s or early 1970s involved bleak stories of children unable to speak or communicate with the world—television news broadcasts in blurry black and white that portrayed autism as a kind of living death to a soundtrack of teardrops splashing from a musical saw. Autism does limit the capacity of some people to speak, but they are very much alive, and usually listening and observing intently. I recently saw a news story about a non-speaking autistic woman who was valedictorian of her high school class and who used voice technology to deliver an eloquent and moving graduation speech.

If you were born mid-century, you might later have seen the movie *Rain Man* and learned something about "autistic savants," people who do complex mathematical calculations instantly, or can tell you what day March 2 fell on in 1264, or have total recall, or play Beethoven perfectly and without lessons. These are impressive people, but we do not all have their particular skillset.

If you are my age you would have eventually heard people claim that autism is a form of brain damage caused by vaccines or environmental exposures. It is not. Autism is genetic, and useful enough to humanity to have survived natural selection. *Someone* needed to discover gravity. Someone probably even needed to destroy Twitter.

As years passed, you, the baby boomer, would learn something of "Asperger's," the "syndrome" named after the Austrian doctor who first described highly intelligent children with a medley of social and cognitive differences. I first heard about Asperger's from a client whose son was diagnosed with it. I remember being dubious. He seemed like a normal enough kid. The term Asperger's is falling out of favor. It is no longer a separate diagnosis, and there is historical evidence that Hans Asperger cooperated with the Nazis to preserve his career and even referred children to a clinic where some would be murdered.

But no matter when you turn or turned sixty-five, you can now find a lot of new, interesting information about autism online, most of which is far less negative than what I'd seen just six or seven years before my "diagnosis," and some of which is downright positive. Maybe it represents a new outlook on neurodiversity. Maybe it represents the pride of neurodivergent people, who are finally taking control of their own narrative. At any rate, soon after my visit with the therapist I found an article online posted by the Asperger/Autism Network, or AANE, talking about the "strengths" of Autistic people.[3] That was new for me, and welcome.

What I call an article was really a list of bullet points. I read it with excitement but also caution, because I didn't know if it was grounded in science or just the creation of some optimist—but whatever the origin, the list felt like me, especially in the context of my work, where all these strengths came into play. Reading it, I began the slow process of accepting the mantle of autism.

The first part was about intelligence and special interests.

"Average to very high intelligence." Check! The latter! That's me, for sure. The nuns told me!

"Good verbal skills; rich vocabulary." Indubitably.

"Ability to absorb and retain large amounts of information, especially about topics of special interest." I rest my case with four words: Charles Edward Anderson Berry. I've made a lucrative career out of absorbing and retaining large amounts of information.

The list continued with the *"Ability to think in images."* Here I was initially less certain. Dr. Temple Grandin, the autistic agricultural engineer and professor, has written about thinking in pictures, and has described her thoughts as being like full color movies, with sound, run on a VCR inside her head.

I do not have that VCR in my head. I dream in vivid and lifelike technicolor, but my visual memories are mere hints of dark, grainy, slightly moving pictures that I can summon but that I can't study or look at. As soon as I "see" them, they are gone.

But though I don't look at my thoughts or memories, I once used the visual image of a "peach" on an old t-shirt as a sort of mental file folder for an intriguing drawing of a gas tank and shield—a drawing that would reveal its secrets to me years later in a startling epiphany. Does that count as thinking visually? In my work I saw details in old, blurred, high contrast photocopies that had evaded other people for years, and later I used my visual sense to make those discoveries easily visible to others. Does that count as visual thinking? And back in my Africa days, I used my talent for chalkboard drawings to teach English vocabulary and grammar to Togolese school children. All these stories in due time.

Another thought about visual thinking: part of my ability to search quickly through reams of documents is based on the image those documents present. When looking at unfamiliar documents for the first time I don't look for words so much as shapes—I learn to recognize the shape of a crash test report, for example; or minutes of a particularly important group; or the pinched, scribbled handwriting or single-spaced typing of a truth-telling fanatic. So the visual shape of documents becomes important to me. But when I do search for words, those words often pop from the page, the way Chuck Berry's name used to pop from the pages of Variety and Billboard magazines I found at the library. When in the zone, I simply have to tell myself in advance which words I'm looking for and my brain finds them, or they find me, with little effort on my part. I also remember how the unpainted metal door of an add-on fuel tank on a neighbor's truck presented itself to me in a heartbeat as soon as I needed it, even though I'd never given it a moment's thought until then— just something I walked past every day with no thought or understanding about what it was. Again, I will tell you about these things in due time.

So though I cannot watch videos in my head like Temple Grandin, or even focus for more than an instant on visuals in my mind or memory, visual images and visual memories are a huge part of my thinking and have been good to me.

The list said autistic people could be "*self-motivated, independent learners.*" Like so many autistic "traits" this is something that could apply to "neurotypical" people as well as the neurodivergent, but it definitely applies to me. I've taught myself pretty much everything I know, including enough law to pass the bar exam. I taught myself how to play music well enough to get on stage, though I can't read a note and have trouble telling bandmates what notes I'm playing. More recently I became interested in neighborhood birds and taught myself to recognize them.

The list said autistic people tend to think "outside the box" and come up with novel solutions to problems. I've done both my entire career. I have used innovative methods to investigate my legal cases; to create exhibits for motions, depositions, and trial; to find witnesses; and to present my cases to mediators. Once I even helped organize a continuing legal education class for paralegals and younger attorneys that we called "Thinking Outside the Cubicle." When I look back at some of the materials, I might have called the class "Thinking Autistically."

The next section of the article had the title "Strong Focus." Its first bullet point was the "*Ability (in some cases a preference) for spending time alone.*" That is certainly me. I love and need my family and my best friends, but I also love and need to be alone. At the time of my diagnosis, I had worked mostly from home for more than 15 years. Before that on three occasions I was given a suite of offices to myself on a separate floor of our office building—sanctuaries where I could organize both my thoughts and the thousands of documents that we had obtained about Doug's pickup truck. Someone at my office must have understood that, like Greta Garbo in Grand Hotel, I wanted to be alone.

Under "focus" the webpage said autistic people might become interested in "arcane or off-beat fields of knowledge." I again rest my case with Chuck, but I wouldn't have to. Throughout my life I have found dozens of arcane and off-beat interests. The article said that sometimes special interests can be channeled into productive careers. Yep. Exploding pickups. Bad airbags. Bad bottle caps. Another bullet point talked about autistic people's ability to concentrate for long periods of time on reading, experimenting, and writing, which describes a large part of my life.

Some of the points were more personal. The list said autistic people don't waste time on activities that appeal to neurotypical people. True for me. I don't go out with the boys. I rarely watch sports that don't involve a hometown team. I hate shopping (except at music stores and bookstores). I don't do clubs. I don't do sports that involve more than one person. Working with lawyers and listening to them talk, I'm often amazed by all the things they do or have that I don't do or care about: skiing, boating, horse racing, gambling, random sporting events, expensive cars, expensive clothes, cigars, fine wine, partner meetings, lawyer associations, legal conventions—all of it bores me.

The next section of the article was about attention to detail. I would prove this repeatedly in Doug's case when I spotted previously unseen details in the photocopied images of old photographs. Decades later I would use patterns in reported complaints to prove that a certain car tended to accelerate on its own every model year until it was reprogrammed.

Less glamorously the list said autistic people might have the ability to accurately perform repetitive tasks. I'm not proud of this but I can do it and often volunteer to do mind-numbing tasks because I know I'll be the best person for the job. Twice, recently, I volunteered to spend hours with spreadsheets indicating which items we wanted. I have spent months of my life in document warehouses painstakingly looking for needles of truth in stacks of photocopied hay and in later years have spent days and weeks of my life opening nonsensical and irrelevant digital files one painful file and PDF at a time. I do it because it works.

The article said autistic people might have a strong work ethic and a commitment to quality and accuracy. Yep, that's me—if I'm doing what I want to do.

The list continued with various character traits that also struck me as true for me. For example, under the heading, "Unique humor," it talked about things like playing with language to create puns, enjoying sarcasm and satire, and relishing life's absurd moments. What a relief after my earlier research which described autistic people as humorless robots. There were sections on essential honesty and a sense of justice. We all want to be honest and fair, but I'm sometimes honest to a fault and have been known to bring people down by going on about some unfair political or social situation—my idea of small talk.

There were other, similar lists, and all were much more useful and meaningful to me than the negative descriptions of autism I'd found during my earlier foray into online research, and more recognizable to me than the opaque and pejorative language of the diagnostic manual. I could remember using each of these traits in my work on Doug's case and in scores of cases that followed.

9

Little Professor, Little Priest

I want to say there's not much in my earliest years to indicate autism. In pictures I look like a typical buzz cut kid from late 1950s and early 1960s. I'm generally smiling a goofy but happy smile, surrounded by family.

Of course, I operated a rosary repair service at age seven or eight, so that might have been a clue.

When I was born, my poetically inclined dad wrote, "Girls three, boys four, not a bad box score" on the signboard outside his business. We are seven, though Stevo passed long ago. At the time I was born we lived in a small flat top stucco home in Sacramento. Paul, Rooney, and Maggie are the oldest. Stevo was in the middle. I was the youngest, tagging along after Ann and Danny, or pursuing one of my small business enterprises.

I got into the rosary repair racket after I broke my own hand-me-down set of black beads and my mom introduced me to needle-nosed pliers. I remember feeling grown up as I carefully bent the broken link back into a closed loop. That was the extent of my actual repair work, but I sprang into action, made several fliers, and put a sign on my door. I would have forgotten this particular example of entrepreneurship but for Ann, who has forgotten nothing.

I was a holy and religious child but not immune to the lure of sin, especially in pursuit of religious commerce and craftsmanship. Once, during a rare "family rosary," (we knelt in a big circle and prayed it together,) everyone ran out into our backyard to investigate some noise. I stayed behind and deliberately yanked apart our brand new, giant-sized, glow-in-the-dark family rosary so I could come to the rescue and repair it. My father was not pleased. I still remember the day he came into our classroom to sell children the glowing rosaries as part of a church fundraiser. The rosary had greenish, glow-in-the-dark, diamond shaped beads and the storage case was a foot tall plastic Jesus statue—in other words, a terrific piece of art that today would be worth real money in any secondhand store with a sense of humor.

Many autistic children are lonely. They go to school and find themselves shunned for one weird thing or another. Maybe they do some funny repetitive motion. Maybe they talk too loudly. Maybe they talk too much about telescopes or Chuck Berry. I never had many friends at school, but our home came with enough playmates that I was never lonely. I remember hiding out for a few minutes in the bathroom when shouting and laughter at dinner became overwhelming.

We didn't have air conditioning until I turned nine, so in summer we'd leave the hot town of Sacramento and spend a couple of months in a two-bedroom cabin at Lake Tahoe. Life there was idyllic. Most days we'd visit the beachfront home of a woman who was some sort of relation to my dad. There were inner tubes and a rowboat and a giant prehistoric plywood paddle board. One of the inner tubes had my full name and middle initial painted on it in giant, careful white letters. The lady who owned the house also had a classic wooden speed boat, a long white Cadillac, and a fragrant pantry stuffed with boxes of crackers and other savory delights. The speedboat boat smelled like gasoline, fish, lake water, and bourbon, and sometimes she would take us for a ride into the deep parts of the lake where the water was inky blue. Otherwise, the kids would swim and play in the water while the older folks sat on a shady front porch and drank cocktails—drinks that sounded delicious to me.

Sometimes my mom would take us on hikes into the Desolation Wilderness. Her courage amazes me. Seven kids, all peering down the nearly vertical chute of Mt. Tallac, Tahoe's most dramatic peak.

My father ran a small business selling garden supplies and installing lawns. The business moved back and forth with my dad from Sacramento to Lake Tahoe, and probably stopped with him for drinks at every bar on Highway 50. I don't think the business made much money, but it kept him active and alive—though one of my earliest memories of Daddy trouble was him lying on his back on the floor of the cabin's eating porch while everyone teenage and up went insane with panic.

We knew how to have a good time. On Friday evenings we would drive to Stateline to count the motel no-vacancy signs and look wondrously at a scandalous shop called Tahoe Togs, which had (purportedly) once displayed a topless swimsuit. Other days we would drive around looking at lawns my dad had installed. It only occurs to me now how similar this was to counting exploding pickups on the way to the zoo.

All seven of us attended Catholic elementary school. The important one for our family was a parish my parents helped establish. It is still there—a pretty concrete church building painted white, with a red tile roof and stained-glass windows. The school rooms followed the same general design. The nuns called the open-air walkways between classrooms "cloister walks." At the more Protestant Catholic school that Ann and I attended next, cloister walks were given the irreligious, nearly atheistic name "breezeways."

For a couple of years, I was obnoxiously good at school and earned the blue ribbon of "Honor Student." I was initially brokenhearted because less honorable students were awarded silvery religious medals, which seemed like better prizes to me. Ann and Danny found me in front of the school, sad about my blue ribbon, and explained I had actually "won" the big one.

I have heard some autistic children described as "Little Professor." It's a characterization Hans Asperger himself came up with. I'm afraid that was me. In third grade two eighth grade girls assigned to sit with our class during lunch (called "presiders" in the vocabulary of the school; these two were homely and undoubtedly unpopular, and thus resigned to presiding over third graders during lunch recess) put me through my mathematical paces while the other kids were outside doing what real children do— i.e., playing. The presiders called me a "wizard," which made the Little Professor in me shimmer with pride.

The only recess activity I recall in second and third grades was walking shoulder to shoulder with two other boys and chanting, "we don't stop for no-body" in monotone voices as we mowed down classmates who failed to get out of our way, so my suspicion is that I was not only Little Professor but also Little Jerk.

The Lord will forgive me, however, because in addition to being "Little Professor" and "Little Jerk," I was a "Little Priest." I was possessed by intense religious fervor and righteousness. Though I intentionally destroyed rosaries, in the end it was All for the Glory and Honor of God, or, as we wrote in florid letters at the top of each piece of schoolwork, "A.M.D.G.," a Latin acronym that means the same thing.

One nun told my class a story designed to instill more such fervor, along with an unhealthy *soupçon* of racism. She explained that once upon a time in Vietnam, communists found a priest teaching *The Lord's Prayer* to a group of schoolchildren. According to the nun the communists demanded that the priest deny God. When the priest refused, the communists cut off his the tongue with a bayonet. The communists then demanded that the children deny God. When the children also refused the communists poked the children's eardrums with (this nun being incredibly precise and imaginative in her racist propaganda) chopsticks. The nun told us that we should be prepared to suffer similar glory if asked by communists to deny God. What scares me as an adult is that I was entirely ready to submit. I prayed with my resurrected rosary for the strength to have my eardrums punctured, A.M.D.G!

In a less violent demonstration of faith, I became the youngest altar boy at two churches by learning to assist with the Latin mass at age seven. I memorized my part of the mass from a small card that I wish I still retained. *Dominus vobiscum, Et cum spiritu tua. Etcetera.* The priest's words were in black and the altar toddler responses were in red, or *vice versa*. I wore red or black dresses and white blouses, got to pour wine and water over the fingers of the priests, and also got to both light and snuff candles. Both latter tasks were done with a long brass and wood tool that had a bell for snuffing and a thick, protected, extendable wick for lighting. I was so short that I had a hard time reaching the candles at the back of the altar even with the long lighting and snuffing tool. I remember the congregation laughing as I stood in front of the altar and stretched in, trying to light the tall candles lined up in the back. Finally a priest came out and told me to do it from the back of the altar, which I managed to do.

Danny and Ann mocked my piety with a hymn Danny wrote that the two chanted to a Gregorian melody:

> *Peter is an altar boy*
> *Peter fills our hearts with joy*
> *Peter prays on bended knee*
> *Peter says his ro-o-sa-ree-ee-ee-ee-ee!*

I've encountered autistic people who were teased mercilessly at school. I wasn't. The only teasing and bullying I got was for my lack of athletic prowess, but it would never rise to the artistry or cutting edge of Danny's work, so the words could never hurt me.

In addition to being a Little Professor and Little Priest, I was a household media magnate. I edited "newspapers" and wrote and published "books," both novels and fictional non-fiction. I was a little weakling but published an illustrated book on muscle-building. I wrote a science fiction book called *The Fish with Arms and Legs*. I published a newspaper, at least once. I still have several issues of my handwritten newspaper, *The Burgundy News*—all from the same day. In another life I might have been an Irish monk who copied manuscripts. Instead, I created three issues of *The Burgundy News* for March 27, 1965. (Lest you think I was autistic enough to know about Burgundy France, or O'Neil enough to drink Gallo Burgundy at the age of eight, we lived on a curvy little street of flat top homes called Burgundy Way.) I remain proud of the editorial content. The top story of the inaugural and final issue of *The Burgundy News* was the murder of civil rights activist Viola Liuzzo by KKK members in Alabama. Her name never left my memory. Another story included hand drawn photographs from the Ranger moonshot that were taken "about 3 minutes before compact." I carefully transcribed the error in each of the three issues.

After being awarded "Honor Student" two years in a row (the highpoint of my academic career) I skipped mid-year from third to fourth grade and became dishonored and somewhat dishonorable. By skipping me mid-year, they cast me from the relatively secure social position of class dweeb onto the bloody rocks at the bottom of the 4th grade social hierarchy. I became an outcast, or at least recognized myself as such for the first time. My new classmates looked at me with suspicion because I had skipped and because I was bad at playing sports—a skill not required in first, second, or third grades. Fourth graders were assigned a small patch of asphalt with a long diamond painted on it and would use it for kickball. I stood near the diamond and looked longingly towards the part of the playground where primary students played, as usual, without me.

I moved overnight from honor student to barely okay student, chiefly because I moved instantly from simple multiplication, at which I excelled, to long multiplication and long division, which I had never contemplated. My mom helped me through that crisis, but I was never a top student again.

Our school was run with military precision by black-uniformed nuns who rang a brass handbell five times to halt recess. When that bell rang, we were expected to freeze until moments later, when a final clang set us free to line up single file outside our classrooms. Kids would not just stop moving, they would leap into frozen, baroque poses, arms, and legs akimbo, like some Bernini saint in ecstasy, while the nun who rang the bell surveyed her prisoners, looking and listening for the slightest muscle tremor or whisper.

My 4th grade teacher was a four-foot tall, black-robed tyrant with a Latin name. Let's call her Mother Melanoma. I'm sure many remember her fondly. I don't. Once, I tried to give myself a dash of pizazz by signing my homework with the name "Pete" instead of "Peter." Shorty took this as an opportunity to ridicule me in front of the class.

"One among us wishes to be called Pete!" she said, approaching my desk while waving the scandalous sheet. Then, in a line prescient of George Herbert Walker Bush's declaration of "This shall not stand!" she proclaimed:

"This shall not happen!"

Her words had great effect. It was the first and last time I ever referred to myself as "Pete," but it was not the last time one of Jesus's crackpot wives singled me out for ridicule.

The final infamy for me in fourth grade was the annual boxing match. The boxing match was a big deal. They set up a real boxing ring in the old, concrete gym. Everything had the exotic smells of sweat, leather, and canvas. Hundreds of people and parents came. In my mind, now, the adults smoked in the gym and snuck bourbon from flasks. There was noise and excitement.

All of us trained for the event. It was my first time, since it only involved fourth to eighth grade boys. The boys all suited up in glossy shorts and big fat gloves and leather head gear and fought each other to bloodless draws. Every time without fail.

Until it was my turn. I had to fight a legit fourth grader. Puny, but legit. And not that bright, so for all I know he was a legit fifth grader. Since I looked a bit like my older brother Danny, (my dad called us "twins, four years apart") I had the fans on my side as I climbed through the ropes to my destiny. I could hear them shout, "Little O'Neil! Little O'Neil!"

I don't remember the fight itself, but my annihilation must have been convincing. To my knowledge I was the first, the last, and the only boy at our school ever to lose a bout at the boxing match. All other matches ended in ties.

Clumsiness, alas, and lack of hand-eye coordination, are often part of the autistic experience. No blue ribbon for me that night. Not even a St. Christopher medal.

I next demonstrated my sporting inability by playing in the local little league. Every time a teammate got a hit he would run to the assistant coach and ask what his average was. ".345!" the coach would say with a manly grin, or ".454!" I remember the numbers being big and juicy.

I sometimes hit the ball halfway to the pitcher or third baseman. After being called out I would walk optimistically to the coach and ask the same question the other boys asked. Every time the coach told me, "Sorry, Peter, I haven't calculated it yet."

Autistic people often have trouble reading facial cues, but even as an eight-year-old autistic boy I could see from his evasive frown how badly Coach felt about not having done the math.

Finally, one day I got an actual double, or at least there were enough errors on the other side that I made it to second base. When I got back to the dugout Coach was smiling. I can still see it. "What's my average, coach?" I asked, dutifully. ".052" he said with a relieved grin. Since I was just learning long division and hadn't got to decimals or percentages I was perfectly happy with the number.

My father, on the other hand, was a former semi-pro baseball player and U.C. Berkeley track star and would have been less thrilled by my season high .052 batting average, but he was spared actual knowledge. He came to just one of my games and stood scowling with his hands in his pockets a few feet to the left of my terrifying post in right field. The bad thing about being the worst player on the field is that they stick you in a position where nothing happens until, suddenly, something *does* happen, and you have to (a) locate the ball (b) pick it up and (c) hurl it into the dirt a few yards in front of you while run after run scores.

Although I played right field that day, when we got home Daddy complained grumpily that my position was "Left Out."

Perhaps I lacked training. Daddy only played baseball with me one time. There is still a photo somewhere of me dressed in full, oversized baseball regalia—probably an older brother's uniform, since I never rose to a level where I was given more than a T-shirt with a team name on it. In the picture I have a big, goofy grin because of dress-up, so I know that our moment of actual sport had not yet happened. We were in the backyard. Daddy stood a few feet away and threw a soft little pitch that hit me in the eye. I, of course, started to cry, whereupon Daddy waddled away in angry disgust at my tears while my mother, who had played catcher, swabbed them. Thus ended our joint baseball career and any chance of preceding the Griffeys.

My mom, on the other hand, stuck with me. She could "throw like a boy" before it was normal for most women and she tried to teach me to do the same. I'm not sure she succeeded. She was another star athlete. When she met my dad she had never played the game, but they became badminton doubles champions in Sacramento, and later, in her forties, she became a truly fine golfer—the type who shoots in the high 60s and low 70s and wins amateur championships. Mommy came to most of my games, which I've since discovered can be an act of considerable bravery and drudgery involving hours of boredom, terror, and meanness on the part of other parents. I played one more year of little league after we moved. That year I earned an infield position and maintained a batting average above .000 all year long. The highlight of my baseball career was watching an infield fly ball come in my direction while another, meaner mother snarled loudly over and over at me to "*Catch* it! *Catch* it! *Catch* it!"

I did.

At school I was so bad at sports that gym teachers ridiculed me. Our gym teachers were all jerks and criminals and could have been nuns if they had been women. I don't say this lightly. At one school our gym teacher was fired the day his wife showed up at school with black eyes and a swollen face. We all saw her. A few weeks later he was arrested for raping a thirteen-year-old girl. Before his imprisonment he used to watch boys and girls change into gym shorts, and inflicted discipline by lining us up in our underwear and knocking each of us on the head serially with his giant ring. Once he yelled at me during a football game then spent several agonizing minutes kneeling with me, caressing me, and insisting I tell him he was a bear. I refused.

When we picked teams at recess or in gym class kids usually picked me last or next to last. Luckily for me, there were kids who had it worse. I was cute, smart, and in a pinch could be funny, so I was occasionally saved from ultimate humiliation.

My ineptitude allowed me to be a hero on one play during a recess flag football game. My team needed a third reception to get a first down, and someone worked out the perfect trick play—a play that involved me. "O'Neil can hike the ball, then step over the line, turn, and catch it. No one will ever expect that!" I received repeated instruction. "Just step over the line and turn around. Just turn around! And catch the ball." Sure enough no one expected I'd have an actual role in the game and somehow I caught the ball.

You can gauge the magnitude of my athletic deficits by the fact that my two most memorable moments in sport involved actually catching a ball.

My parents were older when I was born—my dad fifty-five, and my mom forty. They'd been married fourteen years. Both my parents graduated from good schools—U.C. Berkeley and Stanford—but my mother was the brains of the operation. She had an eye for real estate. Before I was born my family lived on seven acres on what was then the outskirts of Sacramento. My dad ran his business there and installed a community baseball diamond. There are old home movies in fading color showing parades of cars from the late 1940s and early 1950s arriving for opening day of the little league season. He built it and they came.

Around the time of my birth my parents leased those seven acres to a Chevrolet dealer named Lew Williams. This fact would inject some mystery into my career decades later when we took the deposition of one time Chevrolet General Manager Robert Lund. That story will come in due time.

The lease pushed my parents firmly into the middle class and they moved our family into a flat top home just behind the dealership—nine people, seven of them kids, in three bedrooms and 1200 square feet. As long as we were in that house life, for me, was uncomplicated and happy. But before the lease ran out, my parents sold the lot to the same dealer. That pushed them into the upper middle class, and we moved again to a swanky neighborhood about a mile away, with giant lots and houses that seemed to ramble forever. It was such a fine suburb my father called it "the country."

We moved into the big new house on my ninth birthday. For some reason, my sister Ann, my dad, and I were the first to move in. The three of us went over at night to camp on paper wrapped mattresses before the rest of the family arrived. That night would be an epiphany for me.

Ann and I were all giggles and excitement as we entered through a back door and walked down a long, dark hallway with cork floors and dark modern wood paneling. Daddy followed behind. My room would be in this dark, newer wing. The paneling was foreboding, with wood grain that looked like shrieking ghosts.

At the end of the hall the floor sloped a bit into the older part of the house. Daddy, who undoubtedly had already had a few drinks, was surprised by the slope and dropped his whiskey bottle. It broke into a thousand tiny shards on the cork floor, which was laid over concrete.

This is the very moment I recognized Daddy had a problem. I must have known for a long time, but that night it hit me like a freight train. What I remember is kneeling on the floor as he angrily directed my work cleaning up the bits of glass and the stinking liquid. Daddy was pissed in more ways than one. In 1965 there was no such thing as an all-night liquor store so he had few options except to shout and bear it. I resented him barking orders. I resented the shards of glass. I resented the smell of whiskey soaking into the cork. As I knelt on the floor picking up bits of glass, I understood for the first time that the familiar sharp smell of bourbon was at the root of Daddy's problem.

For Ann, it was probably worse. I have learned, since writing this, that for her this was not the end of innocence, or the moment that she learned about Daddy's problem—it was the moment she learned that a move to a new, more luxiurious house would not erase the it.

Over the next five years things got a lot worse. Daddy no longer worked, so there was time for lots of drinking and that's what he did. He made tall glasses of Diet-Rite, Old Crow bourbon, and ice that he carried through the house slowly with a shaking hand, the tinkling sound announcing his approach. He disintegrated in front of our eyes, becoming a laughingstock for the remaining kids. The laughing saved us. In high school I would write a song called "Skeleton Key." It was based on a quote from George Bernard Shaw who said, "If you can't get rid of your family skeleton, you may as well make it dance." We did exactly that.

The skeleton was less funny when I had to change its wet under-wear as a ten or eleven-year-old while he slurred the words "you're a good boy," or when five or six of us would team up in a fruitless effort to pull him off the floor, or when ambulances arrived, or when priests came with balm and prayers only to find him revived and raring to go. (I wrote another song called "Daddy Lazarus.")

I stayed at my second Catholic elementary school from fifth through seventh grades and made some progress socially in 6th and 7th. That was the only elementary school where I stayed in one class for three straight years. It seemed to help.

In sixth grade I worked up the courage to ask one of the prettiest girls in class to "go steady." I bought a hideous purple enamel ring at the local White Front store (I found it tasteful) along with some chocolate stars. I wrapped them in purple tissue paper and managed to sneak the package into the girl's desk under the nose of our wonderful teacher, a gruff, bald World War Two veteran who pretended not to see. She responded with a note agreeing to go steady but added, "We have to keep it a secret!" They say autistic people are prone to taking things literally. I kept the secret so literally and so well, even from the girl, that she called off our romance with a kind note a few weeks later.

I earned social points in seventh grade by "winning" two fights against bigger, taller, stronger boys—one of them the biggest, strongest kid in the class. This is another way that being the youngest of seven kids helped me. For a couple of years my brother Danny was a terror. When I was 11 he was 16. I remember laying on the ground while Danny, enraged, squeezed my neck with the apparent goal of extinguishing life. This unfortunate experience became happier when one of the neighbor kids laughed at my predicament. Suddenly brotherly love and loyalty took over. Danny let go of my neck and chased the now screaming neighbor kid back to his house. He laughs best who breathes again enough to laugh last.

The seventh graders who wanted to fight me were bigger than me, but they weren't Danny, so I stood my ground and hurled feisty insults at both kids as they each struck out swinging and missing. I was declared winner of both fights, at least by the excited outcasts and misfits who became my retinue afterwards.

That year, for the first time, I started to find a place among the "cool" kids. My friend Kevin and I went trick or treating with two of the cutest girls in class, Janice and Mindi. Later I was accepted into the upper echelons of cool by being allowed to buy a Beatles album for our poor nun, a nice young woman who sometimes showed up to class in tears, and who was obviously being tortured by her elders. We conspired to make her feel better. The king of cool pulled rank and bought her the brand-new *Magical Mystery Tour*. I was happy to buy her *Sergeant Pepper*, which I knew was older but better. A few days later the young nun was disappeared by the convent, and we never saw her again. I hope she quit the order and went on to have a wonderful life, but for all we knew they snuffed her.

The same nuns that tortured her tortured me. The "superior" sister put me in detention all day because she didn't like my shoes—black ACME boots she called "Beatle boots" despite the rounded toes. I sat in the "vestibule" of the principal's office all day long. My mom was so angry she sent me back to my original school the following year.

I liked the idea because Danny had done it, and because it meant long bike rides to school every day, which I spent studying new cars in the dealerships along that strip of road, but it was not the wisest decision. I moved from junior dating and the edge of cool at the one school to the very bottom of a slippery social ladder back at the other, where I no longer knew anybody but the puny kid who beat me in the fourth-grade boxing tournament.

My first day in eighth grade my home room nun, Sister Catherine, proposed a "popularity bulletin board" where she would rank us top to bottom. As the newest member of the class I knew exactly where I would wind up, but I had already figured out who the "most popular" were, (Barbie and Adonis,) so I dutifully put their names on my secret ballot.

I only had three acquaintances that year, all outcasts. The juvenile delinquent smoker and I would meet up behind the Catholic girls' high school next door after school and smoke Camel cigarettes. A very effeminate, very tall boy with bad acne stood and talked with me a bit during recess, since we were not invited to play sports and had no desire to do so. My third acquaintance was the boy who beat me in the boxing ring. He had remained roughly the same size and still had, roughly, a fourth-grade intellect, so I probably should have asked for a rematch, but instead he became the closest thing to a real friend I had that year. The main thing I remember is that he wanted to explore the local creek system in the sort of plastic swimming pool boat that was popular in those days.

I can see the headline:

LOCAL BOYS, LIKELY AUTISTIC,
PERISH IN CHICKEN RANCH SLOUGH.

I had the coolest bike in the school, inherited from my mom, who found it abandoned somewhere—an old English racer, all gears removed, spottily painted in flaking silvery-gray, and topped with tall handlebars from a Schwinn Stingray. It was, in the language of the day, *bitchin'*. So bitchin' that Adonis and his sidekick would steal it every day at lunch time. To my credit I asked them to stop, and to their credit, they stopped when I asked.

It was a bad year. The nun who wanted to create the popularity bulletin board hated me. One day she made fun of me in front of the class for reading Eldridge Cleaver's *Soul on Ice*. She should have given me extra credit for reading an adult book about race in America. Another time I politely asked if I could get a drink of water and she said, "Yes, and I hope it has arsenic in it!"

Revising this chapter I now see that this woman's hatred for me was likely a response to her perception of some difference in me that she simply didn't like. I caused her no problems. I was quiet in class. I got decent grades. I behaved well at school. But she clearly valued popularity, and thus, neurotypicality.

So I reacted in a way that I now see was a thoroughly autistic response to mistreatment and the misery of being in her class.

I stopped going to school all together. I cut class for more than a month. Every morning I'd call in sick from a pay phone. I rode my bike to all parts of Sacramento and its suburbs and spent my days doing exactly what I wanted. I enjoyed my last day of freedom looking at minibikes for sale at a lawnmower shop in the far suburbs. The minibikes were the cool, expensive ones with front and rear suspensions. I got home and found Ann laughing gleefully.

"We know all about you!" she sang, tauntingly. Peter, who no longer prayed on bended knee, was still the object of singsong torture.

It turned out my mom didn't believe the principal and went to school to wait for me to exit my class. She came home in tears.

Somehow the school let me graduate. Remember, my parents helped found this church and school, sent seven kids there, donated generously, and raised money for the church and school for decades. A less connected kid who did the same thing would have been flunked or suspended. I was allowed through to graduation.

Things can go south for you in a heartbeat if you are an outsider, but my lucky streak continued.

If I was on the autism spectrum, no one told me, and if I was an outsider, I didn't worry about it much. Life at home was pretty crazy and would become crazier as more alcoholics joined the party, but it was also full of life, laughter, love, art, music and acceptance. It was a good start, and one I'll always treasure despite the trauma and craziness.

And although it would get crazier as I moved into high school, it would also get better, because I found the exact right right school—Peach Tree.

10

Finding Myself in a "Diagnosis."

As I autistically studied autism, (we do our research,) I recognized dozens of quirks and traits in myself that I had known and spoken about most of my life. Some had served me well. Others, not so much.

The *American Psychiatric Association's Diagnostic and Statistical Manual, Fifth Edition,* or DSM-5,[4] is the diagnostic bible for mental conditions. I became aware of the DSM early in my legal career because many of our clients suffered from post-traumatic stress disorder. The DSM-5 calls my neurotype Autism Spectrum Disorder, or ASD. I resent the term "disorder." I prefer to think autism is just a difference, often a good one, and a difference that has served humanity well enough to survive natural selection. *Someone* needed to discover relativity.

The DSM's diagnostic criteria for ASD are divided into parts A and B. Part A is about social abilities—or in the words of the book "Persistent deficits in social communication and social interaction across multiple contexts." In my view, the DSM-5 suffers from persistent deficits in *written* communication, with language that is obtuse, clinical, pejorative, and hard for laypeople to understand. I had to buy a book by another autistic person that translated the DSM into normal language to start making sense of it—but I understood "deficits in social communication and social interaction" immediately. I've had them my entire life.

Rebecca considers me a misanthrope. I am not a misanthrope, but it's true that I like people best when they come solo or in small batches. I don't do casual friendship well. I don't ask coworkers to lunch—nor do they ask me. I rarely go drinking with the boys. I hardly even know the boys.

Except for playing music, which for me is necessarily collaborative because of limited skill and a bad singing voice, even my hobbies and interests are solitary. I like to read, write, and listen to music. Most of my life I have jogged long distances, alone. Now I walk for miles, usually alone. I used to hit golf balls at the range and might have enjoyed golf except that I'm intimidated by foursomes.

I was the same as a kid. One of my hobbies was stargazing. It still is when I can find dark, clear skies. You can't get more alone than to sit under the night sky with a companion that is a hundred million light years away.

Part A describes other aspects of my personality—difficulty with eye contact, and, at times in my life, difficulty understanding gestures.

Part B of the diagnostic criteria is more specific and describes "*Restricted, repetitive patterns of behavior, interests, or activities.*"

One subpart of B is a cinch—what the DSM describes as "*Highly restricted, fixated interests that are abnormal in intensity or focus,*" or what are sometimes called "special interests." My special interests are a huge part of this story and my life, and the first big one is obvious to all who really know me. As the great 1970s funk singer and songwriter Betty Davis screams at the climax of "They Say I'm Different," (a funk blues anthem for the autistically inclined blues fan,) "Chuck Berry! Chuck Berry! Chuck Berry!"

The other parts of part B were initially harder for me to recognize. "Stereotyped or repetitive motor movements, use of objects, or speech." I want to say I don't do any of the well known autistic "stimming" activities like rocking or flapping my hands—but I have a lifetime of habits that probably qualify as stimming that include drumming with my teeth, playing solitaire, noodling aimlessly on the guitar, and breaking twigs into tiny pieces as I sit on the grass or walk. In the past I used my thumbnails to make elaborate patterns on empty Styrofoam cups. (Happily for the environment, sadly for me, I don't encounter many Styrofoam cups these days.) All these habits involve "repetitive use of objects," and I have recognized all my life that these activities help me become or remain calm.

Another section of part B talks about "Insistence on sameness, inflexible adherence to routines," and includes "extreme distress at small changes." At the start of my exploration, I felt certain this wasn't me. I acknowledged having my own gentle routines. I like a slow start in the morning with coffee and news. I like a slow end to the day with streamed television, a book, and sleepy time tea. But I don't suffer "extreme distress" if I break those routines—just moderate distress and a healthy level of irritation.

Eventually I recognized what my family has always known. I have my special spots at the table and around the house. Rafferty knows how irate I can be if I see him occupying my spot on the red couch. And I clearly value stability. I've lived in just two houses since I turned 27, and have had some version of the same job at some version of the same place with some version of the same people ever since that time, too.

The final section of part B talks about "Hyper- or hyporeactivity to sensory input or unusual interests in sensory aspects of the environment." Once again, it is hard to find myself here, though the author of a book on late diagnosis of autism mentioned that a distaste for haircuts might qualify, and that is definitely me; I have had exactly one professional haircut since 1980 and I remember everything about it with distaste, from the light touch of the haircutter's fingers to her breath and body odor. (I have similar memories of earlier haircuts.) The rest of the time I cut it myself—a skill I taught myself during my years as a Peace Corps Volunteer in West Africa but perhaps didn't master. I also hate loud interiors such as restaurants designed to amplify the clatter of plates and conversation. I recently fled an art show in a small gallery because the hubbub at the crowded opening was too much for me to handle.

The better sources of information for me were outside the confines of the DSM-5 in books, articles, videos, and Facebook posts written by autistic people.

First and foremost—I've always felt different, an outsider. Every autistic person I have encountered describes this feeling. I'm never sure where I fit with any group that is not my family, but I know that it's off to the side, and I often feel uncomfortable, though I've learned to participate when I have to. My anxiety dreams are often about finding myself in a group, usually at work or at school, and feeling awkward.

I've often been made to feel like an outsider, too. I remember countless times when some gregarious person shakes my hand and settles down to talk to me and I watch them gradually come to the conclusion that "this guy is a little weird."

I don't like eye contact, though I've gotten better at it with time. It's something I think about while it's occurring. Same with small talk. These are classic autistic traits. I'm better than I used to be, but I notice a tendency to make my small talk about deep and disturbing stuff like politics, religion, climate change, or racism, and I notice as people gently draw away from the subjects that interest me or redirect the conversation to smaller, lighter subjects that don't.

I rarely smile to the satisfaction of others, and when I see a picture of myself trying to smile, I always hate it. This, too, is commonly cited as an attribute of autistic people. I have practiced smiling in front of the bathroom mirror, always to unhappy, strained effect. Toothy smiles, which I admire in photographs of others, are particularly hard for me. When I practice in front of the mirror my lips look like they are under the control of some unseen dentist who is using an unseen device to pull my lips from in front of my teeth. I'm often criticized for failing to smile in pictures, but I know better than to even try. On the other hand, if something causes me to naturally smile, I have no problem with it, or with a photograph of the result.

As a very young college student I suddenly found myself very much alone and couldn't figure out how to break the code of sociability. I'll write more about that later. And although I think I always understood facial gestures such as smiles, frowns, and winks, I didn't always understand them in the context of me. Why did she wink at *me*? More about that later, too, and consistent with being autistic.

Parties and gatherings wear me out. Sometimes after a gathering where I've been more gregarious than usual, I fall into a brief depression. Other times I just need to escape. This, too, appears to be common for people on the spectrum, in part a consequence of the energy required to be gregarious or to appear "normal."

I've told several people over the years that I had to "learn to operate my hard to operate persona" to get by in the world. I had to learn to recognize social cues, to respond appropriately, to make eye contact, to make small talk, and to take chances socially. Oddly, I have never had difficulty operating within the context of my work. I easily take over meetings, joke with experts, and play hardball with opposing counsel—but if there is a drink afterwards, I might have a hard time.

My first marriage and first long-term relationship were with a person from another country and culture. I have read that this is common for autistic people. In another country and culture our quirks and differences are harder to spot. While living in Africa I had to learn a whole new set of rules for dealing with people socially—new handshakes and greetings, new rules for dating, new rules for eating and talking. More about that later, but I think the experience made it easier for me to do new things generally.

I have read that some autistic people hang onto bad relationships long past their expiration date. I did that with my first marriage.

Clumsiness and a "funny" walk are common attributes of some, but not all, autistic people. Some autistic people have poor spatial abilities. I am the only person I know who occasionally bumps into the walls of a long hallway, but I read a post of another autistic person who does the same thing. I hate it when a hiking trail crosses a creek and requires me to balance on a log or big rocks. I walk without much arm movement—something that's been pointed out more than once on more than one continent. I was bad at sports as a child and didn't get better with age. My early memories of sports and PE are traumatic enough that I still refuse to join in the neighborhood Turkey Bowl football game.

I talk to myself constantly, especially when walking or driving alone. Rather, I talk with people constantly—friends, family members, enemies—but they are not there. These internal monologues help me process ideas and feelings and get ready for the next real-life conversation. I liked the early days of Covid because wearing a mask outside allowed me to move my lips without anyone seeing—and when I shared that with people on an autistic social media site, several people agreed. When I'm talking to myself in the car, I quiet down at stoplights so people won't think I'm crazy.

I prepare for important conversations by rehearsing my part in detail. Another autistic trait. I even prepare for tiny, nearly meaningless exchanges. Before I go into a shop I often walk myself through what I will say to the clerk. "Can you tell me where to find batteries? Can you tell me where to find batteries?" On the job I prepare every question of a deposition in advance. I often leave the script but writing what I expect to ask helps me be prepared to "wing it" once the deposition begins. When I wanted to learn to speak Italian better I began talking to myself in Italian. It worked! I'd work out how to say what I wanted to say in advance so that when I finally spoke to someone I was ready.

I have a terrible time recognizing people out of context—even people I've worked near or lived near for years. I go into a sort of panic if I see someone that I might know approaching, because I'm so often unsure. This, too, has been mentioned in writings about autism.

Sometimes people talk about a flat or "robotic" way of speaking as a sign of autism. I don't think I have that, but when I record my voice to make settlement films, I speak in a monotone drone in what I admit is an effort to sound like the narrator in the PBS documentary series Frontline. I don't know if I speak that way all the time, but I don't think so.

People on the spectrum talk about "melt downs." Although I'd like to deny it, I have had a few "melt downs," though not many; but when they happened they took me completely by surprise and shook me to my core. I couldn't explain them even to myself. And, of course, I remember my single parent meltdowns, where I lay in the dark to restore my cool. What feels more familiar to me is the concept of autistic "shutdowns." I know that when I've had my limit I can fall into stoney silence, need absolute quiet, or perhaps a guitar to noodle on.

Verbal instructions are hard for me to follow—another autistic trait. If I ask directions, I usually only try to grasp the general direction of travel and the first turn. Everything else becomes a blur. Rebecca, a marathoner, likes to give me detailed descriptions of her runs. I just nod as she describes street after street and turn after turn. I absorb none of it.

I recently saw a documentary from the late 1950s where a smart little girl was asked to go to the cupboard and get "three sheets of paper, scissors, and paste." She agrees. She's then asked what she is going to get. "Paste," she says. That's me with too many directions. "Yes, of course. Straight ahead three blocks to the second signal, then turn left, then straight for about six blocks and left again after the laundermat."

What do I remember?

"Straight ahead."

Luckily, this doesn't happen to me in court. If a judge gives an oral ruling I follow every word of it easily—perhaps because I have been prepared in advance by the briefing and arguments.

I have a hard time processing two verbal streams. Probably autism again. If Rebecca speaks while I'm typing an email (which she often does) I will not hear a word she says for the first several seconds and she will be annoyed. If she speaks while I'm reading a news story I hear nothing until I break the spell of the written words. Likewise, if my son speaks while I'm watching the news, I lose track of the news entirely. Difficulty with auditory processing is a common feature of autism.

A similar thing happens with music. I know many people study and read while listening to music. I can't. My mind follows the music instead of the words on the page. But while I hear music well, I rarely hear or understand the lyrics, even in songs that I've played with bands hundreds of times. This can annoy our singers, but it shouldn't. I listen intently to the singing, just not the words.

I want to be respected but I'm mostly uninterested in status. I have read that disinterest in status is a common autistic trait. My clothes are mostly old and cheap. I drive older, economical, low status cars. My primary interest in money I've earned is the freedom it provides. I'm equally unimpressed by the status of others. When I was a paralegal, I remember a lawyer scolding me for not treating his partner with proper deference as my superior. I had only spoken the truth. Later, when I became a newbie lawyer and began to attend attorney meetings, I spoke up immediately, sharing my opinions on whatever matters were under discussion. I was scolded for that, too, and quickly noticed that the other younger attorneys mostly limited their remarks to the words "I concur." I often didn't concur and kept speaking my mind.

When I was a young man of 22 and should have been out collecting girlfriends I wore a gray cotton shirt Chairman Mao would have admired and—get this—glasses that I mended with tape. Shocking that my collection of girlfriends was so small.

I talked about some of this with my therapist. I emphasized the things that didn't seem to fit, like insistence on routine or sensory issues. I told her I wasn't bothered by the diagnosis, but that I didn't want to take something that wasn't mine. My therapist laughed. She told me that I had checked about 11 autistic boxes in the few minutes we took to discuss the issue.

11

Infection

I hear about it on the car radio. It's February 12, 1971. I'm fourteen. I am with my mom. Maybe Stevo told her about Chuck Berry, too, or maybe she's concerned about the recent upheaval in our lives, because she encourages me.

"You should go," she says.

My parents have just separated. My father, who is 70, and weakened in mind and body by decades of alcoholism, has been exiled to a nice apartment where a home health attendant named Jose takes care of him and urges us to take him back. "It's wrong to leave him this way" Jose tells me when I visit. Daddy is on the bed, drunk. Jose wears starched white and looks at me sternly. He probably left his own father in a village a thousand miles away. I'm stung but remain strong. I figure my dad left me, opting instead for gallons of Old Crow that he mixes with tall, tinkling bottles of Diet Rite Cola.

Only Ann, my mom, and I live at the Orangevale house, but an earthquake in Los Angeles has brought my oldest sister, Rooney, home for a visit. (She doesn't know, but she will never go back to her husband or to Los Angeles.) I ask her to take me to the show. I'm too young to drive. Ann, who is two years older than me, comes, too. We arrive downtown late but have no trouble parking next to the concert hall. That should tell us something about the size of the crowd we will encounter.

The show is at the Memorial Auditorium, a beautiful old place, built of brick and terra cotta, set among trees and green grass in the center of downtown Sacramento. The place reeks of wrestling, boxing, bad opera, and old rock and roll shows.

We get to the lobby ticket window a few minutes after the scheduled start of a three act show. A local group called Slo Loris is supposed to be opening. A kid named Little Dion is the second act. We aren't in a hurry because we only want to see Chuck Berry, and the ticket lady isn't in a hurry because she is not the sort to be in a hurry. But while she counts our change, blues guitar leaks through the auditorium doors.

"Has the show started?" we ask. She's grumpy even though nobody's there to bother her except us. The lobby is empty.

"He started about five minutes ago" she says, without looking up.

"Who started? Chuck Berry?"

"Five minutes ago."

This is alarming news. Chuck Berry is supposed to be on top, the headliner. He's the reason we came. We push open the auditorium door and there he is, seemingly alone on stage, just him and his guitar, singing the blues to a nearly empty auditorium.

That is the moment of infection. If it had happened differently—if I had entered the sort of jam-packed crowd that Chuck Berry usually played in those days, with thousands of people dancing and clapping; if we had been forced to find places for ourselves in some far corner and crane our necks—if had happened differently, I think that my life would have turned out differently. No dreams. No blog. No obsession.

But the huge room is empty—a few hundred people in the front rows, and a few hundred more along the sides and balconies. We walk straight to the seventh or eighth row. There's no need to sit down. There's no one behind us. And the sheer emptiness allows me—forces me—to focus all of my imagination on this man.

And there is Chuck Berry, tall, lean, wearing jeans and an orange shirt, hair slicked back, eyes half closed, high cheekbones tilted at the mic, singing something slow and sad and woeful.

He isn't the man I saw on television. This is someone thoroughly real, alone in a third rate town, backed by a local band, playing to a crowd that hardly qualifies as such. I'm clobbered by the melancholy of it.

His guitar is a cherry red Gibson. It sparkles under the lights. He bends powerful clusters of notes, two or more at a time. It's loud and raw. His voice is mournful and a bit scratchy. It is one of my first introductions to the blues.

Forty years later old posters on the internet will tell me that Chuck Berry played at the Memorial Auditorium at least twice before I saw him there. On August 24, 1957, he costarred there with his idol, Louis Jordan, and singer "Sugar Pie" De Santo. Louis Jordan wasn't just a musical hero for Berry. Jordan's guitarist, Carl Hogan, gave Berry the outlines of Berry's signature guitar intro—the four bar lick that opens "Johnny B. Goode," "Roll Over Beethoven," and about half of Berry's live songs. De Santo—a tiny, beautiful woman with a big voice and stage presence—endured even longer than Berry. Chuck played another show at the Memorial Auditorium on his 31st Birthday, October 18, 1957. (Birthday shows became a tradition. I would go to several half a century later in St. Louis.) I was alive for the 1957 show and like to think hints of the music blew towards my house to plant the first seeds of infection. It was a star studded show with LaVern Baker, Clyde McPhatter, The Everly Brothers, The Crickets, Eddie Cochran, The Drifters, and Frankie Lymon.

In his autobiography Chuck is unkind to Sacramento. (He's not alone in this.) Describing the 1957 tours he says, "It seemed that all the senior citizens were in Sacramento, all the parents were in Fresno, and San Francisco was oriented to natives and beatniks."[5] I find it hard to believe that any senior citizens showed up at the rhythm and blues review in August, or the rock and roll bash that fall. My wild guess is that, 15 years after the fact, Chuck was not so fondly remembering my first Chuck Berry show, on February 13, 1971—a sad show played to a nearly empty hall that felt like an abandoned senior center, or maybe a hospice.

So, we walk into that empty hall and he's playing the blues. Who knows what the song is? Perhaps it's the Tampa Red / Elmore James classic, "It Hurts Me Too."

"When things go wrong, go wrong with you, it hurts me too."

Maybe it's Little Walter's "Mean Old World." Or maybe it's Chuck's own "Wee Wee Hours."

Whatever the song, he knows he's alone here, in an empty hall, in a drab town, with a mediocre band of young local musicians. The band members are scared, but they're trying. And so does Chuck Berry. He pushes through a full set, clowning, dancing, doing splits and the duck walk, getting the small crowd up on its feet for most of the show.

He tries to get the local guitarist to solo. The guy smiles humbly and plunks a single note. (He probably still regrets that impotence.) Chuck laughs and gestures "Why?" But it's the kid's loss. All Chuck Berry needs is his guitar, an amplifier, and a crowd, however sparse. He plays songs I know only somewhat, by cultural osmosis: they're rocking in Boston, and Philadelphia, PA. He plays a couple of songs I think of as Beatles songs and suddenly realize are not. He finishes with "Johnny B. Goode," bowing as he backs off stage, still playing a guitar held upright in front of himself like a religious offering—and then he's gone, like a cool breeze, the band still rumbling away, and finally a story from the emcee about a mix-up in schedules and another show that night in Los Angeles. If there's another show, Chuck Berry probably booked it from a back stage phone when he saw the receipts for that night in Sacramento. We figure he just wants to get out of our geriatric cow town as quickly as possible with whatever small bit of cash it has yielded.

We watch the other acts for as long as we can stand it, but it's a steep downhill slide. The band that backed him returns for some acid rock. When the diminutive Little Dion, perhaps ten years old and dressed in colored tights and a floppy hat, launches into "It's a Man's World," we leave.

12

Special People, Special Interests

The diagnostic criteria for autism includes "highly restricted, fixated interests" of abnormal in intensity. In the literature of autism these are often called "special interests." You may have seen examples on television. The boy who knows everything there is to know about insects. The boy who talks non-stop about Antarctica. The young woman who talks a lot about animation.

For me, of course, the big one— *"the big, big daddy of them all,"* as rock impresario Bill Graham described him on a live album—was Chuck. But Chuck wasn't my only childhood "special interest." As a child and teenager I seemed to be constantly searching, trying things on for size—pigeons, horse-shoeing, panning for gold, photography, astronomy, and telescopes. Only two of these interests stuck. Just yesterday I bought a fifty-three-year-old Newtonian reflector telescope that was built during my astronomical heyday. I am only the third owner.

I've owned a lot of telescopes over the years and tried to build one from scratch when I was a teenager, but I bought my first good one after my mom died using the first bit of my inheritance from her. I was 51. My mom had always supported me in whatever interest I was pursuing, so I wanted to honor her a bit by returning to my roots. Over the next few years I relearned the stars and the constellations and began to track down the faint but beautiful galaxies and star clusters that make up the Messier objects.

In those days Seattle hadn't yet installed bright, white, blinding LED street lights in my neighborhood, so on certain clear dark nights I could set up in a shadow on my front lawn and find distant galaxies, star clusters, and nebulae. If neighbors walked by they would often want to take a look, and I'd show them, even though I knew they would probably not be very impressed by the faint smudge of silver I was gazing at. Rebecca usually can't even see what I'm looking at, but those faint traces of fuzzy, distant, ancient light thrill me to the core.

As I begin leaning towards retirement, I have found new interests. One day midway through the Covid pandemic a noisy, shrill bird caught my ear. I went out onto a small balcony behind our house to investigate. A little purplish-brown bird was standing and screaming on the electrical wire leading to our house. As I watched, a hummingbird came out of the nearby crabapple tree, hovered in front of the brown bird as if taunting it, and darted away. For the next hour or so I watched the two birds exchange places on the wire, wondering if it was good spirited play or a case of real life angry birds. It took a few days before I properly identified the brown bird as a song sparrow and the hummingbird as an Anna's hummingbird, but I got there. Then, as if by magic, I found a picture book of garden birds in one of those free book boxes kind people put in front of their homes. I sat down with it in a nearby park and another little bird landed in front of me. It looked like it was wearing one of those executioner's hoods from movies about the Middle Ages. I searched the book and learned it was an Oregon junko. By now I know every common bird in the neighborhood, and when something interesting wanders in—a western tanager or a spotted towhee—I recognize its uniqueness, learn its colors, and look it up. I own a couple of new bird books and have a phone app for bird identification. I've gotten to be quite efficient at it.

But the reason I'm writing this book is because for 30 years I have earned good money through my special interests. Each time I got a new case that involved a defective product, that product became my new obsession. One day I wouldn't know anything about Ford pickups with in cab tanks; the next day they were everywhere. One day I cared nothing about supposedly child proof bottle caps; the next day I couldn't care more.

Looking back on a lifetime of legal cases and the work I did on them I am often as dazzled as when I find one of those distant nebulae in my telescope and wonder what it represents. When I open an old file (a single case file often fills dozens of boxes) I am amazed by the work, energy, instinct, and imagination I put into each case.

For a time, two people—Paul Whelan and I—accomplished work that entire law firms have tried to do, and we did it better than most. When my sister Ann joined the team, I was able to relax my obsessiveness and let her take on a huge portion of that burden. Ann latches on to a research problem and spends hours, days, weeks, and months working on it, often finding case-settling gold.

I wonder what a person like me or Ann would add to whatever business or profession you are involved in? I wonder what our obsessive natures would bring to your table or add to your bottom line? I wonder why eighty percent or more of autistic people are under or unemployed?

13

My Early Teens

I'm perhaps fifteen—in high school, at any rate. We've moved away from my dad to a beautiful Victorian farmhouse on the very outskirts of town. I've got a piece of paper and a ballpoint pen. I fill a page with a large square. That's my future real estate. At the bottom is a straight country road. I use my pen to plant trees and shrubs along the road for privacy.

I draw a long, curving driveway from the road to a small house. My house. I surround the house with more trees for more privacy. There is room inside for me and the mystery woman who will accompany me. I draw a room that I know is filled with guitars, drums, a keyboard and a four track reel to reel tape recorder. I have vague plans for a lo-fi band called Fuzzy Martin and the Statics. I will use cheap amplifiers and instruments to produce the low quality sound.

Out back is a small wooden structure with a roof that rolls off onto raised wooden tracks. It is my observatory. Inside that shed is a large, homemade telescope bolted to a concrete pier.

I draw rows of garden crops. I am self-sufficient.

I put a gate on the access road. I am safe.

But while the goal is solitude, I am frightened enough of the country and the pickups that hurtle past on that dark road that I draw outlying cottages for close friends and family. I give each its own gravel road.

I knew myself well at age 15—a person who needed both solitude and the love and support of family and a few good friends. I was autistic but didn't know it. And perhaps a bit wary of bringing too many people into a life that had been somewhat crazy.

For years I attributed my lifelong need for solitude to my childhood in an outrageously alcoholic household. There might be some truth to that—it might have been an unconscious effort to protect myself from untrustworthy people.

I recall at age twelve training a classmate to do my paper route. He was going to be my substitute. I'm not sure how or why he got the job—he wasn't my friend. We didn't hang out together. We hardly spoke. He was a chubby, pushy guy, with an awful mom, and with her help (I can still see her sourly pushing him to my front door at the end of the month and forcing me to hand over just about every penny I'd collected) he took nearly all my profits for doing just one day of work each week. (Some customers didn't pay me. I paid my substitute and my distributor, delivered the papers, and at the end of the month when I went out collecting, the deadbeat customers hid from me, sipping desperate gin behind shut doors.) Anyway, one morning at 5 a.m. this unpleasant kid and I were on the front porch folding papers. It was still dark. We were going to strap canvas bags of newspapers to our bikes and ride around the neighborhood and deliver them as gifts to evil deadbeats. Suddenly the front door opened, and there was my dad, in sagging underpants and a t-shirt, swaying, bleary, still drunk enough from the night before to burp and slur his words.

"Wha' tch'ou doing?"

I saw the kid look, bewildered, but with growing understanding, at my dad, drunk at 5 a.m. The boy's eyes swelled with enlightenment.

"O'Neil's dad is a drunk!"

I knew instantly that he'd share this vignette at school.

I once asked a friend named Kevin to spend the night. I'd never done such a thing and I never did it again. It was night and we were in my room when we began to hear howling, banging, and craziness migrate through the house. Kevin was Irish and probably had a life similar to mine. He became very excited. His eyes lit up. He became hyper. He wanted to see what was happening.

I knew all too well what was happening: my kindly old dad was drunk and berserk. I could hear the house erupt in a battle to get him back into his room.

Kevin became diabolical. "What's going on?" he asked, again and again, with a manic grin. He was ready to pop like a party favor. My mom and sister came to my door and told Kevin and me to stay put. I remember my mom's worried face. I suspect my own expression was the same. My father bellowed and howled. There was banging and thunder all over the big house.

That was my last sleepover.

I hung out in the non-fiction part of the library and scoured shelves for anything that interested me. I liked science and practical things. For a few days or weeks, I read all about pigeons and dreamed of building a coop. I read books on astronomy. I'd become interested in some weird topic like horseshoeing, or rabbits, or gold-panning, and try to learn how to do it.

I took my interest in telescopes from my seventh-grade friend, Peter F., whose engineering foundations were more secure than mine. He was a friend I didn't have to worry about. He knew my secrets and I knew his—(chiefly that we stole half a dozen packs of his dad's Tareyton cigarettes and smoked them in a "fort" that we dug behind his house). We could laugh at our problems, even my dad and his drinking. With Peter I could make the skeletons in my closet dance a bit for both relief and amusement.

Peter was a natural engineer and later became a professional engineer. He was the first of many, many engineers I would befriend, at least casually or professionally, over a lifetime. (Engineers and autistic people seem to speak the same language, probably because so many engineers are autistic.) We built mock spacecraft together. He taught me about Estes model rockets. He showed me catalogs from a company called Edmund Scientific, filled with telescopes, telescope kits, and parts. Edmund sold a three-inch reflector for about $30, and a six inch mirror kit for $13. I chose the latter and spent several months gamely trying to grind a telescope mirror using instructions from *The Standard Handbook for Telescope Making*, by Howard Neale, and *Star Gazing with Telescope and Camera*, by George T. Keene. I still have both books, and the unfinished mirror is in my closet. But in middle age I found the $30 reflector in mint condition at a flea market for $15, and later I purchased and built an Estes model rocket with my six-year-old, Rafferty. I also own two really nice telescopes.

Thank you, Peter.

I played drums. I learned some basics on Stevo's set with assistance from Stevo's dastardly friend Dee. (My mom thought Dee, instead of alcohol, was the source of all Stevo's problems.) Then my former brother-in-law, Rich, gave me his old set of sparkling red Kents. Later I sold the Kents and bought a set of used, black Ludwigs. I wasn't Stevo, but I could keep a few beats and do simple fills. Although I participated in a band, of sorts, most of my drumming was done solo, to records or to some soundtrack in my head.

I stopped playing drums when I went away to college, but I kept the Ludwigs and resurrected them in my mid-fifties. The drums are now "vintage" and somewhat valuable. Visiting musicians covet them.

When I was fourteen my mom gave me her old Argus 35-millimeter camera and I roamed our property shooting pictures. We had just left my dad and moved to a beautiful old Victorian farmhouse on the outskirts of town. I still have the negatives. When my mom saw I was using her camera she bought me a darkroom kit that I set up in my closet. (Did you know that Chuck Berry also had a darkroom when he was a young teenager? And a good telescope that he used to perform real astronomical observations?) I made prints of our goat, our house, and took photos of bits and pieces of my room and our property: an ancient, electrically lit sign that said "Income

Tax"; hand puppets that Ann had made; a pair of overalls blowing in the wind; tiny bottle of some product called "Death to Moles." I sent my poorly exposed photograph of our goat to Rolling Stone, which at the time was a folded newspaper and always featured a nice photo towards the front. It was returned with a nice, handwritten note from some kind woman, thanking me. For a time, I bought photography magazines and studied not only the artistically nude women and the Ansel Adams photographs, but also the black and white ads in the back crammed with deals for cameras from Germany and Japan sold in shops on 42nd Street in New York City. I sent for a $33 East German Exa IIA single lens reflex that I could focus and adjust. I still have a postcard from 42nd Street informing me that my camera had been shipped. My pictures improved just slightly. Eventually the camera broke and the enlarger was retired, but I still have both, and the pictures, too. I hang on to important things.

So, whatever I lacked in social skills and social ability, I made up for with curiosity and learning and special interests. It's also clear that they helped to save my life. They kept me company. They kept my mind occupied. It's clear to me now that these interests were precursors to my nearly unquenchable desire to learn everything there was to know about the trucks, cars, bottle caps, and mobility devices that are at the heart of my cases.

My dream of country acreage was something I read and thought about often. When I was thirteen, I was given a pile of wonderful books on subjects as diverse as astronomy, education, and life in nature. I still own most of them. One of the books was Helen and Scott Nearing's *Living The Good Life* about a New England couple who built their own home out of stones they cleared from their land. I read it over and over and studied the pictures, wondering if I could do the same. I also loved a big, silly book called *Living on Earth* by Alicia Bay Laurel, about imaginary hippy skills—how to live in flimsy shelter without clothing. It seemed appealing, in part because the home craftsmanship, which amounted to bent sticks covered with cloth, seemed closer to my abilities than the Nearing's work, but primarily because there were pen drawings of pretty naked women, arms outstretched beneath the sun. I wanted to live among them.

I also loved a book called *Summerhill* about a free school in England where the children had equal votes in everything to do with their education. I wanted to go there.

When my brothers had trouble with alcohol my mother decided that public high schools were to blame. After eight years in horrid Catholic primary schools, she decided I needed four more years of Catholic education at a Jesuit school for boys. (She was a saint, but not infallible with regard to parenting.) I resisted mightily. I knew in my heart that four years at that school would kill me, but luckily, I got Peach Tree instead, a brand new school as good as Summerhill, maybe better, run by an African American woman, Camille Brunberg, who wanted a good school for her own children during turbulent times. Ann went there, too. It was no "free school." Mrs. Brunberg was strict but loving. She didn't give students an equal vote, but she let us argue our points of view. Our teachers were young and smart. The kids were a collection of delinquents, hippies, and misfits who quickly became family. We did cool things. In one class we built a big raft from plywood, two-by-fours, and Styrofoam floats and floated it overnight down the Sacramento River. We made movies. We protested at Dow Chemical. We saw Ralph Nader speak at a nearby college when he was still a hero.

Our high school art teacher once assigned us the project of writing our "philosophy of life." In part I wrote about my future and what I called "Some necessities":

> ... a Steinway piano, or any spinet or grand piano; a record player of extremely high quality; three or more acres of land; a four track tape recorder; my drums, my Silvertone to be; my Teisco to be; my gorilla; a

typewriter; interesting books with pictures; an eight inch telescope; a small basketball court; four cars of varying prices ($62-$22,000); and of course, the girl or woman of my dreams (depending on how long it takes to get my wishes).

It's startling how close it is to what I now have. I have an old Baldwin baby grand. I have a fine record player. I own a four-track recorder but don't use it; technology has changed, so I use a computer to record my songs. I have my drums. I have several guitars, and though I can't justify the cost of the vintage Silvertones or Teiscos that were so cheap and plentiful when I was a teenager, I own a Silvertone reissue, a couple of Gibsons, and a Fender. I still have my gorilla—a plaster one, hand painted by my former brother-in-law. I have plenty of books, a superb eight inch reflecting telescope, and a very good four inch refractor. I own a $20,000 car (they ain't what they used to be), and I am married to the woman of my dreams, Rebecca. All that's missing is the acreage, which I still covet but may never own.

During my senior year in high school a teacher encouraged me to graduate early. "You could start college at sixteen and be a lawyer by the time you're twenty-three!" he said.

I had no interest in becoming a lawyer at any age, but going off to college at age sixteen sounded cool. I should have thought back to skipping into fourth grade and how well that worked out, but instead, I went to college and got my first real education in the downside of being autistic.

14

Acceptance

There is a formal sort of evaluation process for the diagnosis of autism—a several day affair if, I understand correctly, with lots of tests and interviews. I didn't have that, and since I won't be applying for disability assistance or asking for accommodations at work, I don't need it. My diagnosis comes from a psychologist who is herself autistic and came over the course of several weeks. That's good enough for me.

More important than the diagnosis was my own acceptance. So much of what I read, learned, and heard about autism was so familiar that I had no qualms about accepting the diagnosis, but I didn't want to take what wasn't mine. I told my therapist about the white woman who became newsworthy for a time because she headed a college's Black Studies Department by passing as African American. I didn't want to be that woman. So I kept pressing my therapist, asking about this and that and was she certain?

"There's a patient I've been seeing for more than a year," she told me. "Just last week I told her that I was beginning to wonder if she might be on the spectrum. How long did it take me to raise it with you?"

"About 15 minutes," I told her.

Still, I went back and forth. At times I felt a huge sense of relief at finding something that explained aspects of my life that had been inexplicable to me. Other days I was wracked with doubt.

My kids were a big help. There were aspects of autism that I did not think applied to me. Stimming, for example. I had never heard of it, but seventeen-year-old Rafferty knew all about it. He told me about kids at his school who flapped their hands in class.

"I don't do anything like that," I told him. "I don't think I ever have."

"Look what you do with aluminum foil at the dinner table," he told me.

He was referring to bits of foil I remove from a beer bottle or piece of dark chocolate and then spend twenty minutes ironing, folding, and unfolding until I achieve some satisfactory pattern. It's something I do during dinner with company when listening to a large group of people talk and chatter, which in turn reminded me of my old habit of using my long thumbnails to put herringbone patterns into the walls of an empty Styrofoam cup—or what I often do with a paper napkin during a dinner with guests, twisting the corners and worrying the whole thing into the shape of some prehistoric sea creature.

"And look at your deposition notes," he continued. "I'll see two or three lines of notes on a yellow pad and then an elaborate drawing of a Greek temple or some building in Florence." True enough—though he was mostly describing my meeting notes, not deposition notes. One of them—an elaborate pen drawing of a dome like Brunelleschi's, with cars zooming around the base—was framed and hanging on our wall across the room. (For what it's worth, those doodles are usually a sign that I'm actually listening, though perhaps against my will.)

As I thought more about it I decided that perhaps my stimming was pushed into activities like drumming, noodling on a guitar, or hours upon hours of solitaire—a game I have always considered a complete waste of time and yet nearly essential to my mental health. It settles me.

I used to feel the same way about pulling weeds in my front lawn. I've long since given up that battle, but when my knees bent more easily, I consciously enjoyed the mindlessness of weeding to work through a problem or settle myself on difficult days. I suppose running did the same. I have run or jogged all my adult life, but I took up marathoning at 50, and the hours of training kept me sane and calm despite work and teenage daughters. Now that I can't squat easily, and running seems to cause me more and more injuries, maybe I should take up some more classic form of stimming. (It won't be hand flapping. Arthritis and carpal tunnel! Elder autism has its challenges.)

I recognized myself again and again in stories and anecdotes told by autistic people. I found a Facebook page by and for autistic people. Someone asked if other people sometimes turned away if they saw someone they knew approaching. I don't often do that, but I commented that I enjoyed the early days of Covid when we would cross the street if *anyone* was approaching on our side. My rude comment got a lot of likes, including someone who wrote that Covid had lots of benefits for the autistic. I replied that masks made it a lot easier to mumble to myself while walking alone. More likes and laughing emojis.

Another topic took me by surprise. Someone mentioned using closed captioning while watching television shows and movies, because it helped them process the story. This was a revelation. I love complicated, difficult television, but I had to watch *The Wire* twice before I could remember all the characters and really follow all the twists and turns. Same or worse with *Game of Thrones*. Rafferty watched it with me the second time and helped me with names and faces. Whenever I'm watching a show, I have to pause to ask whoever is watching with me if this person is the one who did such and such. Until I really know a character, I have a hard time remembering their face, and it could take several seasons for me to learn the character's name. (I just noticed that on one show I have watched for six years, one of the main characters—the wife and mom—is named "Rebecca." You'd think I would have noticed that, but it escaped me until the last episode.) My family often jokes that my questions show I'm old and stupid. Now I know they show I'm autistic. (And smart!)

Little by little I have tried to "come out" with people I know.

One particularly helpful incident involved a small reunion of people who attended a junior year abroad program in Florence, Italy in 1974 and 1975. I wasn't a junior. I had started college mid-year at age sixteen. I began the Florence program midway through my sophomore year. I was eighteen the entire year. Except for one other guy, who was nineteen, the rest of them were twenty or twenty-one at the start of the year.

My first eighteen months of college had been a social disaster. I made exactly one friend. I also failed to hold on to three serious girlfriend candidates. I intended to do better during the year abroad program. I decided to join in whenever and wherever I could. I went out drinking. I went out dancing. It didn't work. I even blew it with another girl—probably the most serious of the small bunch.

After most of the people left the little reunion, a few of us lingered, and at some point, there was a discussion about how quiet and apart I had been. I decided to tell them about my new diagnosis. "It made it really hard for me to participate socially. I just really didn't understand how the social world worked."

One of my former classmates is a transgender woman. We knew her then as a cheerful and positive young man. She looked at me quietly for a few seconds and then said, "We both struggled with an issue we didn't recognize or know about at the time that made our lives more complicated." I was very touched by this. Her dilemma was much more profound than mine; she had to change her body, her name, and her outward presentation to become who she really was— to become whole.

I never had to change, but I did change. In a way, I suppose, I did the opposite of what my friend did, or I did it in reverse order. She became more like herself. I had to learn to act more like the majority of people. I had to learn how to exist in a social world that I didn't fit into, or that didn't fit me. Before I had any notion I might be autistic

I told my first therapist that it had taken me years "to learn to operate my very hard to operate personality." I learned to make eye contact and small talk. I learned how to get and keep the girl. I learned not to talk about Chuck quite so often. It would take me years of trial, error, and deliberate effort, and I'm still not very comfortable with some of it.

Once my mother told me that she always felt twenty-seven inside. I think we all have an age like that. I have always felt seventeen or eighteen. Perhaps that's because at seventeen or eighteen I was so authentically myself—and so authentically autistic. I wasn't successful socially, but I was me.

So little by little I start to remove the "mask." During my first session with the exact right person, I tried hard to maintain appropriate eye contact, but last week I looked out the window while I talked and felt much more honest and comfortable.

15

Daddy

It's the summer of 2010. I call an archivist for the city of Sacramento. A manager at the Sacramento Convention Center has told me, "She knows everything." I tell her I am researching a Chuck Berry show at the Memorial Auditorium I attended as a teenager. I think it happened in 1971. Can she find the date?

She promises to look and get back to me. The next day I get an e-mail:

> Dear Peter: I did find that Chuck Berry played Memorial Auditorium on February 13, 1971. Also, on November 24th 1971, there was a "50s Rock & Roll Revival," but the listing doesn't mention who played. I can also tell you that 800 people attended the Berry concert, and over 4,000 attended the rock & roll revival.

I attended both of those shows. The Rock & Roll Revival show was a roaring success, with a full house and at least a half a dozen acts. Chuck Berry ended it with a short, victorious set that topped even his friend, Bo Diddley. But it is that first show, on February 13, 1971, that has always haunted me. Now, forty years after the fact, I make a startling connection.

I have always known that Chuck Berry was a father figure to me—albeit an odd one, and as different from my own father as could be. My father was born in 1901, 25 years before Berry. He was fifty-five when I was born. When I first saw Chuck Berry, my father was seventy and doing poorly. Chuck—the "father of rock 'n' roll"—was a mere forty-five.

The only song I ever heard my dad sing was a seafarer's song called "Down Among the Dead Men," which he sang in a descending bass that sounded like a foghorn as the seaman's body sank "down, down, down, down—down among the dead men." (It's hard now not to hear a certain resemblance to "Downbound Train," a traditional pub song that Chuck Berry covered and took as his own.) My dad was no longer thin by the time I knew him, his belly swollen by rib-eye steaks and whiskey; Chuck was perfectly fit. And where Chuck Berry, a non-drinker, was always sober, my dad rarely was.

I was the youngest of his children. When I was little, he was my hero, and a worthy one—a nice man, funny, a former athlete who knew a host of famous and not-so-famous ex-ball players. (They used to come to our house on his birthday and get drunk. We tended to leave.) He was well known in his hometown Sacramento. When he was young someone sent a letter to him from across the state. Instead of an address, the sender glued a picture of my dad to the front of the envelope over the word "Sacramento." He got the letter.

He had so many friends he couldn't remember them all. I remember when some happy guy accosted him after church. My dad talked and joked and slapped his back for several minutes. As we walked away, he asked my mom, "Who was that guy?"

When I was small, he still had his own business, installing lawns and selling grass and garden supplies near the highway. By then it was more of a hobby than anything else, or maybe a place to drink without interruption. Sometimes he took me along. There were huge piles of black peat, topsoil, and rice hulls. Rice hulls are the hard, paper light sleeves that wrap a grain of rice while it's growing. My dad would add them to soil as a sort of mulch. They were slippery, and fun to sink into. There were still nice moments. I remember that we occasionally walked next door to the Shell station for a Bireley's Orange.

At work, and most of the time until he finally retired, my dad wore white t-shirts and khaki work pants. When he retired, he switched to polo shirts, slacks, and cardigans.

Once, when I was six or seven, my dad stopped his pickup while backing out the driveway, and watched my mom wave goodbye to us with a happy smile.

"Pete, your mom is the most beautiful woman in the world," he told me.

"No," Little Priest told him. "The Virgin Mary is the most beautiful." I clearly needed a rock and roller in my life, but Daddy laughed and said I was probably right.

Within a year he was sharing a bedroom with me. I don't know if that move represented a rough form of family planning or if it was motivated by his collapse into alcohol. Probably both. I remember in the bedroom we briefly shared watching him open a high cupboard. His back was to me. There was the "*kss-kss-kss*" of a screw cap or the *thu-up* of a cork. He leaned back to swallow, then turned to smile and wipe his lips. I didn't know it was odd to keep whisky in a bedroom cupboard, but I was learning.

Even in those early days he wasn't always kind, as when he attended my first little league game and stood, glaring, hands in pockets, a few yards to my left as I played the position he called "Left Out." He barked some instructions, and then left. He never came back.

But I felt loved and cared for by him until the eve of my ninth birthday, when understanding hit like a freight train after Daddy dropped his bottle at the new house. The bottle shattered into a thousand dangerous pieces. My childhood shattered, too.

For a few moments my father was an angry bully. He made me clean up the mess and berated me for doing it improperly. I remember the sour smell of the bourbon, the shards of glass, and my own irritation. I was angrier than he was. I talked back to him for the first time.

"It's not my fault! It's not my mess. I didn't break it!"

Daddy stood over me, barking instructions. It was the man from the right field sidelines, fully engaged by the loss of a night's whiskey.

In the rest of our short time together—five more years—Daddy's disintegration continued. He wasn't usually mean but sometimes drinking made him that way. He mocked our weakness when my mother and a few of us kids struggled to pull him off the floor where he lay bleeding into his own urine. I remember changing his wet underpants as he sat uselessly on the edge of his bed and drunkenly thanked me.

Once, a priest performed the last rights. There was weeping until, like Lazarus, Daddy woke on the gurney and then charmed the attendants as they wheeled him out the door. At the age of twenty-one I wrote a song about it.

> *Called from school, emergency*
> *You strangle on your heart*
> *They say it's your last chance to see him*
> *Hurry, drop the phone and start*
> *You run home through a nightmare*
> *And then you run past mother's arms*
> *Who would guess that it's only just*
> *Another false alarm?*

I was at the Orangevale house, age fourteen, when the real call finally came. It was my brother Paul. He had rushed off that morning after a call from the hospital.

I had seen Daddy the previous day. He was happy. He thought the hospital was a cruise ship. I remember him clutching and tugging at his sheets with stiff fingers as he told us about his journey.

"Is he okay?" I asked Paul. I remember almost smiling. Daddy had rolled away the stone so many times we came to expect it.

The phone was quiet then Paul answered, "Peter, he died."

Paul asked me not to share the news until he got home. I knew I couldn't face anyone. I went outside into a small pasture where no one could see me cry.

I didn't know until the archivist sent her e-mail that my father died just weeks after my first Chuck Berry show, at that time when I was immersed and lost inside Chuck Berry's "The Golden Decade."

No wonder I grabbed on so hard to Chuck.

16

Persistent Deficits 101

There is, of course, a Chuck Berry song. In "Oh Baby Doll" Chuck sings about "the old alma mater" and remembering how things were in high school. I always listened wistfully, wishing I had the sorts of memories he describes in the song. I didn't. It's the funny thing about Chuck's songs—I loved them, but they celebrated a teenage world I was rarely part of, and that I was fully aware of being outside of.

But now it's time for college. It's time for a real education—an advanced degree in what were, for me, the harder parts of autism.

In a book called *The Nine Degrees of Autism* the authors describe a path from the birth of an autistic person to a productive and useful autistic life. They describe nine degrees or stages.

The first degree is simply being born. We are born autistic and remain so.

The second is knowing we are different without understanding why. For me that phase lasted sixty-five years. I always knew I was different. I have always been proud that I lived my life my own way. I don't pretend to agree with people when I don't. I don't hang out. I make almost no effort to fit in or do the popular thing. The social world often confused me, and it often hurt not to be warmly accepted by others, but I accepted it as a part of my life.

The third degree is where the rubber meets the road, or hits the fan, or both—it's when the autistic person develops secondary health issues. According to the book:

> The key difference between the second and third degrees of autism is that the individual does not suffer initially at the second degree stage; but later adverse environmental factors cause suffering at the third degree stage. Typically, the individual would be a target of abuse and he or she would struggle to cope with normal social conventions.[6]

For some people that adverse environmental factor might be preschool or kindergarten or a bit later, in elementary school. But I was treated like a "wizard" during my first few years at school, then skipped and moved from class to class and school to school. After the first half of third grade I was always on the fringes, but I explained that to myself by all the classroom moves and school changes. I had to keep starting over—that's why I had so few friends.

After eighth grade my mother threatened to send me to a Catholic boys high school. I know that would have been an "adverse environmental factor" for me. I can't think of a bastion of neurotypicality more formidable than a late 1960s Jesuit high school. But luck intervened: we found Peach Tree—the exact right school, a tiny one where half the kids were misfits, most of us were smart, and all of us were accepted.

I remember trying to make fun of one clean cut, athletic, all-American boy at Peach Tree. He was six foot two, fit, and looked like the young Glen Campbell.

"He sure loves that car," I told an older girl I liked, using a mocking tone about the way he took care of his classic American muscle car—something like a Pontiac GTO. It would be worth fifty or sixty thousand today.

She gave me a searing glance.

"Yeah, fast cars aren't as cool as *telescopes*, are they?"

And they say we don't understand sarcasm. I shut up and learned something new.

The Nine Degrees of Autism analyzes the transition from the second to the third degree.

> Theoretically, it could be possible for an autistic person to live most of his or her natural life at the stage of second degree autism. The prerequisite is a favorable environment, which allows individuals to stress their self authentically and to pursue their special interests without restriction.[7]

And that's exactly what I had—a favorable environment—until January 1973, when at age sixteen, having learned nothing from my abrupt, mid-year switch to fourth grade, I made the abrupt, mid-year switch to college, and suddenly found myself lost and alone, and struggling to cope with my new social situation.

My mother and my sister Ann dropped me off at San Jose State University. I had high hopes and had packed a pair of high-top red Converse sneakers that would seem normal today but stuck out brightly at the time. I wore them only once and then wrote a song about them.

> *I got me bright red sneakers,*
> *got a silver and gold bow tie.*
> *I got me ruby colored glasses,*
> *got a duck-ass, and Maybelene eyes.*
> *I got my fingers loaded with diamond rings,*
> *I got me silver cuff links— they're beautiful things,*
> *I got it all for you girl, but I can't say "Hi."*

It's funny to look back. All my songs were about being an autistic misfit. I just didn't know.

Ann helped me register for classes. We did it last minute, walking around the gym and signing me up for every social science class that ended in "ology." "You'll need all of these anyway," Ann told me. That would be the extent of my college advising until seven years later when I finally walked into an advisor's office at the University of Washington and asked if I could graduate. It turned out I could, and then some.

After helping me purchase books my mom and Ann left. Ann went to the much nicer university across the mountains in Santa Cruz. I would visit her later in the year and be shocked by the beauty of the campus, the architecture of the dormitories, and the quality of the food. I lined up at the cafeteria for "Ham Hawaiian" and she lined up for grilled New York steak. I lived in an urban wasteland and she lived in a redwood forest overlooking the Pacific. My dormitory was a 1950s red brick box. Hers would have been comfortable in the pages of Travel & Leisure.

At any rate, once my mother and Ann were gone I was alone, and alone I stayed.

I remember walking onto campus on a bright California winter day, seeing people everywhere in small groups laughing, talking, sharing, walking. Some played guitars. Some played frisbee. A few kissed. Some lay side by side in the grass.

I remember immediately understanding I had no clue how to join any of them or how to find a small group of my own. I felt immediately hopeless and overwhelmed.

So instead of exploring friendships and love interests, I started wandering the streets of San Jose at night alone. I walked and taught myself to smoke cigarettes I purchased from a machine outside a downtown drive-in.

My single room didn't help. I could go in and shut the door. (I would learn later in life that leaving a door open sometimes helps.)

Music *did* help. I played drums but didn't want to make that much noise in a dormitory, so I brought an old Japanese electric guitar that someone left at our house. I found a book on how to play blues at the local public library and got to work. The book emphasized simple patterns for playing blues that made immediate sense to me. Within an hour I had learned some of the patterns and licks and had figured out which strings to "bend" while playing. Pattern recognition is an autistic strength, so it makes sense to me now how quickly I understood what I found in that book. Since I already knew the structure of blues music well, at least by sound, it was easy for me to feel how the notes of the blues scale fit together and where it was appropriate to bend those notes. (In other words, I had absorbed enough of the music I loved that it revealed its simpler secrets to me!) Every now and then I'd stumble on a new lick and play it over and over, delighted. The next summer I would pick honeydew melons with Danny and Ann and buy myself a Japanese Telecaster copy and a tiny but fine Fender tube amplifier.

When I think back, I see music was one of the few ways I drew people to me during my college years, but never for long. Before starting college I had learned a few chords on my mother's electric organ, and at San Jose I used those chords to fuss around on a piano in the dormitory lobby. Once or twice, that attracted people to talk to me. One African American guy found me struggling with something that was sort of bluesy and came over to talk to me about the blues. I learned he was a guitarist. He, of course, learned I was a disciple of Chuck Berry. But then he surprised me—he knew things about Chuck Berry that even I didn't know and shared a lesson I never forgot.

"Chuck uses super slinky strings because he likes to play two notes at a time and bend them," he told me, mimicking Chuck's big hands on an air guitar. Noted! This made perfect sense to me. I could hear those bending "double stop" notes as he spoke, and the next time I sat down with a guitar I started to play two notes at a time and bend them as best I could. When I do that today, I still think of this tall, dark stranger and how our brief interaction influenced me. He was, it seems, the exact right person. It didn't occur to me to shake his hand, or ask his name, or ask him to teach me a few licks on the guitar, or do any of the other things a person might do when meeting someone new. As the DSM-5 says: "deficits in social communication."

Music connected me with a couple of other folks at San Jose State, though never very deeply or for long. The guy across the hall had a drum set. I knocked on his door and introduced myself, but what I remember most about him were an unsatisfying drumming style and a polite lack of interest. Perhaps he had social deficits, too, but of a different and opposite sort. He didn't invite me to sit down and try his drum set. Instead, he interacted with me in the skeptical way I have come to expect from some people I meet, starting out friendly and then backing away with an appraising look as if they see something a bit odd in me. I recently looked him up online and was pleased to see he became a beloved educator of high school kids in his hometown. He won't ever look up the skinny kid across the hall.

A gangly, geeky, and sweet music major used to come talk to me every time I was at the piano or reading the free newspaper in the same lounge. We knew each other because she roomed with my chief love interest, a girl named Donna. More about Donna later, but from this distance it's clear I should have focused my attention on Donna's music major roommate. The first time she found me playing the piano she laughed and told me my little rock composition was ugly. I was working on the lead-in to a song I wrote called "Bathroom Rock Star." You've heard of acoustic blues. "Bathroom Rock Star" is autistic blues.

I'm a bathroom rock star—chicken walk in front of the mirror.
Yes, I'm a bathroom rock star—chicken walk in front of the mirror.
You know my music's so good that it's inaudible to the human ear.

"Chicken Walk" was my own terminology for Chuck Berry's famous "Duck Walk," which I hadn't yet learned a name for. I came pretty close.

The girl probably had a point about my musical introduction, and based on her bluntly honest but not unkind way of talking, she may have well been another undiagnosed autistic person. What I know for sure, looking back from the age of Medicare, is that she was a far better prospect for me than her little hottie of a roommate, Donna. This girl sought me out and talked to me every time she saw me. Did I recognize she might be interested in me—a similarly gangly, geeky, and sweet guy? Nope. Did it occur to me that I had an entree with this nice person? Nope. When it came to things social, I had no clue. If I am ever given a chance to travel through time, I won't try to save the world. I'll go back and try to save that clueless boy.

I also remember stopping to listen to a guy playing jazz guitar in the main grassy square on campus. I asked him who his main influence was. He told me Wes Montgomery. That was the extent of our conversation, but that brief snippet nevertheless puts him among my top ten acquaintances at San Jose State. I bought a Wes Montgomery record soon thereafter, and I remember the young player—one of my college buddies!—whenever I see Montgomery's name or photograph.

The same brief musical interactions happened when I continued my haphazard education at other universities. At Humboldt State University, three or four years later, I found a beautiful, new Steinway grand piano in a big room off the main dormitory lounge. Nobody ever played it. By then I could play blues in the key of C pretty well, and I often sat and improvised. Once a jerky white guy poked his head into the room and ordered me to "stop playing that horrible shit!" (He's undoubtedly now a famous Republican politician.) It was actually pretty decent shit, so I ignored him and kept playing. Within minutes a black guy came in and said, with a bit of surprise, "You're playing blues!"

"I'm trying to," I told him.

Clearly a musician himself, he took time to teach me something about the music I loved and was teaching myself to play.

"Blues is kind of like Gospel music," he told me. "You want contrast. You want to play down low, and way up high, and everywhere in between. You've heard B.B. King, right? How he gets up high on the frets? You want to start getting out of the middle of the keyboard."

Once again, I made no effort to learn who this guy was. I didn't ask his name. I didn't suggest we get a beer at the little campus lounge. I didn't invite him to listen to my growing collection of interesting blues and soul records, or to sit down and show me some licks on the piano. I listened, though, and absorbed his lesson, and think of him often during my struggles on the piano, where I still mostly play the same notes the easy way, with both hands close together in the middle of the keyboard.

What's interesting now is how little effort I made to keep these conversations going. All together (subtracting the gangly girl) they probably lasted 20 minutes—and yet they were a big part of my college social life and I've never forgotten them. I never asked a name. I never told them mine. I never suggested we get together to play music. I just didn't know better. The social world that surrounded me was a complete mystery. People came and people went. I had no idea how to find and keep my own people—even when they came right up and started talking to me.

Since the advent of the internet, I have developed a habit of googling the places I have lived and the years I lived there. I'll find my village in Togo. I'll look for photographs of Florence, Italy in 1974. A few months after my diagnosis I googled "San Jose State University 1973," and found a 135-page yearbook for the dormitories there. Who knew they made such a thing? I scrolled through it in wonder, looking at the photographs of young people having fun at college. I only recognized three people: our resident advisor (who I think used to worry about me); my eventual roommate, Stan; and me—lanky, awkward, hair well below my shoulders, eyes downcast, a faint trace of not yet shaved mustache. To my surprise, I had an actual, toothy smile, though my eyes were aimed down at the floor somewhere to my left.

The yearbook was both fascinating and horrifying. It was horrifying because in my mind, at the time, I turned all the happy young people smiling from the pages of the yearbook into my enemies. In my mind they were boring, horrible, shallow, stupid, and mean. In my mind they had spurned me. I wrote nasty letters to my family about them, and once tried writing a nasty essay about them. I still have it somewhere.

But in my Medicare years I can see they are sweet and innocent. They are kids. I was just a younger kid, autistic, undiagnosed, and poorly equipped to interact with them. Calling them horrible, stupid, and mean was my best defense.

To be frank, though, I didn't really want to interact with the guys. I wanted to interact with a girl. But I was poorly equipped for that, too.

I had few role models. My mom and dad were long past displays of affection by the time I was conscious of their existence, and I never saw my brothers with a girl until Paul, the oldest, brought home one he would marry.

The other thing I lacked was a friend I could share with who might push me a bit. "She likes you! Ask her out!"

And I had a strange and sad logic about girls. I told myself, correctly, that I would be a good boyfriend—attentive, loving, caring. On the other hand, I told myself no girl I wanted would have any interest in me.

The sad thing is that several made it clear that they did.

17

Art, Love, and Product Liability

I have given a number of continuing legal education talks to lawyers and their staffs about how to investigate cases and do discovery. I made it personal. I often began with the line "I never wanted to become a lawyer. I wanted to be this guy, but that didn't work out."

And at that moment I used my PowerPoint to show a photograph of Chuck Berry I'd taken from the cover of Smithsonian magazine, elegant in his white suit with black lapels, doing his famous "duck walk" with an older model Gibson guitar.

It's interesting now to see how, even decades before my diagnosis, I somehow recognized the connection between my work and my autistic "special interests," and that I managed to fit both Chuck Berry and exploding trucks into a single 30 minute lecture.

I enjoyed watching the puzzled faces of my audience as I explained that I'd never imagined myself as a lawyer, that I had always wanted and expected to be an artist of some sort—a musician, a writer, a painter; that I really didn't care which.

Then I would show them a photograph of Seattle artist James Washington, Jr., whose wonderful stone sculptures can be found in public places throughout the city of Seattle. Washington's work explores nature and spirituality. I would show a couple pieces and explain how Washington didn't make massive changes to the rock—that he tapped and chiseled lovingly until he found whatever had been hidden there—usually some meek and vulnerable animal, like a lamb, or a baby bird still huddled in the shape of its egg. I explained that I had once been lucky enough to visit Washington at his home and interview him for my college newspaper, and that he'd told me, "If you love a thing, it will give up its secret to you."

And then I made my pitch. "Law schools teach you 'to think like a lawyer.' I want to encourage you to think like an artist—to think like James Washington, Jr.—to love your clients, and your cases, and your work, even the old photocopies and wrecked pieces of old crashed cars, until they give up their secrets to you."

I might have said, "I want to encourage you to think like an autistic person," but I didn't know. That's for the next class.

My way of accumulating knowledge and understanding has never been to undertake a thorough or systematic study. If I am trying to learn something I don't start at the beginning and read to the end. My way of accumulating knowledge and understanding has always involved returning again and again until connections light up inside my brain like magic and secrets are revealed.

Just the other day, in a road design case, a defense attorney pulled out a document I'd never seen in an attempt to prop up her case. I'm not convinced she understood the actual significance of the document, at least from our point of view. At first it frightened me because it appeared to support her client's argument. A few hours later, with no work on my part other than letting the new information commingle with the old information inside my brain, the meaning of the document "popped" for me. I suddenly understood it, and how it connected with other evidence in our case, and the new document fell into place among the other documents like the smoking gun that it is—for our side, not for the side that introduced it. The document helped prove everything our experts were saying and that the defendant was trying to deny. It was just the latest example of this phenomenon of a sudden, "popping" sort of clarity—a document suddenly giving up its secret. I'll tell you others when we talk more about my cases.

Several months into my therapy my therapist told me she works the same way—she listens to the stories her clients tell her and files them away until, suddenly, two or more of the stories connect to reveal some deeper meaning.

The stories give up their secrets to her.

18

College Girls

I'm in a car again. It is 2010. Rebecca and I are returning home after a nice dinner out. She might be a little tipsy. She is at least tipsy enough to believe she can finally pry loose information about a subject I have mostly avoided for several years now: my early love life—or really, the lack thereof.

In 2010 I have avoided this subject for decades. I was married to my first wife for more than seventeen years. I never thought to ask about her prior love life, and she never asked about mine. The subject came up with Rebecca once or twice but I made it clear it was not something I wanted to talk about, at least beyond telling her that there wasn't much to say. Rebecca, for her part, seemed to have had an endless stream of boyfriends and suitors. I never particularly wanted to hear about any of them, but that didn't stop her from telling me. She lived with one guy in a basement. She travelled to Florida to meet another guy's parents. There was a guitar player in there somewhere with nice hands. I could go on. With no good stories of my own, I just let her talk.

But this day she leans back against the car door with a lazy smile and says, "Tell me about your college girlfriends."

I am suddenly dropping in a free fall into unutterable darkness.

After twenty odd years of marriage (odd being a double *entendre* here) I thought I was past this. I thought I was passing as normal in a normal world.

But I never had a college girlfriend—at least not a real one.

The college girls in my life skittered past like leaves on a windy day, sometimes catching for a moment or two, but never long.

I didn't discriminate. I only had one real college friend, period—my roommate Stan. We are still friends today, communicating by text and email even if we only see each other every ten years or so.

I spent time with a few other people, but not much time and not many people. On a year abroad in Italy I sometimes went for pizza or beer with guys from my *pensione*, and during my last month or so in college I became friends with a fellow English major, but that basically meant we once split a six-pack by the railroad tracks along Puget Sound and once attended an art event together. I suspect he was gay at a time when it was difficult to be openly gay and that he had hopes for me—but I was not good at reading the social tea leaves, so who knows?

In college I wasn't particularly interested in guy friends. I had Stan. I had Greg, left over from high school. That was enough and suited me fine. I didn't want to hang with "the guys." I didn't want to talk about football. I didn't want to gossip about girls or their body parts.

What I wanted was a girlfriend. A real girlfriend. Someone who would be in my corner.

I sometimes imagined her. Dark hair, bangs, smart in a quiet way, funny in a quiet way. I imagined her being off to the side a bit, like me.

How those two shy people were supposed to meet was not clear, but one night I wound up making out with her, for about an hour, before I let her skitter away.

I was sixteen or seventeen. I forget if it was my first or my second semester in college. Somehow I found myself involved in a drinking game in the dormitory lobby. How this happened, I have no idea. Other than a dance where I stood and watched the band, (I would later see them appear with Chuck and back him,) this was the only social event I participated in during my first three semesters in college.

The drinking game turned out to be a drinking and kissing game. I forget the rules, but if one thing happened you drank and if another thing happened you drank and then kissed the person on one side or the other. As it happened, the girl on my left had (and still has) the honor of being the first girl I ever kissed. (She would soon become the first girl I ever kissed who grew to despise me.) The girl on my right was (and remains) the second girl I ever kissed.

At first things proceeded evenly. I kissed one, I kissed the other. I kissed equally. I was thrilled to learn how easy it was. Then the kisses to the right started getting longer and longer and provoked howls and catcalls from the larger circle. The ones to the left became downright perfunctory, served cold and with contempt by my fellow gamester. Love is a fickle thing.

When the game was over the girl to the right led me to one of the Swedish modern couches that lined the room and we stayed for quite a long time.

She was probably the ideal girl for me. She was pretty. She had the bangs I had imagined. She was shy and quiet but aggressive enough to get me over to that couch. With due respect to the girl on my left, she was also, hands down, the best kisser I'd ever encountered.

I'm not telling this story because there is anything unique or newsworthy about two teenagers making out. I'm telling it because of my own weird reaction, which I now find uniquely horrifying.

I have no idea who this girl was. I never asked her name. I never asked for her phone number, or which dormitory she lived in, or where she was born, or even her astrological sign or major. When it was time for her to go she told me and I said "okay." I didn't offer to walk her back to her own dormitory and I didn't offer to walk her out of mine. I didn't suggest we see each other again. I simply watched her walk away.

In the weeks or months that followed I saw her now and then, usually outside the cafeteria the dormitories shared. She would smile, shyly and sadly. I can't vouch for my own response, or whether I smiled. As I recall, she was as alone as I was each time I saw her, but it never occurred to me to stop her and ask her name or to amend that aloneness.

People on the spectrum often have trouble understanding rules of social engagement that neurotypical people find easy to decipher. What I can say from the here and now is that I didn't know what any of it meant. If this pretty girl spent an hour making out with me did that mean she might like me? That she might want to get to know me better? Did it mean I could ask her name? Did it mean she might like to see me again? Should I walk her back to her dormitory? I don't remember asking myself any of these questions. For me it was just something that happened, an interesting, enjoyable, isolated, and completely random incident. I made no effort to explore its potential. A pretty girl took me to a couch for an hour, and when she left, she was gone. She was the first leaf that blew past and momentarily entangled itself with me, the first of too few.

I'm not sure that being autistic can completely explain or forgive the weirdness of letting this young woman slip into and out of my arms so wordlessly and easily. I was thoughtless and rude not to walk her home or ask her name or suggest another meeting. It was abnormal and nearly insane. But though it provides no excuse, autism is part of the answer. I had a lot to learn about the neurotypical social world, and it would take time and experience. So, I try to forgive myself. And if this sad episode sounds familiar to anyone, especially a quiet, sweet, formerly reddish-haired woman who went to San Jose State University, I ask *her* to forgive, too. I knew not what I did.

Oddly, though, girls kept coming—not many, but enough to provide a more normal boy with opportunities to find love.

Donna was a stunningly pretty, mixed-race woman of Polynesian descent. She was also smart and funny. When she brought her brown plastic tray to the cafeteria table where I routinely dined alone and asked to sit down across from me, I knew immediately that I was lucky. We hit it off instantly. She began with a silly comment about my overuse of black pepper, and we continued with scathing commentary about the dullards who surrounded us. It was a common theme of mine in college—when I struck out socially it was the other people's fault.

From my perch in the 21st century I see progress. I learned Donna's name. I pursued her. We did things together. I visited her room. I took her to a funny Egyptian museum. We laughed at the sarcophagus that looked like Donald Hollinger from the old television show, *That Girl*. (Danny's observation, not mine.) We watched the World Series and the Watergate hearings together. We liked each other. I know she liked me because she was a first-class flirt and I can still see her face. I now recognize what her face was trying to tell me.

But at the time I was much less sure and had no idea how to proceed.

I remember how close I came. We were walking out of the dormitory together. Her jeans were inches away. Her bottom was spectacular. Her hand was there to be taken. But I didn't know when or how to reach for it. I didn't know what she would allow, and I didn't know how to ask. I don't think most boys would have hesitated an instant to reach out a hand, and certainly most neurotypical boys would have known what to do.

I've learned enough now to know she would have happily taken my hand—I just didn't know then. So, one day, weeks into our friendship, I saw her come into the building with an older guy, obviously from a date. We exchanged the briefest of glances. I must have looked stricken because she looked at me with concern. I went to my room and spent the first of many nights listening to gut bucket blues and feeling them.

To my credit I tried again. I invited Donna to a Charlie Chaplin film. She sat next to me and laughed at the movie while I fell deeper and deeper into myself and into depression, not laughing, hardly seeing the film at all. On the way home I apologized for becoming so quiet.

"It's okay to be quiet," she said.

But I never saw her again, or made any further effort to see her.

So, it turns out that a girl named Terri is the third girl I ever kissed. I only know her name today because of words written in her hand in one of my college notebooks the day after my first full on sexual encounter.

Do you know that I don't even know your name!

I wrote mine and she wrote hers. It would likely never have occurred to me to ask.

We had become friends in our natural science class. It was one of those large, lecture hall classes and I'm sure she is the one who initiated the friendship. We were in the same lab group. We became lab partners and giggled and laughed as we scratched rocks and did all the little experiments that lab partners did in that class. It's funny now to think what good friends we seemed to be and how much I now see that she was flirting with me, leaning close, touching my arm, letting her hair touch me too. She was another astonishingly pretty young woman, tiny, with long brown hair. My luck knew no bounds. Her ethnicity was ambiguous. My guess now is that she was Native American or Filipina, and a year or two older than me. Her glasses made her even prettier in a geeky sort of way. But no matter how close she leaned in as we did our experiments in that lab, it never occurred to me that she might have a romantic or sexual interest in me. I was blind to it.

After my diagnosis, 48 years later, I read the book *look me in the eye: my life with asperger's* by John Elder Robison, an inventor and self-taught engineer who was diagnosed in early middle-age. When I got to page 167, I had a shock of recognition. Robison was talking about his years working with rock bands, including KISS, years that, of course, included many groupies and fans.

> Did any of the girls try to pick me up? I'll never know. My sensitivity to other people's actions was limited enough that any attempt to pick me up went unno-

ticed. I often felt lonely when I saw couples together, but I could not see any way I could change my own situation, so I just plodded along.[8]

That's me. What interests me now is that even then I knew the teaching assistant who ran our lab group—an older graduate student—was jealous of me and my situation, and I liked that. But it never occurred to me there was good cause for his jealousy. I just knew that a spectacular girl was paying lots of attention to me, and that he wanted that attention.

One day Terri asked if I wanted to see where she lived. Sure, I said. I have a single frame of nearly photographic memory of the two of us walking across campus together on a sunny blue day. In my mind we were going "to see where Terri lived." (Except that I didn't know her name.)

She lived in a big old house, some sort of boarding house or maybe a sorority. I quickly got the impression that only girls lived there. Terri took me to her room and showed me her bed. After showing me her bed, she led me a few feet north to her chest of drawers and opened one drawer to show me her contraceptives. A "normal" person would understand. I just nodded my head. A minute passed. Terri gave me a short but detailed lecture on the contraceptive practices of each of her roommates. Interesting. Who knows what happened during that minute. I imagine I was there nodding my head. Finally, Terri let out an exasperated sigh, grabbed that nodding head, pulled it to her level, and kissed me.

I liked that part, and the third girl I ever kissed quickly became the second girl I made out with.

But this was the early 1970s. Terri gave me about 60 seconds to enjoy making out and then stopped, let out another, louder gasp of exasperation, and started unbuckling my belt.

I will spare you further details.

I describe this because of how each step took me so completely by surprise.

If I had watched the scene progress in a movie, even then, I'm sure I would have seen it all and thought, "He's a dope!" But as a participant I really *was* a dope. I saw none of it coming. Each gesture from this girl took me completely by surprise, and it would keep happening.

I have learned since that there is a name for this. Social imagination. The ability to imagine or guess what people are thinking or what might happen next. I've read that autistic people often lack it or have to learn it by trial and error.

Terri was quite advanced in learning. I should have grabbed on for a master's degree in sexual relations, but I let her skitter. Still, we kept meeting up in class and giggling over our science experiments.

She even asked my name.

19

The Peach

When I began to explore how a so-called "disorder" enhanced my ability to master facts and connect the dots in complicated legal cases the first thing I thought of was the "peach." I don't know if it has any connection to autism, though it clearly has something to do with the way I process information and mark it for future use. At any rate, it presented itself and I paid attention.

What I'm talking about wasn't really a peach. I knew that from the start. I immediately recognized that what I mentally tagged as a peach was a rough sketch showing the cross section of a gas tank and a steel gas tank shield.

This was in early 1993. We had just filed Doug's exploding truck case. I had gone to Washington, D.C. to meet the great automotive safety advocate Clarence Ditlow and get some basic information about exploding trucks. Clarence was a remarkable individual who ran an important automotive safety advocacy group but puttered around in an old General Motors version of the Toyota Corolla. He met with me personally for more than an hour and gave me a notebook with basic documents uncovered in prior exploding truck litigation. Most of the documents were highly technical but the one that caught my eye was the sketch with some words and letters scribbled on it. This simple drawing was the only thing in that notebook that shouted, "Here I am!"

For reasons I can't explain, the first thing I thought of when I saw the drawing was a pretty half peach my sister Rooney painted with acrylics onto the front of a white t-shirt. The only connection is that both images had roughly concentric shapes. The peach had its dark pit, the yellowish fruit, and was outlined by the darker, reddish skin. Rooney designed the shirt for Peach Tree High School. She hoped the school's director would print the design on shirts for the students and supporters of the school. That didn't happen, but it was a lovely design.

In early 1993, it had been more than 20 years since I saw Rooney's shirt and peach, but it was what I thought of as soon as I opened the notebook and saw the drawing, and it was what I would remember a year or two later when the significance of that drawing leapt out to grab and shake me.

The gas tank shield drawing was someone's quick sketch, probably on a napkin. The lines skittered in places as if the napkin had bumps that made the pen bounce or skip. The sketch had been photocopied nearly into oblivion, and someone had stamped diagonal lines across it and put the word "CONFIDENTIAL" in the center of this particular copy.

Like the peach it showed a cross section with loosely concentric features. At the center was a slice of fuel tank with little loopy lines on either side that I knew were seams that connected the top and bottom halves of the tank. The tank was the pit. The tank was mostly encircled by something identified as "CRS" that covered the top, bottom and the left side forming a loose ring around the tank. I knew the expression "cold rolled steel" and understood immediately this outer skin was a shield made from that material. The shield was the skin of the peach. There was a squared "C" shaped thing on the right that I knew was supposed to represent the truck frame.

The words "A probable easy fix" and "Ale" were scribbled beneath the drawing.

As a future lawyer I liked the words "probable easy fix" because I knew a jury would understand them. A bad design needs a "fix," and this one was "easy."

And here it was, sketched on a napkin.

From my current vantage I see this moment of recognition as the true beginning of my legal career. My best and most important work was beginning the moment I saw this drawing—a drawing that I would file away mentally as the half peach my sister had once painted on a t-shirt. It was a drawing that would soon help me solve a wonderful mystery and pin awareness of this bad design on one of the top engineers and administrators at General Motors.

20

Why the Smile?

Another issue for some autistic people are the faces themselves. For some of us faces can be hard to recognize, and facial expressions are hard for some of us to decipher.

Take, for example, the wink and the smile.

I am another year along in college. I am still smarting over Donna and still puzzling over Terri. I am at a new school—the second of five universities I will attend before earning a degree. It is a junior year abroad program in Italy that I join as a sophomore, so I am dropping further behind chronologically. I will be eighteen all year long, while all but one of my fellow students start the year at twenty or twenty-one. I nonetheless try hard to join in. I go to the cafes where my classmates get coffee during the day or party at night. I go to the disco where they dance. For the first time I know the other students, at least by name. I know their faces, too. In fact, because I am acting mostly as an observer, those faces will always remain etched into my memory at a brain stem level. I sit more or less alone in whatever crowd has assembled and study them as they have fun together.

One night I learn my fellow students are going to the disco again. By now I am able to ask women to dance. I watch the eyes of several young women search the dark corners of the ceiling while I dance with them.

But one young woman I ask to dance doesn't look into the corners. She looks straight at me, the whole time, with a big, goofy smile. There is actually nothing goofy about the smile, but for me it is a conundrum. I wonder, "Why the smile?"

The song is "Dance to the Music" by Sly and the Family Stone. It is three minutes long. When it ends do I stay with her to talk? Of course not. Do I offer to buy her one of the expensive little drinks? Nope. Do I offer her a cigarette or do anything at all to answer my own question, "Why the smile?" No. I go back to my place and wait for the next song and the next dance.

It's interesting that for nearly 50 years I remember these two images: the generic image of other young women looking away, and the specific image of this young woman looking straight at me with a big smile. I clearly knew it had meaning—I just didn't know what the meaning was.

Once again, if I had seen this in a movie, I would have understood, even then. "She's smiling at you, fool! Maybe she likes you! Talk to her!"

But in the context of me it made no sense. My only thought was "Why the smile?"

That same night, during slow dances, I tell girls a joke I have made up about how young Italian men dance. The style is cool and understated. The man slips his left hand behind his partner's shoulder. The right hand dangles to his side with a cigarette. His feet, about a foot apart, barely move.

"It's because they grew up around the David," I explain, referring to Michelangelo's famous statue, which stands in a similar pose about half a mile from where we are dancing.

Most of the young women I practice this joke on make some sort of polite, bored, breathy sound, but without interest. The young woman with the goofy smile laughs hard enough that her back shakes beneath my fingers. I can still feel it. Do I take that as a sign? Do I gather useful information from the fact that she understands and perhaps appreciates my odd humor? Of course not. I go back to my place. But again, I never forget.

Late in life I've met several of my former classmates from this school. In some cases I have spoken with them for the first time. It is fascinating to me because forty or forty-five years later I am "suddenly" able to deal with them—to ask questions, to talk, to laugh, to enjoy them as people. They often burst into fugues of memory, laughing about outings to Pisa, weekend trips to Rome, crazy nights on the town, a Chinese restaurant they enjoyed together, the wacky actions of a particular person, or who loved whom, for how long, and when, and how they broke up.

My own memories are mostly things like pizza and beer, at a zinc counter, alone; the frescoed stars at Orsanmichele, alone; a street near the Ponte Vecchio, alone; Botticelli's Venus, standing naked on a half shell, surrounded by deities, handmaidens, and whitecaps, while I stand before her longingly, clothed, and alone.

I could go on and on. San Miniato. The Bargello. Santa Croce. San Lorenzo. I'm proud I investigated the city constantly, and in depth, but I did it alone.

In the midst of this aloneness, that smile, that laugh. Clearly, they meant something to me even then, because I filed them away as permanent memories. I just didn't know what they meant, or what to do with them.

My memories are soundless images, dark and blurry, scratched like an old piece of movie film. They move, just a bit, like those silly iPhone "live" pictures, or like a portrait in Harry Potter. I can't look at them, but the few I have are accessible to me somehow, fleetingly, somewhere near the visible spectrum.

I once counted up the memories I have of this particular young woman and found something like a dozen.

Let's call the dances memories one and two. Memory three takes place in the little cafe where the students from my school get coffee between classes. The owner likes our patronage and lets us sit upstairs for free instead of adding the usual *coperto* to the cost of a coffee or tea. I like it up there. The juke box songs are etched as deeply into my brain as the faces of my classmates. "Kung Fu Fighting." "Smoke Gets In Your Eyes." "Can't Get Enough of Your Love." An over-the-top Italian ballad called *"Bella Senz'Anima"*—beauty without a soul.

Mostly I sit, read, and observe, though I have memories of two other young women from the school, both worthy of my interest and attention, talking to me in the cafe. Even from this distance I have no idea if these other young women were interested in me, but I remember one smiling and laughing as we talked, and another granting me a confidently sexy smile.

I was not confidently sexy. The best I can hope for from my perch in the here and now is that I appeared mysterious in my silence. But since I lacked the ability to read the social tea leaves, I have no idea if what was being served to me by those two women were friendly cups of Lipton's or something steamier and more interesting.

I looked good enough. I began the year with hair down almost to my waist. I cut it to my shoulders on the advice of my sister's Italian boyfriend, Gianni, after various Italian men harassed me, and I had no language to respond. It worked. I cut it to my shoulders and the men shut up. I wore a leather jean jacket and bought myself an Italian shirt, a pair of good jeans, and some Italian boots. From this distance I looked good. It's not impossible the two other young women who talked to me at the cafe were at least marginally or momentarily interested. I had no idea then, and no idea now—but I know that if the same thing happened today, or at least later in life, I would try to figure out if they were. Then, I didn't. I just watched and waited—for what, I didn't know.

One day the smiling young woman from the disco shows up at the cafe. She's with one of her friends. They sit at the next table. She begins asking me questions about things that interest me—my family, my hometown. This surprises me. Other students ask me "Hey, Pete, what's up?" and I start to answer before I realize they aren't expecting a response and don't care. This young woman is listening and following up with new questions. I don't remember engaging in actual conversation. My guess, today, is that I treated it more like an interview and simply responded. The young woman's friend writhes in quiet but visible agony. She doesn't want to waste time talking to me.

Though I don't remember what I said aloud, I do remember my internal monologue. This is one of several times I remember providing myself this sort of running commentary during a conversation I was supposedly involved in. Think of me as being my own, built-in Howard Cosell. I'm answering questions on the outside, but simultaneously watching the scene play out and talking to myself about it. I remember looking at the nice young woman as she tried to speak with me and thinking, "She is a good person." And I remember looking at her friend and thinking, "She is not."

Nothing occurred to me beyond that. It didn't occur to me that the young woman's questions might indicate she was interested in me. It didn't occur to me to follow up on this potential interest. I doubt it occurred to me to ask her about her own life, family, or hometown. I told myself she was good person, and when our conversation ended, I returned to my book.

It's interesting. I had learned to communicate roughly in a foreign language, but I still couldn't understand the normal language of smiles, small talk, and social cues that had surrounded me since I was a child. I could negotiate a foreign city with ease but had no idea how to negotiate simple human relations.

I was not a robot. When I was comfortable with a person or a group of people, I was funny, smart, kind, gentle, and interesting. I looked like a junior rock star. I could have been a contender. Yet here was a young woman who smiled at me, who laughed at my joke, and who listened with interest as I answered questions about topics that were important to me. Did it register? Not in the way that it might register with a "normal" person. But it registered somehow because I filed away the grainy snapshots for future reference.

This is the part of being autistic that hurt me—the only aspect of my neurology that I see as having been a disability for me. It's also a part of autism that I learned to deal with to at least some degree, with the help of time and an assist from another culture. Even today I'm bad at small talk and niceties, and even today I would have no idea how to pick up a woman at a grocery store or bar, but at least I've learned to listen, to look, to respond, to ask questions, to understand a smile or a touch, to engage. And I've got a woman who's on my side.

Oddly, it didn't hurt as much then as it did when I grew older. In those days I consoled myself with endless exploration of the world around me—the places, the things, the music, the art, the books, the literature. Just not the people—though I observed them constantly.

And yet I had a resilient hope. One of my favorite songs was one my sister Ann gave to me on my otherwise lonely 18th birthday—Jimmy Cliff's "Sitting in Limbo." As a former altar boy, limbo fascinated and terrified me. I saw it as a spooky, joyless place with giant, floating, unbaptized babies. I was in limbo, but I also had a naive faith that what I was looking for would come for me, and that I would move on.

What haunts me decades later is how often it did come.

As part of my effort to join in I sometimes went to a bar where students from my school gathered to drink. Sometimes, if I arrived early, one or another person would talk to me for a few minutes, but once their real friends came, I was left to myself. I would sit watching, alone and silent in a crowd of people.

One night the place was packed, and some noisy extrovert had caught the attention of the whole group. I'm sure it was something funny, but instead of paying attention to the person talking I turned to scan the room behind me.

They were all watching the speaker except one person.

The girl from the disco and the cafe was looking straight at me with a fresh new smile.

And she winked!

I knew what a wink was. Again, if I had been watching this scene in a movie I would have understood what it meant. "Smile back! Wink! Go join her! Do something!"

But in the context of me it made no sense whatever. I wondered "Why did she do that?"

Then, suddenly, she is walking behind me. "Peter, follow me!" she says, and I obey. I have no idea why she wants me to follow. I am simply obeying an order. I am a very obedient person.

We turn the corner into a little washroom outside the *gabinetti.* There is barely space for the two of us. She turns and rolls the dial of the little metal lock, and we are alone. I look down and suddenly understand I am going to be kissed. This surprising turn of events makes immediate sense to me once it has begun. She is a person with whom I feel instantly comfortable.

At some point there is a knock at the door and a female voice tells my new friend it is "time to go." I reach obediently for the door lock and my friend shakes her head. As the voice outside rings like an angry mother, my friend puts a finger to her lips to keep me from responding. When it's quiet we carry on.

I'm not sure of everything that happened that evening. I think we stayed put until our classmates had all gone. I remember two things clearly. Once again these memories are comprised of images I know are there and can see, but that I can't look at for more than an instant. There are, again, a few bits of internal monologue.

The first memory is an image of my new friend walking beside me through the dark, damp streets telling me something that is important to her. Today I have no idea what she was telling me. What I remember is the image itself, her eyes focused intently on a spot above the sidewalk, and my surprise that, "She's acting as if I am her friend."

The other is an image of the sidewalk in front of me. I am walking with my arm around this young woman, and she is talking to me about the important thing. I am listening, but in front of me I see an Italian man about my age walking alone, and I think, "That is usually me. I am the one who is usually walking alone."

That night or morning I walk her home. I have learned that much, at least, since my first kiss. We dawdle for a time on the sidewalk across from her *pensione*.

A "normal" person might have believed he was leaving limbo.

But here's the part that always mystified me: as soon as I was back in my tiny room at my own *pensione*, I returned to limbo as obediently as I had earlier obeyed the command to follow her and leave it behind. I had no idea how to repeat or recreate what I had just experienced. I enjoyed the memory of that brief connection, but from my perspective it was gone and over—the leaf had skittered past.

I think that if I had lived this episode in the age of social media or texting, or even email, things might have turned out differently. Perhaps I would have received or sent a message. "That was fun!" I would certainly have responded to a text message. I was a good enough writer, funny, smart. Perhaps one text would have led to another. Maybe emojis and jokes would have flown back and forth. I would have understood that I was only five minutes away—two or three if we both started walking.

But this was Italy, 1974. I had no phone. The only communications technology available to me was in person, and for me it seemed impossible to approach her at school, where she was surrounded by an entourage of friends I saw as being more formidable than the Secret Service.

So, I returned firmly to limbo.

Until she came to me again.

Same bar, same room, a week or so later. She comes downstairs to find me again sitting alone in a crowd. I have a table to myself. She sits next to me, leans in close, and we resume our comfortable friendship. What had disappeared for me during her absence is suddenly back.

That night we close the place down. Her friends again attempt to intervene. They line up next to us in order of height and popularity. The tall, pretty one again tells my friend it is time to go. My friend ignores her, without responding, without even turning her head. I watch with interest and satisfaction. I can watch in comfort because the tall one never looks at me or acknowledges my existence in any way.

That night we spend a longer time together, wandering the beautiful streets of Florence. I remember being happy when she suggests we walk by the river. We walk past the Strozzi Palace towards *Ponte Santa Trìnita*. The major buildings and the bridges are floodlit and beautiful. We stop for a while to lean against the short brick and stone wall next to the Arno with the Ponte Vecchio is in front of us. In a nearby alleyway, I become a bit proactive. I know my friend has a boyfriend. I must have learned this through talk at my *pensione*. I tell her I should be her boyfriend instead.

She doesn't say anything or even look at me. As an attorney who does some negotiating, I now realize this means she is listening. Then, to me, it simply means "no." But I change tactics. That same week our entire school will leave for a two-week tour of the Middle East. We will visit Istanbul, Beirut, Jordan and Israel—and her boyfriend can't come. He doesn't go to our school.

"How about I be your boyfriend on the Middle East tour?" I suggest.

She nods. "Deal," she says.

I walk her to her *pensione*. I have a ticket away from limbo.

But I broke the deal.

My only memory of my friend on that trip is the image of her at a table surrounded by her popular friends. In my idiotic brain I think the only way for me to join her is to join the whole table and engage in casual small talk with people who don't know me or like me. That is what I see other people do, and it's what I think I must do if I want to talk to her. It doesn't occur to me that I could ignore them all, lean down, and ask if she wants to go for a walk.

She would have gone for the walk. Over time I have learned how the world works. But then I had no idea, so I threw in the towel and spent the rest of the year alone.

Happily, our story wasn't over.

21

Stevo

The best pictures of him are a couple of black and white photographs that my sister Maggie took and printed. His eyes are deep and dark and sad. His face, covered with long stubble, is scarred from car crashes and fights.

His psyche was scarred by jail. He was locked up frequently for stuff that wouldn't get you in trouble now—once for two tiny marijuana plants in his bathroom window, miniature seedlings with tiny pale leaves on a stem. I saw them and can testify.

He was the middle child in a family of seven children and didn't naturally fit with the older kids or the little ones. His closest associates were the other middle children, Danny and Maggie—but Danny and Maggie were swingmen who could play two positions. Danny would be with Stevo one day and the next he'd drop down to dominate Ann and me. Maggie could hang with Stevo or with the older kids. Stevo didn't have that luxury. He was stuck in the middle.

Stevo was a musician—a self taught drummer who played in a string of local Sacramento rock bands in the mid-to-late 1960s. They battled other bands at local shopping centers and played teen dances at the Cottage Park youth center. Although I never heard one of his bands, it occurs to me that they undoubtedly played Chuck Berry songs, and I would love now to hear Stevo play "Roll Over Beethoven" or "Bye, Bye, Johnny." He was good enough to play in the minors. His group once opened for Sly and the Family

Stone. Stevo played Sly's drummer's set during sound check and got caught. Sly's drummer wasn't pleased. But Stevo could shrug off such stuff. He was certifiably cool.

He was also tough as nails. He once walked home from a car crash on a badly broken foot. Another crash left the circular gash in his cheek. Stevo could fight when he had to, but we saw him cry when a new arrest meant he might graduate from county jail to state prison. Hard time scared him.

Like my father, he was locally famous. He once borrowed a moped and led a pack of Hells Angels through town on their Harleys. Once Danny came across a crowd of young people outside of a concert hall chanting, "Stevo! Stevo! Stevo!" He didn't know what they expected, but watched as Stevo rose, told the crowd he wasn't "in the mood," and then quieted them by taking a quick bow.

Stevo enjoyed my dad even during Daddy's precipitous decline. He'd sit and talk with him during those last years when there seemed no point in doing so. As Stevo got older, he and my dad would sometimes drink themselves into insanity and run amok inside our house. Stevo thought it was funny, which it sometimes was, but more often it was a sort of hell. I remember Stevo laughing as my father chased him through the house with a plastic pitcher of my dad's pee. That night Stevo hit my mother over the head with a plastic TV table.

I told my mother we needed to move out, and the very next day we did.

But Stevo could also honor my mom. "You were a mother and a father to us," he told her one day, staring into the distance, a little drunk.

He had, at times, a quick wit. In a grocery store newly equipped with closed circuit cameras Danny, Stevo, and our sister Rooney took turns mugging in front of the camera. Danny and Rooney did quick bows. Then, while the other two watched the monitor, Stevo stood in front of the camera, looked right, looked left, and stuffed a pound of bacon under his jacket. His humor was goofily weird.

When the A's moved to Oakland there was a joke going round. "Are you a Giant fan or an Athletic supporter?" The joke was the notion of a being a jock strap, but Stevo got as big a kick from the idea of a "giant fan." I don't know if he envisioned a giant electric fan or a folding ladies' fan, but he was ahead of the artist Claus Oldenburg, who designed a giant kid's baseball mitt outside the A's stadium.

In other ways he was a dummy. On a trip to Europe with Paul, Gina, and Danny, Stevo didn't seem to grasp that people in other countries spoke other languages or used other money. In London the others left Stevo in a hotel and returned to find him gone. When they inquired at the desk the clerk responded: "Oh, you mean 'Fuck your fucking hotel? Fuck your warm beer? Fuck your fucking accents?' Oh, and 'Fuck your fucking Queen?' Yes—I remember him. He's no longer a guest at our hotel."

But Stevo was a gifted philosopher of pop culture, sports, and politics, which he understood in a deep and instinctual way, and which he liked to teach, lecturing us in the living room or from the front seat of a moving car. Blazing south one night on Highway 99 in California, Stevo held forth on song after song on some 50,000-watt rock and roll radio show, discussing obscure hits and forgotten performers. Paul would test him in "Name that Tune," twisting the volume knob off as soon as a song began. Stevo was unbeatable. He recognized songs from a single beat or note, then could expound on the author, the band, the roots of the music, the time he saw it performed, or the time he drank wine with the performer.

He was a savant.

He was unconcerned with contemporary fashion or taste. In the late 1960s it was unusual to hear a long haired tough guy defend Frank Sinatra or Tony Bennett, but Stevo did it with force and eloquence. I remember him describing the serious chops of Jackie Gleason and Mickey Rooney. He lauded Sammy Davis Junior. "He's a Nixon supporter!" we said. "He's an entertainer," Stevo told us. "He can dance, sing, act, tell jokes. He does it all!" (Just yesterday I read a nearly identical assessment of Sammy Davis, Jr. by the great bluesman and entertainer, Bobby Rush. Stevo would have loved Bobby Rush, and I suspect Rush would have appreciated Stevo.)

Because of the difference in our ages Stevo and I weren't very close, at least early on. I remember him trying to roughhouse with me when I was six or seven. He was trying to have a good time. I didn't like it. He was thirteen or fourteen and smelled different, and I was the prissy Little Professor who told my dad that the Blessed Virgin was more beautiful than my mom. But little by little, as I grew closer to him in age, our relationship grew. I remember that he gave me a red plastic gum machine with real gum. He bought it right in front of me. He told me it was for Danny. I told him that it was an excellent gift, then opened it on Christmas Eve.

A few years later I began copying Stevo on the drums, sneaking in to play his beautiful blue set any time he wasn't at home. His friend Dee caught me playing along to "Love Me Do" and taught me my first real beat.

I remember once asking Stevo what he wanted for his birthday. He told me to get him the original album by The Monkees. I did so proudly. The Monkees, in those days, were right up my alley, the most popular group among sixth graders at my elementary school. But just before I presented it, Stevo opened a package of new records by The Grateful Dead, the Paul Butterfield Blues Band, and The Jefferson Airplane. By the time he opened my slim little package his interest in The Monkees had been erased by these newer, hipper gifts. I was ashamed, but Stevo was nice about it.

It was Stevo, of course, who gave me Chuck Berry. And years later it was Stevo who filled in important blanks in my own knowledge.

Chuck Berry's first hit, "Maybellene," was recorded a year before I was born. I'd never been conscious of hearing one of my hero's hits at the time it was new. I barely knew the songs the first time I heard him. But Stevo told me that Chuck Berry's "No Particular Place to Go" was a hit back in 1964 when my mother packed six of us kids into her station wagon and drove us to Missouri to visit our eldest brother Paul. Stevo said that our mother didn't like us to hear it, because of its suggestive lyrics, and would turn it down.

As we got older there were more moments. Once he came to my apartment and I played him a tape of a song I'd written. It was a funny blues written from the perspective of an alcoholic. Stevo listened and laughed. "Who's singing?" he asked. "That's me!" I told him. "That ain't you," he said. Later, as I drove him home (Stevo frequently lost his driving privileges) he told me we should start a band, and that he'd play drums. We never did it, but I was surprised and honored.

I remember a couple of incidents at Stevo's apartments. Once Stevo and I shared a six pack. It was the first and last time we drank together. I got a little drunk and fell asleep on his couch. Later his roommate came home. The roommate was a rough biker type, but he and Stevo spoke in gentle whispers. "Who's that?" "My little brother. He had a little too much to drink."

At another apartment—an old place downtown—a neighbor began to yell at us. At some point I touched her shoulder. She called it an "assault." Two police officers arrived. They were nice but told me the woman was technically correct. Stevo intervened on my behalf and the officers left us with a polite warning. "That was close," he told me, and then explained that his pocket was full of heroin.

Stevo kept trying to get clean. Unlike my dad, he found Alcoholics Anonymous and enjoyed the meetings. He felt at home with the stories of drunken chaos. When Stevo's crazy friends would catch up with him he'd move, always switching apartments, always hoping that a new home would lead to a new life.

I remember once when he was looking for a new place. I was home that summer washing dishes at a restaurant. Stevo had no license or car at the time and asked me to drive him this way and that across the sprawl of suburban Sacramento. "Let's check out Fair Oaks Boulevard," he said. Every time we'd get close to some destination, he'd change his mind about the neighborhood and tell me to take him to some opposite and far off corner of town. "Let's try Del Paso

Boulevard. I like it out there." I dutifully turned. It was a huge waste of time, and fun—a couple of wasted hours I will always cherish.

In the middle of that night my mom flung open the door to the guest room where I was sleeping and switched on the light. Her face was serious. She ordered me to get up. I had never seen her so stressed or so forceful. She was all business. "Get dressed! Stevo's at the hospital!" As we drove she told me that Stevo's friend had called her. He didn't say if Stevo was okay—only that she had to go to the hospital quickly. Then he hung up.

"He was crying," she told me.

We rode grimly. You can sense the worst. We entered a dark waiting room with fish and shadows and sleepy, worried people. A doctor came in. He looked exhausted. He mumbled what he could. I watched my mother wither in grief. I've never felt as helpless or as useless.

In the next couple of days, we learned only the sketchiest details of Stevo's death. He was dragged out of a bar by the bouncer and pushed into traffic. It was essentially a homicide.

I quit my job at the restaurant and moved to Seattle, where my brother Paul lived. Maybe it's just a coincidence that when Stevo died, my interest in Chuck Berry faded for a while, too.

Probably not.

And maybe Stevo wasn't autistic, but I bet he was.

22

The Paper Haystack

A few weeks or months before my first session with the exact right person, a friend I used to work with emailed to ask when I would write a book about my cases. My response was: never. I had once tried to write about a favorite case and client and found it stressful and a bit depressing to relive the years of conflict and struggle the case involved—lies, dishonesty and obstruction from the defense, years of appeals, and many disappointments (before a rousing victory).

Besides—although I considered each case a sort of work of art, I didn't think I could explain that to others. When lawyers talk about their cases other lawyers call it "war stories." I didn't want to tell "war stories," and I doubted what interested me about my work would interest many other people.

But then I learned I was autistic, which put the war stories in a new light. My so-called "disorder" was suddenly a hero, planting its flag on the backs of negligent corporations, both private and public. So, here's a war story, or maybe the story of my first skirmish—a case where autistic persistence and an autistic eye for detail settled a big case.

The case involved a child's serious adverse reaction to a diphtheria-tetanus-pertussis, or DPT, vaccine. Our client was a boy who received the shot as an infant and had a seizure immediately after his injection. He later developed a seizure disorder and suffered a serious brain injury as a result.

In this age of vaccine deniers I recognize the irony of launching my autistic legal career with a case that alleged a vaccine had caused brain damage, but let's be clear that we weren't claiming the vaccine had caused autism, and that I don't consider autism to be brain damage or even a disorder. The boy was not autistic. Our case involved an FDA-recognized "bad batch" of a highly reactive whole cell DPT vaccine that had caused numerous adverse reactions before it hurt our client. A respected pediatrician and a university professor were both ready to testify the vaccine caused our client's injuries.

By that time, I had cut my teeth on a handful of toxic tort and product liability cases. One of my early strengths was that I knew nothing about law or civil procedure. If an attorney asked me to do some interrogatories, I would ask someone what "interrogatories" were, (they are written questions to the other side,) and then write a set from scratch. Most people recycled old ones. But, in truth, my boss, Paul Whelan, only asked me to do things a few times. After that I figured out what needed doing and did it.

Knowing now that I'm autistic, I could not have had a better mentor. Paul was a legend in Washington State legal circles—especially for his work on product liability cases. He was a quick study, great with judges and mediators, and was liked and respected by opposing counsel. He had taken on the lead industry in Idaho and the asbestos industry in Washington and then, with a little help from his autistic friend, me, he became one of the top automotive product liability lawyers on the west coast. He was different from me in most respects—gregarious, cheerful, a charmer, and a flirt. He enjoyed the good life. He wore expensive clothes and drank expensive wine. He owned a series of boats that got bigger and bigger. He drove a series of Mercedes once he gave up on big motorcycles. He had a series of marriages, too, until he met Kathryn, with whom he remained happily and proudly married until his own death parted them 30 years later. In his later years, after decades of hard work, he often showed up at the office around 10 am, read the paper for a while, visited with whoever showed up at his door, and after doing a bit of work, left around 3 pm, heading to his boat and hollering at all the worker bees to "Go home! Go home!" But he was an incredibly smart lawyer, a great delegator of responsibility and, if he liked and trusted you, a gifted manager of people.

Luckily, he liked and trusted me from the start, and never had to manage me. That was key. Paul freed me to follow my often-quirky instincts and gave me a safe environment to do so. He never told me what to do, and rarely told me not to do something I wanted to try. Instead, he provided a kind of safety net. I'd bring him my next goofy idea, and if he said "go for it," I knew I'd be okay.

(I once had one manager who told me exactly what to do. I worked at the Jolly Tiger restaurant in Sacramento in the weeks before Stevo died. I was the dishwasher. My assistant manager was a bossy little runt about my age. He ordered me to take the blue plastic strainer from the men's urinal and run it through the same dishwashing machine that washed the cups, saucers, plates, and silverware. "You want me to take that thing out of the urinal and put it in the dishwasher?" I don't remember having to have a food handler's permit on that job, or a toilet handler's permit either. "You're the boss," I told him—a concept he surely relished. I ran the urinal strainer through the dishwasher every shift until the night Stevo died, and then never returned. My brother-in-law Ty sued them for the wages they refused to pay me.)

We lassoed the DPT case in true Paul Whelan style. The referring lawyer was in a small town about ninety minutes away by car. The lawyer invited us down to audition and meet the family. Instead of driving, Paul decided to charter a twin engine plane at Boeing Field—a decision that probably doubled our travel time. Now, instead of a ninety minute drive we had to drive to an airport, find the charter company, check in, fly 90 miles, de-board, and get a ride into town. But it was impressive! Even the lawyer who had to pick us up the airport and then drive us back to the airport a couple of hours later had to chuckle and admire the extravagant lunacy of it.

On the DPT case I began what would become my standard practice: I called lawyers and paralegals around the country who were handling or had handled cases involving the same product and asked for whatever advice they could give me. Once I had accumulated some knowledge myself, I did the same thing in reverse—I shared everything I could legally share with anyone handling a similar case. It is the best way for the little guys to be successful fighting giant corporations.

At some point the drug company invited us to a document production in New York City. Since this was 1986 or 1987, the documents were produced as paper copies, numbered on the bottom and produced to us by the ton in a windowless conference room at a very fancy New York law firm. It would be the first of many giant document productions I participated in. We got one chance to look at the documents and select what we wanted.

Before leaving for New York City, I called a lawyer who had handled a case involving the same "bad batch" of vaccine. The lawyer was careful not to divulge any protected secrets. Like most product liability cases, these DPT vaccine cases were litigated under protective orders. You notice I haven't divulged the name of the vaccine manufacturer. I could, legally, but I won't. The lawyer I spoke with was similarly careful, but he told me this much: "Peter, there's one document they don't want you to find. Our case settled because we found it. It will be part of your production. Find that document and they will settle your case."

That was all I needed.

The vaccine in our case was bad for two reasons. First, it was a bad batch or lot of vaccine—something had gone wrong in the processing. The company's own technicians found odd particles inside the vaccine vials. The FDA flagged the lot as causing a large number of adverse reactions, some, like ours, quite serious.

But it was also "bad" because it used whole cells of the bordetella pertussis bacterium. The whole cell vaccine was known to produce adverse reactions, some minor, some more serious. The manufacturer's internal documents acknowledged this.

A few years earlier a different company made a version of the vaccine using fractionated cell particles. The fractionated, or "acellular," vaccine was recognized as causing fewer adverse reactions. Unfortunately, that company stopped making the better vaccine. However, when they did so they offered to sell rights to produce their superior vaccine to the other vaccine manufacturers—but the defendant in our case declined to buy it.

Then our really bad batch of the bad vaccine got onto the market and our kid was catastrophically injured.

So off we went to New York City.

Paul, being Paul, tried to book a room for himself at the Plaza, but Paul was born on December 25, and as luck would have it, there was no room at that luxurious inn. He and our co-counsel settled on the somewhat less exalted (but equally comfortable) St. Regis, and I found a $60 hotel much closer to the midtown law firm where the document production would take place. My place was perfectly comfortable. (This became a pattern for me on business travel. I did my best to save our clients money whenever I could by looking for good deals and skipping expensive hotel breakfasts.)

The documents were produced at a mid-town law firm with fancy oak paneling and lots of employees. The three of us were escorted to a conference room with a big table and no windows. Every now and then clerks would arrive with carts stacked with paper. Foot tall stacks were set on the table twenty or thirty at a time for us to review. When we finished one set, they brought another. The pages were numbered, and we had special pink carbon paper sheets where we logged our requests for copies in duplicate.

I didn't worry about Paul. He was smart, and in this instance, he was slow. He had no real interest in fanning through ream after ream of photocopies.

I worried more about our co-counsel. He was smart, too, and seemed intent on proving this to us. Every couple of minutes he asked me some impossible question that interrupted my work.

"Peter, have you seen the December 12, 1964, memo from Duckwiler?"

Sometimes I had, sometimes I hadn't, and more often I had no idea—but every time I was annoyed by the interruptions. Responding, or having him read the document to me, wasted precious time.

I first learned that I loved huge document dumps on this trip. I could plow through the paper faster than anyone, and I was confident in my ability to spot the important ones. Years later I would try to teach my process to other lawyers and paralegals, but I now understand I was born with a unique ability to spot patterns and detail. Score one for autism. As a sixteen-year-old college student I used to go to the San Jose municipal library and pour through old copies of Billboard Magazine looking for the name of my childhood hero. His name would pop from the page, every time.

The same thing occurred with these neat stacks of old photocopies. For all intents and purposes they were haystacks, designed to hide the glittering needles that would win or settle our case among mind-numbingly dull corporate and laboratory documents.

I wanted to make sure we found the document the lawyer told me would settle our case, and even without a diagnosis I was certain I was the person best equipped to find it.

I see now that the reason I was able to move through those stacks so quickly was that I was using my ability to think visually. Think back yourself to one of those corny television cop shows where we watch a monitor as the computer looks through thousands or hundreds of thousands of images to find the right one. It's a bit like that, though at a more human pace. I quickly learn the look and shape of meaningless documents—hum drum reports of no consequence—which make the more important documents pop. Suddenly there's a memo that looks different. Suddenly there's a name of a person you've learned was in the thick of it. Look more closely. I took nearly all the emails, all the complaints, and anything in a pinched scribble. I took minutes of any meeting about quality. I stopped to read the more interesting looking memoranda.

We looked at paper for four straight days, from 8 am until 5. We went through hundreds of neat, foot tall stacks of documents. I found lots of good stuff. I hoped the others were finding good stuff, too. I wanted to doublecheck their work, but couldn't, because it would have been rude.

Sometime after lunch on the fourth day the clerks came in to remove the last batch documents we'd gone through. We were talking about our departure plans—flights and an airport taxi.

The head clerk looked bored. "There's one more load of documents. Do you want to look at them?"

A taxi beckoned. A drink at the airport.

"Sure," we said, without enthusiasm.

They brought in the final batch, smaller than earlier ones, perhaps a dozen stacks total.

And in one of my piles, there it was.

It popped like the name of Chuck Berry from a forest of print! It was a detailed and chilling calculation of benefit to risk, from the corporate point of view. I no longer have it, of course, but the gist of it was something like this:

> We have an opportunity to purchase the rights to produce the better, less reactive acellular vaccine. It will cost XX thousands of dollars to purchase the rights and gear up for production. In the alternative, we can continue to produce our own more more reactive whole cell vaccine. Continuing to produce and sell our more reactive vaccine will injure babies and result in lawsuits. Over X years there will be X lawsuits resulting in X dollars in legal costs, verdicts and settlements. Since the cost of purchasing the rights

(XX) is greater than the anticipated cost of future lawsuits (X) we recommend against purchasing the rights to produce the safer, less reactive vaccine.

Evidently they put this document in the last batch, hoping we would be too tired to look or long gone. That was somewhat devious, but I am touched by the essential honesty that gave it to us at all—two or three pages among hundreds of thousands, but I bet quite a few people and lawyers would have simply left it out of the pile.

It was not the last such cost-benefit document we would see in our product liability cases. We would find similar ones in Ford and General Motors fire cases. But it was by far the most explicit, and finding it meant that our case would go no further. Within a short time, and prior to any additional discovery, we would resolve the case for an amount that would make the cost-benefit document's authors blush—far more than they evidently thought possible, and far more than it would have cost to purchase the right to produce the safer vaccine. So even from the corporate point of view, the cost benefit analysis failed the corporation. From our client's point of view, the failure was even more egregious. He suffered needlessly because a corporation decided it was cheaper to injure children and pay legal costs than to produce a safer vaccine.

I'm not arguing against vaccines. Their benefit is real. As a former Peace Corps Volunteer I've had dozens and dozens of them, sometimes with painful reactions, and three years after we settled our vaccine case my first born, Jade, received the exact same vaccine as my client, though presumably not from a bad batch. But I'm happy to say—perhaps because of lawsuits like ours—my youngest child definitely got a safer, less reactive, acellular pertussis vaccine, and that maybe my very autistic persistence and eye for detail played a role in that.

But I was only getting started.

23

Better Off Dead

From the moment I arrive in Togo, I know I have stumbled into something wonderful. We arrive at night, and as we leave the airport I stare at the long, dark roads and streets lit by the kerosene lamps of a scattered few, then dozens, then hundreds of street vendors. People walk in the dark streets, sometimes with a flashlight, sometimes not. I had caught a glimpse of the variety in clothing during a change of planes in Senegal—men in jeans and t-shirts, or long Muslim kaftans, or slacks with western shirts, or shirts cut straight along the bottom, or traditional suits sewn from bright African or Dutch fabrics and heavily embroidered at the collar, sleeves, and hems. Here the dirty shorts of working men are added to the mix, along with elegant *kenté* cloths worn like the toga of a Roman emperor (or the kenté of an Ewé king); and despite the darkness I begin to learn that women in 1980 Togo mostly wear two- or three-piece *complets*—a blouse and skirt made from beautiful cloth, often intricately ribbed by the tailor, with a third piece of the same cloth as a wrap and to hold the baby. For the younger women and girls it might be simply a traditional skirt or cloth wrap and a modern blouse. Other Americans on the bus are laughing and talking to each other. I am glued to the window absorbing everything I see.

The next day I take my first excursion, leaving our late colonial era hotel to walk a mile or so to the *Grand Marché*. The Hotel is Le Benin, five or six stories tall with a formal tropical garden, a swimming pool, and lots of tall palm trees. Lizards, about a foot long, do pushups in the dirt paths. Across the two lane highway is the Atlantic Ocean and Beach Club Benin, where in coming years I will enjoy expensive thirty cent beers while watching giant waves crash onto the beach. I will learn that in the mornings the beach provides toilet facilities for many residents of the Kodjoviakopé neighborhood, but whatever they leave there washes away. Despite that, I'll swim in the big waves when I get a chance.

Most of the streets leading to the market are made of sand and dirt. Cars, trucks, motor scooters, and bicycles are everywhere, often honking. Taxis, I will learn, have a fixed rate of about thirty cents a carload to go anywhere in town, providing some of the world's best and most convenient public transportation. Highlife and reggae music blare from every small, open-air bar where people sit drinking Togo's fine German style beer. On the sidewalk a fat woman serves up giant plates of breakfast—rice, beans, eggs, noodles, meat, sauces, fish, peppers, what have you. There is a kind of chick pea called *azikokwi* that will become a favorite of mine. Months from now, when I am getting skinnier and skinnier in Better Off Dead, I will use plates of this street-side breakfast smorgasbord to restore myself whenever I come to the capital. Today I just look.

As I get closer to the *Grand Marché* the crowds of people become more and more dense. Children call me "*yovo!*" and turn it into a song. "*Yovo, yovo! Bon soir! Ça va bien? Merci!*" Vendors fill every available bit of real estate at the sidewalks' edge, their homemade wooden tables stacked with cigarettes, matches, mosquito coils, playing cards, cassette tapes, Quaker Oats in a can, canned coffee, canned sardines, canned mackerel, canned margarine, canned milk, nail polish, soap, laundry detergent, hair products, birth control pills, machetes—the list literally could fill pages. Little children wander the street with a few boxes of matches or tiny cans of tomato paste balanced on a tray or basket on top their heads. A man with an umbrella cap sells "*essi glacéééé,*" which I can see is "cold water" sold in bulging plastic bags tied shut and torn at the corner to shoot an ice cold stream into your mouth. It is stunningly hot and humid. Cold water would be good now, but as a newcomer trying to stay well, I don't dare drink any. Closer to the market food vendors spread vegetables and yams on mats on the ground, and money changers wander offering *francs, naira, cedis,* and dollars in whatever language they think might work with me.

The market itself is extraordinary—a three story concrete box, almost like a downtown parking structure but without ramps. It's so crowded now you have to push your way forward or be pushed along by the people behind you. It is nearly overwhelming. The first floor is devoted to food—probably an acre of big wooden tables covered in tomatoes, okra, onions, garlic, yams, cassava, potatoes, greens, lettuce, fish, beans, nuts, peanuts, seeds, carrots, along with busy butcher tables where every part of the unfortunate animals who arrived there this morning is on display or being actively disassembled by knife and machete—and nearly everyone I pass yells, "*Yovo?*"

I climb the concrete stairs and everything changes—I am suddenly in a sort of cathedral of cloth, with stall after stall displaying hundreds of varieties of printed and woven fabric folded into flat bolts and piled high along the three walls of each shop. The women who run these stands and import the cloth from places like Holland and Jakarta are said to be (or at least to include) some of the richest and most powerful individuals in Togo. They are called "*Nana Benz,*" after the cars they own. Someday, soon, as a full-fledged volunteer, I will stand behind a *Nana Benz* at the bank while the cashier rapidly counts stacks of bills as high as the stacks of paper that will be at my future document productions. If you have seen Chaplin's *Monsieur Verdoux* you have seen this particular bank clerk, whose fingers fly through the eight inch stack of bills like a buzz saw. (Even faster than I will fly through documents a few years hence.) Every *Nana Benz* calls my new name. "*Yovo! Yovo! Viens ici!*" Some jokingly offer me their daughters in marriage. I smile and thank them. I'm suddenly a catch.

I climb another set of concrete stairs and find just about everything else that is available for purchase in Togo this year: bicycle parts, hardware, tools, hinges, locks, door knobs, rebar, concrete, shortwave radios, enamel plates and dishes, cooking pots, cast iron cauldrons, charcoal stoves, playing cards, cookware, plastic buckets, zinc buckets, plastic bowls, plastic sheeting, hoes, machetes, flashlights, batteries, kerosene lamps, mosquito coils, mosquito netting, monkey skulls, feathers, small bones, antique trading beads, cheap modern glass beads.

And finally, after an hour or so, I return to the *Hotel Le Benin* where an air conditioner awaits, and where I collapse on the bed and process what I have just experienced. This is, I now recognize, a happy autistic shutdown. I have reached my limits. I process. I hear again every new sound I have heard and see again every new thing I have seen and smell again every new smell I have smelled. I close my eyes to a rush of all my senses, an experience not too different from the final scenes of the film 2001, where the lights streak past as the astronaut enters the unknown. I am overwhelmed and exhausted, but very, very happy.

For the next two and a half months we are in training. We start in the hillside city of Atakpamé. We are staying at a girls' *college*, or middle school. We sleep in a large dormitory where beds are separated by cotton fabric. We take blessedly cold-water showers, still being careful not to let a single drop of the tap water enter our mouths. Our training has two main components. In the morning we learn to teach English at the teacher's college. Our primary instructor and mentor there is a man named Kodjo for whom every school child snaps instantly to attention. The other main component of our training is French language instruction. People who already know French start to learn one of the local languages.

Something happens that surprises me now. For the first time since high school, I am part of things. I am far from the center of things, but I am part of it all. In the evenings I go to local bars with other *stagiaires.* We talk and joke. A cute girl with short red hair takes an interest me. It has been a while since such a thing has happened and I am pleased. She takes me to a little bar where we sit at an open window and watch the world of Atakpamé walk by. We drink cold beer and a local white lightning called *sodabi.* I foolishly buy a couple of Marlboros from the woman outside who sells them one by one for a few cents apiece and I am suddenly a smoker again, after several years of abstinence. I am becoming a human being again, too.

I become friendly enough with enough of the Americans but start to take even more pleasure from talking with our Togolese French teachers. One striking young teacher takes a couple of us on a walk through Atakpamé and, for the first time, I find I am actually speaking French. We talk about politics, life, and culture in our two countries. By the time we finish training a month from now in a different town, I will be on my way to fluency, at least in village-level Togolese French.

The second month of training takes place in Sokodé, Togo's only majority muslim city. Sokodé has a completely different feel from Atakpamé. Atakpamé is built on hills, and if you blur your eyes a bit the rusty, red corrugated steel roofs and golden yellow walls can almost make you believe you are in some Tuscan hillside village. Sokodé is flat and red.

Now we live in houses spread around town, six or eight people in each house, and meet up for training at a school down the road. First, we have to teach our fellow trainees who will pretend to be students. When I stand in front of them and do my lesson, two of the popular girls pretend not to understand, making big gestures of confusion. They did no such thing during their own lessons, which, evidently, were beyond reproach or criticism. I know that what they are doing is unfair, but what can I do? One of these women lives in my house. She hates me. She will tell me so one day, but only after she has gotten to know me and has changed her mind and likes me.

"You are not at all who I thought you were," she'll tell me.

There's a lesson there. Sometimes you have to get to know someone before you can hate them or like them. And sometimes a person who is a bit different takes a little longer to understand.

But the next day real children are in the classroom, and the tables turn. My assignment is to teach "big, bigger, biggest." I am ready. I walk to the blackboard, which is a smooth panel of concrete, painted black, that protrudes an inch or so from the concrete block wall.

I draw a chicken.

"What is this?" I ask. There are always some smart kids in the room, and they are the same on every continent. I call on one who is frantically shaking her raised hand.

"Eet eez a cheeken," she tells me confidently and with great pride.

"Yes! It is a chicken!" I say, and then turn to another girl.

"What is it?"

"It eez a chicken!"

"Is it a *big* chicken?" I spread my hands to the size of a beachball. More hands raised and shaking. I call on a boy.

"Yes, eats *big* chicken!"

"It's a big chicken," I say, nodding.

Then I draw a much bigger chicken. They all laugh. My cartooning skills are good—a potential fall back if lawyering fails me. This chicken is the size of a wolf.

"Big chicken!" I say, pointing to number one. "Bigger chicken!" I say, pointing to number two.

They are all chiming in now so after we have talked about the relative size of the chickens, I have children stand, two at a time.

"Is Koffi big?"

"Yes, Koffi is big!"

"Is Mawulé bigger?"

"Yes, Mawulé is bigger!"

And when we've got those two words down, I start at the very top of the blackboard and draw two giant chicken legs that spread into claws at the very bottom of the blackboard.

"The biggest chicken!" I say, and then draw a planet featuring the giant continent of Africa. "The biggest chicken in the world!" And they all repeat it giddily.

"Thee beegest cheecken een thee world!!!"

I have won the day and feel vindicated. The two popular, neurotypical girls who scorned my practice teaching a day earlier watch the delight of my students with jealousy, dismay, and confusion. They are supposed to win, every time, but their own lessons with real students did not go well.

I bet every one of those children (now in their fifties) remembers my lesson to this day. I hope my two tormentors do, too.

When we finally finish training, it is time to pick our assignments. We each get to submit three choices. I choose a village I visited during training and two that I've heard good things about. As far as I know, every single volunteer gets their first or second choice—except me. I am the last to be assigned and am given the name of a town I've never even heard of.

At first it is only a rumor. Several of my Togolese French teachers surround me and tell me, "Peter, don't go! They have assigned you to a terrible place! The people there are wizards and witches! They are experts at magic and poison! They will kill you. Even the town—the town is called 'Death is Better!' Don't go!"

I am given my assignment by two middle aged Togolese men. One works at the Peace Corps office. The other is a middle school director on the rise. Years later I will read that he became an important government minister.

I tell them what my Togolese friends have told me—that they say I should refuse this assignment. The two older gentlemen shake their heads, smile, and make small clucking sounds. The future minister speaks glowingly and like a politician.

"It's prejudice, Peter. You'll love it there! It sits atop a plateau. The climate is mild, the best in the country. And the *college* is run by my friend, a fine and progressive man. He has a car. He will take you into the city. You are very lucky to be assigned there. The teachers you talked to are just ignorant and superstitious."

Then, somewhat dampening this optimistic pitch he adds:

"Just go to work, teach your classes, and then go home. Don't talk to anyone and you will be fine."

To close the deal he adds, "Above all, don't talk to any of the girls!"

In my own mind, the name "Death is Better" begins to transform into "Better Off Dead."

The future minister explains the name to me. It is a proud one. Once upon a time a group of people were escaping from the evil king Agorkoli. When they arrived in the beautiful hills and saw all the fine agricultural and grazing land, they decided not to run any further. "Death is better than running," they said, thus naming the town.

I will be the only American and the only foreigner in Better Off Dead. Every other volunteer will either share their town or village with one or more other volunteers, or at least have someone very nearby. My closest American neighbors will be 30 or 40 miles away, which, I will soon learn, can mean half a day or more of travel. Contrary to his friend's promise, my school director will drive me to the big city just once.

I point out to the future politician that every other volunteer got their first or second choice. "Why not me?"

"You are always calm, Peter. Some of these others, they could not make it in Death is Better—but you will do fine!"

Oh! Thanks for noticing my autistic difference!

So off I go—dropped off after dark on a rainy night. After a day or two shopping at the *Grand Marché* in Lomé I am equipped with a couple of brand new kerosene lanterns, a small foam Peace Corps issued mattress, a bucket, a shortwave radio, the materials to build a water filter, a little hibachi kind of thing, a *bidon* of kerosene, a gas stove, a canister of gas, and a few other essentials. I am also given a luxury item—a small, rusty, broken down, kerosene powered refrigerator. I will only be able to get it to work for a week or two in the next three years.

We are supposed to be given basic furniture by our Togolese landlords. It is part of the contract. I will later visit the homes of volunteers who enjoy running water, electricity, couches, armchairs, tables, dining sets, and huge, comfortable beds in every room. Me—in three years I will never receive a stick of furniture from my landlord, a wealthy man who visits me often, shrugs and says, over and over for years after it is true, "Monsieur Peter, what can I do? The government has not paid rent."

If you're reading this now, landlord, go fuck yourself.

As I say, I am dropped off in darkness during a storm. The chief's son lets me into my house. It is brand new, the color of concrete, and still unpainted, inside or out. It will still be unpainted three years hence when I leave. When the chief's son sees the dark, unfurnished rooms, he feels badly enough for me that he sends for a child-sized steel and Formica table and a child-sized steel and wood chair. I am ready for kindergarten. I struggle to fill and light my kerosene lamps for the first time, and when I am successful, everybody leaves. I lay my foam mattress in middle of the concrete living room floor and fall asleep to the sound of rain drumming on my brand new steel roof. The bats have not yet made a home in my attic.

I wake to the sun, which rises every morning at about 6 am. I open my eyes. Ten feet away, five or six small faces fill my one glass window. When I sit up, they giggle, scream, and run.

I am determined to make friends.

During our training, a departing second year volunteer dispensed some good advice. She encouraged us to seek out important people in the village and do our best to make friends with them.

"These people will really help you when the time comes that you need some help. So, when you meet them, invite them to visit. And be ready for them. Have some beer or soft drinks and some snacks."

I try. I have just finished three years where I was more alone than I ever have been or ever will be, but suddenly I am *Monsieur Sociabilité*. I walk through town like the stranger in an old western. Eyes follow me everywhere. Babies see my bizarre skin tone and hair and burst into inconsolable shrieks of terror. I shake many, many hands. I ask about people's jobs, wives, homes, and children. I buy rounds of beer and *pamprankou*—a fermented drink made from raffia trees that smells to me like Cheerios left too long in a bowl of milk but that has advantages beyond the gentle buzz it provides.

"*Ça fait bien pisser!*" says the elder Mr. Dando, with a happy smile.

The remark is as befuddling to me as when Terri showed me her contraceptives. I smile, nod, and finish my calabash, confused but at least confident in the knowledge that I will "piss well" tonight.

Lots of people introduce themselves to me. Lots of people accept my offers of drinks. I like to watch them pour a drop for the ancestors before taking their first sip. I learn the pleasure of *sodabi,* the homemade gin distilled from palm wine.

The two villagers who are friendliest to me are the Dando brothers. Both Dandos have children in the school where I will teach. One of the Dandos is the "catechist"—the man who guides the Catholic congregation through Sunday services when a visiting priest isn't available to say an actual mass. I will learn that in addition to being a devout Catholic, he is a firm believer in the local gods. He gives me some hope when he asks if I speak the local language. I tell him no. "You'll learn it. When you play with the girls, they will teach you!" I listen with interest. Maybe the future government minister was wrong about the girls. I invite both Dandos to my house. "How about Sunday, after mass?" I ask the catechist.

"I will come!" he responds dynamically.

I prepare for the visit. I buy soft drinks and beer, peanuts and cookies, and even a bottle of Johnnie Walker Red Label Scotch whisky, which, like Quaker Oats and Marlboros, is available tax free everywhere in Togo, including Death is Better.

I wait. He never comes. I crack open the bottle of Scotch and follow a shot with a slug of warm beer from the bottle.

This sad scenario repeats itself a dozen times. I invite various teachers and "*fonctionnaires.*" *Ils ne viennent pas.* I invite the Dandos again and again. They don't come.

In Seattle I had been alone for a reason. I invited no one. Here I am doing everything I can to be more sociable. The foreign language and culture somehow free me to do so. I am becoming a new person, but with the same old result.

Even the teachers at my school don't visit. They are friendly at work, but aside from my school director (friend of the future minister) they never come by, despite my invitations, and even the director only stops once or twice to say hello and check on me. So even though I am learning to reach out to people, it is not working. It's like the pretty young woman I invited to the basketball game, but 100 times over, and makes no sense to me.

I decide to finish the school year and go home. In letters home I call Death is Better "Better Off Dead."

Then one day some newly minted teachers are assigned to our school. I see them congregating with the other young teachers in front of a house on the main road where several teachers live. I decide to make one last effort to be friendly with my colleagues.

One of the new teachers is an excitable man named Dadjo. Dadjo has an almond shaped face, facial scars, and heavy duty black-framed, Bo Diddley-style glasses. He shakes my hand with gusto and snaps my middle finger as he lets go.

"And do you all hang out with *Monsieur Pita*?" Dadjo asks the other teachers.

A quiet, polite teacher who has been around since the start of the year shakes his head and gazes at me.

"Mr. Peter likes to stay by himself."

This pisses me off. How can he say that after all the efforts I've made, for the first time in my life, to meet people? How can he say this after I've waited, time and again, for him and others to respond to my invitations.

"I like to stay by myself?" I repeat, nearly hissing. "That's not true. I invite you to my house all the time! You never come!"

I think these are the first angry words I speak in Africa—but I've had it.

The professor looks as befuddled as I feel, and a bit sad at being so maligned.

"I come to your house every day," he responds, shaking his head. "The front door is always closed."

And then I see it—a vision of startling clarity—how so many doors in the village are wide open so much of the day, with only beads or a sheet of light cloth to keep out the hot sun and flies.

How visitors approach those open doors clapping their hands to get the attention of people inside.

And how I, like any good American, go home every day and shut and lock my front door.

I understand, for the first time, that I simply haven't known or understood a cardinal rule of Togolese sociability.

I return home and leave my front door open. All afternoon and evening I am besieged by visitors. The teachers. My neighbors. Children from school. The Dandos. Dadjo.

And it is like that every day for the remaining two and a half years I live in Death is Better.

After learning about autism and the difficulty many autistic people have understanding neurotypical social rules, social cues and facial cues, I see this as a nearly perfect parable. My inability to understand how the social world works has had definite consequences. I failed with girls in college not because I didn't care, and not because I didn't want to be with them, and not even because they didn't want to be with me. Each of the young women I've described here obviously did, at least for a time. I just didn't understand the rules. I didn't understand how things work.

But little by little I am learning, not only the rules in Africa, which are new for me, but the general rules of sociability, which are more universal—and Africa and its people will be a huge part of that education.

24

How I Experience the World

I'm walking through my own neighborhood. It's something I have done for decades, but more frequently since the start of Covid. If I'm with Rebecca, or Rafferty, or Leila, I concentrate on being with them. If I'm with the elderly Peanut, we move so annoyingly slowly that I concentrate on the screen of my phone while Peanut concentrates on smells dogs have left near the sidewalk. But if I am alone, which I often am, I am drawn first to the details. A tiny series of trebly bleeps tells me that a troupe of bushtits is crossing my landscape. I find dozens in a small tree preparing their move to the next bush, which by their stealth and speed, appears to entail an element of daring. Do bigger birds represent a threat? Then a little grinding sound draws my eyes further up into a taller tree where a lone hummingbird sits like a tiny Pinocchio surveying his or her territory. Suddenly other hummingbirds catch my ears and eyes—two of them, one hovering with a humming sound just a few feet away. The birds take me on a 365 degree tour of the trees and gardens I am passing. I see the white flicker of junkos from behind. A wren hops bravely near my feet and doesn't try to flee. I look up to see the baby Madrona trees at one neighbor's house and wonder if they are natural or if someone managed to plant them, because I would like a madrona tree.

I keep walking. Further ahead I see movement in the Saint John's wort, the yellow flowers of which are alive with small bees. A few days ago, the same blossoms were visited by giant bumblebees that hovered near them like fat little bison.

I've begun to understand that I see the world differently than most people. I start at the most detailed level I can perceive and work my way out to a bigger picture. No wonder I loved the bizarre paintings of Hieronymus Bosch as a child. But happily, I don't stop at the details. As a young teenager I loved nature walks with rangers in the National Parks who showed us how the tiniest plants and animals affected the larger ecosystems and even geologic features around them. I like how things work together to make a whole, which itself is only a part of something even larger.

So, for me a tree is, first and foremost, the needles, or the leaves, or the bark, or the birds or bees that draw me there; and only then do I look at the tree as something bigger—a shimmering, green tower of leaves and branches quaking and sparkling in sunlight.

The same for my cases. Before there is liability, there are documents—hundreds or thousands of them: complaints, emails, test reports, police reports, photographs. As I start through them, I have very little notion what I will find, but through details a larger story emerges. To make the story clearer, even to myself, I begin to organize the most interesting documents chronologically. The bigger picture, or bigger story, becomes even clearer, ultimately revealing a more important story of longstanding and repeated negligence.

If I have the case long enough, I begin to connect pieces of the story in new, more meaningful ways. The connections present themselves in flashes of insight. I sometimes struggle to explain them to my coworkers for a time, but I understand them myself and I know I have found something important.

One brilliant young attorney who briefly helped us with our first exploding truck case, proposed simplifying our presentation to a purely legal one, which might have worked; but for me the real story of the corporation's negligence and its disregard for the lives of its customers and those who shared the road with them, could only be told through dozens of smaller decisions and choices that I saw reflected in documents that showed how the company repeatedly chose to continue tweaking and selling a truck it knew to be dangerous. In other words, the bigger, more important story could only be told through the details.

Sometimes the details become overwhelming. Right now, I am haunted by a hundred little chores I've been ignoring, ranging from taxes and bills, to blackberry vines, and clutter. I'm forever conscious of these issues, but paralyzed by them, too. I think perhaps my inattention to those details and my inability to take care of them is a different side of the same picture. We can talk about it later.

25

Better Off Alive

Living in Better Off Dead changed my life considerably. I had little choice but to fit in—or at least do my best to fit in. I was the only American for thirty miles in any direction, and thirty miles usually meant several hours waiting for a taxi to fill, and then several more hours on the road, stopping to pick up any person we found waiting on the roadside, whether there was room in the car or not, along with whatever they were bringing to town—anything from huge bags of coffee, cocoa, or maize, to squawking goats or a basket of live chickens.

Rural taxis were amazing. Most were jalopies with bad brakes and cracked windows sewn together with wire. One local driver, Tsombé, drove a newer Toyota Corolla and could easily squeeze seven to nine adults and several infants and children into it. I liked to ride with Tsombé because his first trip was at the crack of dawn and usually filled up immediately so you didn't have to wait. I'd be in Atakpamé within half an hour. As a foreign guest I was usually given a position of some honor in the front seat—but never so much honor that I rated shotgun. Instead I was usually told to squeeze in next to Tsombé with my butt on the parking brake handle and Tsombé's right hand reaching between or against my knees to shift gears. Seatbelts were out of the question, since only Tsombé got a seat to himself. Two adult men would be to my right, and a boatload of men, women, and children would be in the back. Tsombé's car was new, with good brakes. Other taxis not so much. Most were

1970s Japanese jalopy pickup trucks with thousand pound mahogany campers over the bed and cab. All but the luckiest two or three passengers rode in the bed, facing each other on loose wooden benches that would be routinely overloaded. (I remember one long and painful trip when a nursing baby next to me pushed its foot rhythmically into my full-to-bursting bladder for half the distance to Atakpamé.) The already top-heavy pickups were usually topped by towering piles of boxes, luggage, bags of coffee and maize, and uncomfortable goats. As a future automotive product liability attorney I was surprisingly nonchalant about the danger of it all. We routinely careened over mountain roads while the driver pumped the brakes furiously to get at least a few drops of brake fluid into those brake cylinders. Sometimes the driver intentionally aimed the overloaded, top-heavy, and horribly unstable truck at some hapless rodent hoping to bring some roadkill home for supper while the front seat passengers cheered. By the end of my three years all fear had evaporated and I was cheering the attempted slaughter with the rest of them. (Fear would not have been inappropriate. Occasionally we would pass the scene of a taxi disaster where the bones of an old pickup lay twisted in the distance. Passengers would get quiet for a while or make gentle clucking sounds.)

Once I learned the social rules, like not shutting the front door, I made friends in Africa, and from what I can tell my friends didn't think I was any stranger than any other American. We were all strange enough. My exuberant friend Dadjo did tell me that I walk funny, without moving my arms. We were just buddies. My teacher friends and I went out for beers almost every evening. Since I was actually getting paid and my friends were still waiting for the bureaucracy to kick in to get their first checks I did most of the buying early in the year and even later. I could afford it. I made about $100 a month and had nothing and no one to spend it on. We sat around banged up wooden tables in whatever little bar or *buvette* happened to have beer and talked and laughed, chased off flies, and watched the world go by.

I had fun using French. One day Mr. Niwou was hung over, so I told my friends about "the dog that bit you." After that we called beers "*les chiens.*" "*Pita! Tu veux un chien?*" Dadjo or Niwou would ask, laughing, and off we'd go. This was the first time in my life I ran with a crew. One night, talking over our "dogs," Dadjo became solemn and told me "Peter, if I were blind, I would never know you were not African."

Sometimes the teachers fed me *fufu*, rice, or *akumé.* Food in Togo is delicious and varied. There is *Djenkumé*, a dish made from ground maize and red palm oil, with some fried bits of beef inside. In my village *fonio* was a traditional food, a tiny grain prepared with oil and small black beans. *Fufu* is made from pounded yams or taro or even plantain, or some mix of these, and is served with a rich sauce or soup. Like most things, we ate it with our hands. A plate of *fufu* looks a bit like a rising ball of pizza dough. The soup or sauce is usually in a separate bowl or plate to the side and can be made from palm nuts, or okra, ground nuts or seeds, or even leaves from trees like the baobab. There is usually some meat or fish in the sauce. To eat *fufu* you tear off a little ball with your hand, roll it with your fingers, pinch it a bit to create a tiny dish or scoop for the sauce, and then use it to scoop up soup, and swallow. It's delicious. *Akumé* is similar, but prepared with ground maize. Sometimes the teachers prepared these meals themselves, or sometimes the meals were prepared by their girlfriends. In return I fed them homemade chili or homespun *faux* "Rice-a-Roni" that I made with rice, broken spaghetti, onion, and bouillon cubes. (Once some neighborhood boys watched me make my "Rice-a-Roni." They had all seen me do a lot of goofy things. This day they watched as I fry hard, dry rice in a bit of oil to brown it. "*Monsieur...*" they said, gently. "*That's not how you cook rice.*" I had to explain that this is the first stage of creating a very American rice dish, and they watched with fascination as I added onion, broken spaghetti, and finally water and cubes. I can hope they all eat this concoction today.)

I liked visiting the chief, a stately man with a worrisome sore on the top of his foot. He was not simply chief of the village, he was paramount chief of the surrounding villages and the local ethnic group. I had been told not to look directly at the chief, or any elder, while speaking, and of course I liked that, since eye contact was never comfortable for me and I knew I could form my thoughts and speak more clearly while gazing, without focus, at the ground in front of me. The chief was an exemplar of manners and gentility. I remember seeing him dance once, and was struck by the simplicity and gracefulness of his moves. When I visited we talked about a huge range of things, including the walls of his home, made of pounded clay, which were at least double the thickness of most. "This is the way we used to do it," he told me proudly. He told me about the benefits, which included a near constant temperature no matter the weather outside.

Africans taught me manners. Everyone I passed greeted me, whether I knew them or not. "Good morning! How are you? How is your home? How is work? How are the school children?" I learned greetings in both the local language and *Mina*, which was a sort of trading language in the southern part of the country. Everyone in Togo spoke several languages. I was far from conversant in the African languages. My knowledge was limited to greetings and shopping and saying silly things like "I am hungry," but I did my best to use whatever local words I could." "Good morning," I'd say. "How are you? How is your wife? How is your husband? How is your home? How are the fields?" They would answer "yo" to each greeting and then walk on chuckling among themselves about *yovo*.

If I passed a friend or colleague, I learned to stop and shake hands, usually with a loud snap of our middle fingers. It's required to stop, and greet, and shake hands every time you run into someone, even if it is the fourth or fifth time in a day. I learned that I was better at small talk in French than in English, since even small talk is an adventure when you're speaking a language that is not your own. All of this was good training for a person who, for several years, had wandered silently and invisibly through Seattle with limited human contact.

I loved teaching—especially the younger kids. I was in my mid-twenties and some of the kids in the younger classes—essentially fifth and sixth grades—were older and bigger than me, but they still treated me with more respect than I really deserved. One young man named Bilanté was in my fifth grade class. He was a giant, and at least my age. He worked in the fields for a living but still attended class. He had undoubtedly seen more of life than I had, but he always greeted me respectfully and humbly. Off campus I tried to get him to relax and treat me like his contemporary, which I was, but he couldn't. I was his teacher and so he had to treat me as such.

The littlest kids were flat out cute and snapped to attention to please me with a correct response. I tried my best not to use French in class. I was good with chalk and pens, so I used funny pictures to teach vocabulary and grammatical structures. "The Biggest Chicken in the World" became "The Tallest Basketball Player in the World"—a permanent teaching tool on folded paper that always got a laugh when I opened the final page and all we could see are the tallest player's knees and shoes.

Three of the younger kids played big roles in my life. Early on I was adopted by two fifth graders, Dando and Baba. They did chores for me, like bringing me clean water from the creek and helping me to clean up the yard of my house—a job done not so much for beautification as to remove hiding places for dangerous snakes. In return I bought them bicycles from China, clothing, and books. Another boy, Ouadja, lived in my house for a while and helped me with cooking and cleaning. I taught him to make chili, and he made me various delicacies from his region, which was in the north. I will always feel bad about Ouadja, because I fired him after I found out he had been stealing food. This was probably the first time in his life when he had an excess of food available, so I should have turned a blind eye to it, but some stupid sense of "justice" kicked in and I let him go. Sorry Ouadja. (For what it is worth, Ouadja was okay. He simply returned to live with his brother, a teacher.)

Death is Better didn't have running water, wells, or electricity. There were no phones. To isolate it even further, it was at the end of a sort of spur road that broke off the main road over the plateau—so pretty isolated. There was one small store that sold things like soap, perfume, nail polish, cigarettes, canned mackerel and matches. I was one of the store's chief customers, buying toilet paper and whole packs of cigarettes. There were several small bars, most of which sold beer warm and shots of locally made *sodabi*, a drink made from distilled palm wine. On Fridays a market opened at the center of town. A cow or steer would arrive on Thursday evening and for a time stand quaking near the butcher's hangar, undoubtedly smelling blood and sensing doom. Twelve hours later he or she was a collection of bones, meat, and innards that would head towards pots throughout town.

One day there is big news. The chief's son—we'll call him Raymond—has opened a big new bar we shall call Bar Rafic, "RAFIC" substituting for some sort of long and mysterious French-Togolese acronym of Raymond's invention. The bar is essentially four concrete brick walls and a concrete floor, no roof, but Raymond buys an electric generator, lights, and a large electric refrigerator and opens his new bar grandly with a traveling band from Ghana, the country next door. The band is excellent, and for the first time in history Better Off Dead has light pollution. I can see the lights brightening the horizon from my house, half a mile away. Not for the first time there is dancing till dawn. No one complains or worries about the music resounding through the village all night. New Orleans is an African invention, after all, and the same all night reverie enjoyed at Rafic has happened in Better Off Dead for centuries during traditional funerals or wakes, celebrations that last several nights running when a resident of Better Off Dead finds himself or herself better off.

One night I go to Rafic and enjoy watching a pretty young woman dance with an old farmer from out of town. I know he is from out of town, and a small one at that, because he is wearing a suit of African cloth that could get him arrested in most bigger Togolese cities. The suit celebrates the inauguration of Togo's first President, Sylvanus Olympio, who, rumor has it, was shot in the back by the country's current president and then sergeant, Gnassingbe Eyadama. The story is celebrated in Eyadema's own comic book which shows the sweaty Olympio attempting to climb over the wall of the United States Embassy just before he is dispatched to a better world. In Better Off Dead no one cares about the old guy's suit. They can see the old guy is enjoying his night in the "big city." I am enjoying watching both the old man and the pretty young woman who is making the old man's evening so special. She flirts, she dances, she smiles. The old man is in heaven.

But as I watch a drunk man decides to engage me in lengthy and annoying conversation.

Like the farmer, he is from out of town, so I didn't know him, or even his face, but he tells me he was born here and is a member of the chief's extended family and thus a relative of Raymond After a while he takes it on himself to give me a girl.

"These are my shishters," he tells me, slurring his words and bringing two young women towards me, one on each arm. The one on his right I know and want no part of. She is part of the royal family, and has been the girlfriend of just about every teacher at my school.

The other is the young woman I've been watching. I don't know it yet, but she is also part of the royal family.

I tell the guy no.

He keeps insisting.

I keep saying, "No, but thank you," until I finally realize the only way to shut him up is to say "yes". So I point to my future wife. "Okay, this one!" I say, walking away with the young woman who will become the mother of Jade and Gemma, and the grandmother of Leila.

We'll call her Afua.

Afua and I dance, we talk, we drink some of Rafic's cold beer, and smoke cigarettes.

I am Better Off Dead's champion cigarette smoker. Even though they are sold cheaply and without taxes, cigarettes are a luxury. Most people in the village who smoke either buy cigarettes one at a time or grow their own. They treat store bought cigarettes the way an American cigar aficionado might treat a Cuban cigar—a luxurious treat. I buy whole packs of them and smoke all day long.

But this night I run out. I must have said something about it, because Afua disappears. I figure, another leaf has skittered past, but then she comes back with a cigarette for me and one for herself. This is no small thing. We smoke, and then she disappears completely.

The next day I tell my little friends Dando and Baba that I danced with a girl at Rafic and want to find her. This is not breaking news. They already know all about it. Evidently the whole town already knows all about it. Dando and Baba say they will let the young woman know. Later, I get a message that I am welcome to visit her that evening.

Walking at night can be a challenge in Death is Better. There are no street lights, and for the most part there are no streets—just rutted paths of red earth that cross this way and that, formed over decades or even centuries. People with a salary carry a flashlight. People with less money use a kerosene lantern. Men on the prowl, on the other hand, use neither. A married man visiting his girlfriend will turn off his flashlight or dim his lantern in order not to be identified. And it's quite effective. I have watched my friends straining to see who is going where to visit whom and chuckling about it.

Afua lives at her father's house in the oldest part of town—a neighborhood where ancient red walls seem to rise out of the red earth. To get there I will have to take several rutted, bumpy paths that I'm not terribly familiar with. It is a dark night with no moon, so I am relying on my flashlight. I see someone in the distance, maybe 100 yards away. I turn off my light.

"Bon soir, *Yovo!*" the man yells.

Yovo means white person or foreigner. So much for my discretion. With my pasty white skin I am visible to everyone, even in the dark.

"*Bon soir,*" I yell into the darkness.

As I stumble over the bumpy path I begin to laugh, at least inwardly, and mumble the lyrics, "Ain't no mountain high enough, ain't no valley low enough, ain't no river wide enough, to keep me from getting to you." It is a lesson that has taken me way too long to learn.

The first time Afua comes to my house and spends the night the villagers make it clear that my status in the village has changed. She leaves before people are up, but not in time to stop news from spreading far and wide.

Normally when I walked to school the people I passed would ask about my house, my work, and the school kids. This time the added a new greeting in their native languages:

"*Esrowodé?*" some ask in Mina.

"How's the wife?"

Others ask the same thing in the local language.

Things aren't so pleasant when "the wife" and I travel to other towns. Then people assume she is a sex worker and that I am a John and they pummel Afua with insults. I can make greetings and buy things at the market in the local languages, but I can't understand or respond to insults to my girlfriend, so Afua comes up with a solution. In town she wears a third *pagne,* a cloth wrap around her waist, to signify that she is married, or at least partnered. Togolese markets are famous for beautiful cotton prints sold in two meter lengths called *pagnes.* One *pagne* is used to make a woman's blouse, another the skirt—but a married woman or mother wears a third *pagne* as a wrap that is used to carry babies behind their backs. In Togo this is symbolic of marriage, much the way that a ring on the left ring finger is symbolic of marriage here. Once Afua put on the third piece of cloth, we can go anywhere together and be treated with respect.

So Afua becomes my first real, long term girlfriend, and soon thereafter, my wife. I will eventually learn it is not uncommon for autistic people to find love in other cultures. Our quirks are less visible, and we often feel more at ease in a culture that is different.

I won't go much further with our story, except that we had some very good years, and produced two beautiful daughters and an amazing granddaughter. Our marriage ended badly and sadly seventeen years after it began. I've read, too, that it's not uncommon for autistic people to remain too long in relationship that's gone bad, and I am certain we did that, in part because we could not afford to separate when I was a legal assistant. But my years in Togo and my marriage to Afua brought me to a new place. For the first time I was living a life that appeared "normal." I had a relationship, and for many years, a good one. Together we had friends, we owned a home, we had children. Before Togo, I was on the edge of being a lost person, forever alone. After Togo, I felt almost normal. And it wasn't just an act. Togo had taught me a great deal. I had learned there were rules in any culture. I had learned to greet people and shake hands. I had learned to take chances. I had learned how to operate my difficult personality in a difficult world.

In short, Better Off Dead had taught me I was better off alive.

26

Executive Function

When I began studying about autism there was an issue I was pretty sure did not apply to me: problems with "executive function." As I understand it, executive function refers to brain functions necessary to manage time, plan ahead, or carry out complex activities. Since these are exactly the skills I use on the job all the time, I figured executive function was not a problem for me. I am a lawyer. Before that I was a paralegal. Before that I taught English to several hundred kids in West Africa. I have spent a lifetime juggling facts, dates, appointments, schedules, students, clients, what have you. With a paper desktop calendar, I could actually keep track and get most of my responsibilities taken care of.

Of course, I've read that frequently misplacing keys can be a sign of executive dysfunction. If so, executive function is a major problem for me.

But I have long recognized I have only so much capacity for this sort of thing. I will take care of 100 things at work and then willfully ignore chores at home. The dandelions on the front lawn grow tall yellow flowers. I ignore it. The flowers turn to puff balls. I ignore them. The puff balls scatter in the wind and come up next year as new weeds. Ah well.

The same thing happens with bills, taxes, oil changes, and blackberry vines. I've known for decades that when it comes time to pay bills, or do taxes, I'm often too fried by work to bother. I know the unpaid bills are there. I can feel the late fees pile up. But though I care, and though I resent every penny lost to small fines, interest, and late fees, I often don't have the energy or will to face them.

So, I wait until I do have the energy and then pay with interest.

One trick that has always worked for me: when I start to worry too much about what I'm not getting done, I make a "to do" list on the back of a junk mail envelope. (A simple piece of paper won't do. It has to be an old envelope.) I rarely get all the tasks done immediately, but when I see the envelope a week or two later, the tasks have been taken care of.

And although I use executive function on the job, it's interesting to look back at the accommodations, accidental and self-granted, that helped me be a better paralegal and attorney.

As I've explained, Paul Whelan regularly simplified my job so that I could concentrate on my strengths. A couple of times when I was still a legal assistant I forgot minor but important tasks, like calling the court to confirm a motion. I was devastated by every such mistake, but Paul didn't care. He laughed and gave those jobs to a more junior employee so that I could concentrate on what interested me and what I was good at. I no longer had to schedule depositions or file documents with the court, and instead spent my days with the facts and documents that made money for our clients. Paul also reduced the number of cases I was assigned to, keeping me on the big ones with complicated facts because he knew that was where I shined and made a difference.

When I started my own one man law firm I knew that I could survive nicely by settling just one or two cases a year, and that by limiting my work to one or two cases I could preserve my sanity and do a better job. My website says that "[Peter] concentrates on just a few cases at a time so that he can dig deep, focus, and obtain the best possible result for his clients." It was an "accommodation" I made for myself long before I knew that I was autistic.

As I write these words, I know that various bills and obligations are piling up. I can feel the late fees accumulate. I know that berry vines are taking over the garden and that it's once again time to mow the dandelions in front of the house where grass used to be.

But I'm in the middle of a case that needs my attention, and in the middle of a writing project that is consuming my energy. The bills, taxes, and blackberry vines will have to wait.

But it's probably time to find an old envelope.

27

Doug's Case

We first met Doug in a hospital room, months after the fire that burned and melted his skin, and weeks after we filed his case. I still have a snapshot I took of him that day. The skin of his face was not yet squeezed under the clear plastic mask he'd later wear to compress and minimize burn scarring. Dark, jagged, Frankenstein monster stitches zigzagged across the front of his neck. His arms and fingers were wrapped in pressure garments. He had no shirt, and no bed covers above the waist.

The part I remember most clearly was a gaping, open wound across his chest that exposed glistening blood-red muscle. Some sort of contraption was attached to the wound to slowly stretch the skin back together. It was a process that would take weeks and made him look like the goriest statues or paintings of the dying Christ. Doug took it all in stride, quietly joking with nurses and visitors in his raspy voice.

Doug had already spent several months in the burn unit, near death, and suffering through painful debridement procedures in which nurses would scrape and clean his burned skin. Much of the time he was on morphine. He remembered paranoid but horridly lifelike dreams in which doctors and nurses conspired to torture him. He was burned over forty percent of his body, but skin grafts affected another twenty percent. They removed skin from one part of his body to cover a burned place somewhere else. The grafted skin was cut in a sort of herringbone pattern that allowed it to stretch and cover a larger area. It looked like expensive alligator or snake skin shoe leather and covered large portions of his arms. His fingers, for a time, looked to me like fried chicken. It was a look I would grow somewhat accustomed to over a dozen or so cases in the coming sixteen years. I would grow to know and love people who were missing feet, or toes, or ears, or husbands, or a granddaughter.

Those who say autistic people lack empathy must themselves lack perception and understanding. We have as much empathy as the next person, if not more. We understand outsider status.

We filed our case against General Motors without Doug's knowledge, while he was still in the burn unit. His wife, Sharon, acted as guardian on his behalf. His burn doctor supported the guardianship.

Soon after we filed, General Motors came calling in the form of two attorneys we would grow to know well. We thought they might come with a settlement offer, but it soon became clear they were just sizing us up. The older lawyer—the one I would later call the evilest man alive—asked if the gas tank was original or "after market." One attorney from our office blurted out derisively that there was no such thing as an "aftermarket" fuel tank.

"You can't add a fuel tank to a truck after it's sold!"

The evilest man alive shot him a tiny smile that said, "You, son, will be easy pickings."

Although I knew nothing about "aftermarket" fuel tanks, my autistic brain leapt into overdrive. I had a sudden vision of an old truck on my street with an unpainted aluminum or galvanized steel door riveted to the side of its bed. I had walked past the truck for years without paying attention, but my brain had taken it in, and I saw it clearly now. The unpainted metal door was obviously "aftermarket" and probably covered the gas cap of an equally "aftermarket" fuel tank. I had already autistically researched fuel tanks by looking at a parts catalog that included a drawing of the original tank so I knew that it matched the curved and ribbed halves of the crushed tank on Doug's truck.

I spoke up at once.

"I'm not certain, but it looks like an original tank."

The evilest man alive looked at me appraisingly and nodded.

After that meeting the attorney who blurted nonsense about aftermarket tanks was no longer on our team.

As part of "discovery" we served General Motors with written questions called "interrogatories" and "requests for production of documents." In response to the document requests, we were invited to visit and pick through the haystack of documents that GM's lawyers called the "General Motors Document Repository" in Detroit. With these words, GM's attorneys tried to make the "repository" sound like an exalted archive, while in fact it was a drab and cluttered room full of castoff file cabinets. Getting there required a badge and an escort. Since it was inserted deep within the bowels of the General Motors Building in my own mind it became "The Suppository."

On our first visit Paul Whelan took pictures of the piles of boxes and clunky file drawers. The next day one of GM's top lawyers came and demanded the film. Paul chuckled and kept it, and some of the pictures later became exhibits to our discovery motions: this pile of crap, your honor, is the wondrous "General Motors Document Repository."

But clunky as it was, I loved the repository. The repository is where my autistic charms came fully to life. Many attorneys rightfully object when a party tries to respond to specific discovery requests by making you hunt for the documents yourself in a warehouse full of paper. Not me. I always found good stuff.

On our first couple of visits, we were never left alone in the "repository." GM assigned an employee with an old computer to help us "search" for things. His real purpose was probably to keep an eye on us, take notes about our progress, and report our search terms and requests to his superiors. I decided to ignore him except when I wanted to do what many say is impossible—to prove a negative. It's not so impossible when you have assistance. Every time I struck out looking for a document that I knew had to exist—a set of minutes, or a design drawing that was referred to by number in another document—I would ask the man with the computer to search for it using terms I knew would be in the document. When he struck out too, I documented his failed search in a declaration to let the judge know which documents *weren't* in the room. The computer guy became an extremely useful tool.

The General Motors Building itself was magnificent—an imposing fourteen story building on Detroit's West Grand Boulevard. In the early 1990s Detroit was a burned out, mostly abandoned city. Every block seemed to have a liquor store on one corner, a church on the other, and here and there a well-tended house alone amid the rubble. For a good picture of what we saw there, check out Eminem's film *Eight Mile*. Even one of the beautiful art deco skyscrapers downtown was boarded up and empty. But West Grand Boulevard still had a bit going on, including the beautiful Fischer Building, the drably modern New Center building, our funky but formerly glorious hotel, and, best of all, the original Motown building just a few blocks away. I liked the stately General Motors Building chiefly for the glassed in first floor where cars and trucks were on display. (An unintentionally funny display I remember had a giant SUV aimed directly at the drivers door of a tiny Saturn—the car I drove. It was a mismatch.)

On our first trip we spent a week looking at documents and ordering copies of any that seemed worthwhile. Murray Kleist, another legendary product liability attorney from our office, joined us. It was the first of many visits over the next several years and there was a randomness to our selection of documents that would serve me well over the years. Highly redacted minutes from something called The Executive Committee? Take them. A lawsuit from the U.S. District Court in Tacoma? Take it. Crash tests? Take them all. A lone set of Chevrolet Planning Committee meeting minutes? Take it. On our first visit I looked at every document in the room, but over the years the room changed and grew, so we made a point of visiting the repository for at least a few hours on every subsequent trip. Each visit resulted in a new shipment of bankers boxes filled with undifferentiated paper photocopies, and I took on the job of organizing and reviewing all of those documents.

But "review" isn't the right word. As I often explained in continuing legal education talks I gave to attorneys and legal staff, I absorbed the documents, little by little, by a sort of osmosis. I *wallowed* in them. I returned to them again and again. Most of the time, at the start, I didn't have a particular destination—I would simply look and learn, and the more I learned, the more I knew the story of the truck and the ways of General Motors, the easier I could find my way from one document to another and the more certain documents made sense. At first a sheet of paper might just show another sketch of a fuel tank shield. But as I pieced together the larger story and returned again and again to the documents, I would realize in a flash of insight that a sheet of paper wasn't just another shield or crash test, but a very important shield or crash test—one that would add context and drama to our trial presentation. I now attribute this ability to connect far off dots to my autistic wiring and now see that when I tried to teach my methods to others, I was trying to show them how to think and act autistically.

I was blessed in those days to have a big office lined with enormous white plywood shelves. The founder of our firm, Leonard Schroeter, had insisted every employee have a private office with a door that closed. Leonard understood a person needs privacy and quiet. He probably wasn't thinking about autistic people, but he found part of the prescription for my own success. I needed a space where my mind could work without too much distraction. Little by little my shelves filled up with black notebooks full of crash tests, design drawings, planning documents, and weird old memoranda. I had a smart assistant who would organize the documents to my specifications, which left me nothing to do but absorb them. I loved it all.

I was also blessed with time. A few years before we got Doug's case, I had begun to work on major product liability cases, and I had proven myself valuable. Almost as soon as Paul Whelan saw what I could do on big cases he began to strip away all of the minor but distracting and time-consuming duties someone in my position might have, like scheduling meetings or confirming motions. This gave me the luxury of uninterrupted time and the ability to focus.

Like so many things Paul did, this was an extraordinarily insightful move on his part. Autistic people have an uncanny ability to focus, but a harder time jumping from job to job and task to task. Paul didn't know I was autistic, but he knew *me*, and he provided me the perfect environment to thrive. In later years I would be given a suite of offices on another floor, separate from my coworkers, with room to line up trial exhibits, including my collection of shielded and unshielded (and sometimes crushed) 20-gallon gas tanks. Paul knew instinctively that my special talents worked best when I had time and space to work alone. It was another unwitting "accommodation" to my autism. If employers could make a policy of accommodating and encouraging autistic and other neurodivergent people the way Leonard and Paul did, there would likely be an explosion of creative productivity.

Sometimes a stray document or page showed up that was different from the others. Once it was thirteen pages of meeting minutes from something called the Chevrolet Planning Committee. One of the attendees was the famous former General Manager of Chevrolet John DeLorean. The Seattle Public Library was only a few blocks from our office so I went to find out what I could learn about John DeLorean, aside from what I already knew—i.e., that he'd been arrested but acquitted on drug charges, and that he put his name on the sports car used in *Back to the Future*. At the library I learned there was a book about DeLorean, credited to a Detroit writer, but written in DeLorean's voice, boasting of his own legendary status. (My favorite part of the book was a picture of Mr. DeLorean holding a football with the newly infamous O.J. Simpson, who had just run into his own legal trouble.) The book was incredibly detailed. DeLorean used names I'd become familiar with in the documents—Lund, Winchell, Staudt, and others. To my delight the book talked about using the Chevrolet Planning Committee to design the pickup! "And it was the Planning Committee that guided the development of the new 1974 Chevrolet pickup truck line which I think was the finest American light truck ever built."[9] One chapter is titled "How Moral Men Make Immoral Decisions." (Imagine what immoral and amoral men might do!)

I would soon learn from engineers that DeLorean himself was largely responsible for the placement of the fuel tanks outside the protection of the frame rails—evidently in a quest to beat out the competition with an additional four gallons of fuel capacity. The story was there to be found in the pinched, handwritten design notes of the draftsmen and engineers, supplemented by my occasional chats with the old men who had made those notes decades earlier.

Aside from the thirteen pages we found we knew there were no other Chevrolet Planning Committee minutes in the vaunted "Repository." I looked myself and then made the man with the computer help me look. Neither of us found anything. We then did a formal request for the Planning Committee documents, and GM's local counsel, who I'm guessing had never been to the repository himself, responded with rote, boilerplate nonsense about GM's "diligent search" for the planning documents which, he said, were in the "document repository in Detroit, Michigan."

We knew this wasn't remotely true and reminded the local attorney of his duties under the civil rules. He happened to be an officer of the state bar association and a candidate for judge. That's when regional counsel upped the ante. Instead of saying there might be a mistake, the regional counsel wrote us a letter that would become an exhibit to the motion to compel. "As set forth in General Motors response (sic), those portions of the meeting minutes that relate to the fuel storage system on the 1973-1987 C/K pickup trucks are in the document repository. Your statement that these documents are 'nowhere to be found in the repository' is inaccurate."

Like hell. A few days later the attorney called to report that GM had found "a very large volume" of Planning Committee minutes in a basement somewhere in Warren, Michigan. Every couple of weeks they sent us more minutes. After our successful motion to compel they found even more.

Our motion to compel included some of my best "outside the box" work. Autistic people see the world differently and therefor often find unique, new ways to do things. Instead of merely describing the slow arrival of these minutes, I illustrated it visually by spending a few minutes at the copy machine. With the cover open, I set the first thirteen pages edgewise on the glass and pressed "copy." The result was a black field with the edge of a thin sheaf of paper running across it. You could count the pages. Then I did the same with each successive batch of paper, leaving the rubber bands in place for a nice textured look as the piles got fatter and fatter. I used correction tape to label each picture with the date the documents arrived. Although these pictures were worth a thousand words, I used them to punctuate GM's repeated assertions that we now had all the available minutes until, *whoops*, the next, fatter batch arrived. It was funny, visually compelling, and irrefutable, all at the same time. In the end we won our motion and received all the relevant minutes—enough to fill about a dozen binders.

The more time I spent with the documents, the more I saw. I now credit autism for this. I have read that some autistic people think visually. I struggled with this concept, unsure what it meant, but my therapist has pointed out the many, many times in this book I refer to my use of fleeting images stored in my brain—the aftermarket fuel filler door on an old pickup truck that appeared to me when I first encountered the evilest man alive; the image of a peach I used to bookmark a sketch that I encountered; and my ability to connect various images and to see details in them that others do not see—the faint and grainy line representing a fuel tank shield, for example.

I used to love the crash tests. GM engineers would slam the pickups with a car or a moving barrier at anywhere from 15 to 50 mph, filming it all with fantastic lighting and slow motion cameras and documenting it further with before and after photographs. They are fascinating to look at and to watch, so it's no wonder that similar crash tests are so popular on YouTube.

The early crash test reports we received didn't include actual prints of the photographs but instead had photocopies of photocopies of photocopies of photographs. They were hard to decipher, but as I visited them again and again, I began to spot subtle clues. For example, we had heard of testimony from a former GM engineer that some of the early "successful" tests had a steel shield that was never put into production—but no one had seen it. The assumption was that the relevant documents had been destroyed by a secret team of young attorneys who people working these cases called "The Fire Babies." The Fire Babies purportedly collected and destroyed documents relating to the side-saddle gas tank pickups. One engineer testified about shredders in the hallway. But one day, staring yet again at the the grainy, high contrast, over-photocopied photograph of the underside of a crash-tested pickup, I saw a line that didn't belong running parallel between the sheet metal and the gas tank. I also saw that the fuel tank mounting brackets beneath the tank had been extended and ran all the way across the bottom of the tank to this unfamiliar line. We requested copies of the actual photographs of all the crash tests and somehow got them. And *whoop*, there it was, in the photographs, clear as a bell—a steel shield designed to protect the fuel tank in a side impact that was used on that one test but never actually put into production or sold to customers. And no surprise—the crash test with the special shield was the very first side impact crash test of the new truck that didn't leak a drop of fuel.

Later, in the Document Repository, I found the design drawing for this so-called "Safety Impact Shield." The design was credited to two people named Joe K. and T. C. Since I was beginning to recognize various numbering systems Chevrolet used on the documents,

I was able to find the corresponding Engineering Design Order and Design Log. Each new document revealed more nuance. The log was like a daily, handwritten diary of the draftsman as various engineers gave him orders or tweaked his work on the shield.

Once I broke the code and learned how parts were linked to design orders that were in turn linked to handwritten notes, I was able to discover more and more truths about the design and testing of the truck and learn which people were doing the hands on work of grinding out the design. I filled notebooks with their names and wondered who they were, where they were, what they remembered, and what they might tell me about the development of this insane design.

This was before the internet really became useful to me, but by spending large parts of my workdays at the Seattle Public Library I learned the library had a set of regional hard drives with names and phone numbers of millions of people from white pages throughout the United States. And somehow, I found Joe K.! ("K." was a very common name, like Smith or Jones. Finding a man with two such names was very lucky.)

I called him. Like anyone with a job, Joe had war stories, and he gave me a line from the GM drafting room—that "You'd sell your mother for 10 cents a car." The idea was that they were designing something that would sell in the millions, and a million dimes was an amount of money you'd do anything to save.

We took his deposition and walked him through the documents. Or rather, Paul took his deposition using my script and documents I put together. We asked him about "T. C." Joe K. told us "T" stood for Toby, a person he remembered but hadn't seen or spoken to in more than 20 years.

I remembered a little "shopper" newspaper that was distributed all around the newer and older General Motors Buildings. Autistic brains keep track! It was mostly classified ads—so I wrote one:

"Toby C., we want you! $100 to first caller with good information on current address, phone of this former GM Draftsman. Call Peter or Paul at 1-800-XXX-XXXX."

It worked! Within a few days a guy called me laughing. I forget the story—I think Toby's official first name was different—but he got us to Toby, and we sent our new friend a check for $100.

It wouldn't be the last time I used a classified ad in that paper, and it wouldn't be the last time I cold called a former GM employee or executive. I still have a notebook of addresses and phone numbers and some of my scribbled or typed notes of conversations.

I shared what I knew with other lawyers who had cases involving the pickups and they shared back. It was a glorious time. As soon as any of us learned something new, we told our friends. My paralegal friends Beth Glen in Georgia, Cindy T. in Memphis, and Stella V. in Texas. These women were "superparalegals" who worked with big time trial lawyers in their respective states, and we talked all the time. I called attorneys, too—Mick in Texas and Joe McCray in California. See something, say something. We called each other about every little thing we learned.

Beth worked with attorney Jim Butler, who preceded us in the truck litigation in a very big way. Butler and his firm handled a case called *Moseley v. GM,* that involved teenager Shannon Moseley, who burned to death in one of the pickups. Shannon's mother was a strong woman with little interest in settlement, so the case went on to a very public trial on Court TV. Although there had been one prior trial of importance—Joe McCray's *Adams-Esparza* case in the early 1980s—the *Moseley* case changed everything. Before trial one of the attorneys at Butler's firm managed to find himself on a plane next to former General Motors engineer, Ronald Elwell. Elwell was well spoken, good looking, and smart—the type of person who is often designated by a corporation to testify on its behalf—and he had testified for GM in several prior cases. The attorney told Elwell about Shannon's case, and Elwell ultimately swapped hats and testified in deposition and at trial under subpoenas from the

Moseley attorneys. His testimony was devastating for GM. He testified that soon after testifying on behalf of GM that the truck was safe he learned that about a major test program where GM engineers launched passenger cars into the sides of test trucks at fifty miles per hour. Elwell described fuel tanks as being split open like melons. Butler and his firm tried the *Moseley* case to a $105 million verdict, rocking the automotive product liability world.

With that verdict Jim Butler became a hero of mine, so I was honored when he wrote to congratulate me about a letter I had sent to the U.S. Department of Transportation in support of a recall of the trucks. My letter included photographs from GM crash tests that we colored digitally so that formerly hidden fixes and shields were easily visible. (An assistant in our office, Diane, did the colorization and helped make dozens of demonstrative trial exhibits for me over the years. Diane later started her own legal graphics firm.) A short time later I received the letter from Butler mistakenly addressed to "Peter Shields" congratulating me for my work. I was thrilled—even by the appropriate Freudian slip in my name.

I accompanied Paul Whelan to Detroit several times to take depositions. We always had a good time, working hard, then eating well, drinking well, and looking around the city. Because I knew the story of the trucks, I would prepare the exhibits and script the depositions for Paul, then sit next to him during the deposition and pass notes for follow-up questions, or simply whisper follow-ups into his ear.

Paul is the only attorney I have ever met who was able to endure that sort of thing. I know I don't like receiving notes or suggestions when I'm taking a deposition, but Paul liked them and used them. We had started the practice on an earlier case involving tampered sinus medication, and it drove the other side crazy. It drove GM a little crazy, too. I used large, yellow Post-it notes because I could tear them off silently and line them up in Paul's peripheral vision. I whispered a lot of questions, too. Once, when I whispered a string of follow-up questions to Paul, GM's grizzled attorney, the evilest man alive, sneered, "Why don't you just let your sidekick ask the questions!"

Paul's response scared me. "Pretty soon he will!" Paul snarled.

I hadn't revealed to many people that I was studying law in my spare time, and I certainly didn't want to reveal it to that guy—but I did appreciate watching the old lawyer absorb and process that information. It was no secret to anyone at GM that I was becoming an expert on their trucks and therefor dangerous.

I would ship up to a dozen boxes of documents and office supplies back to Detroit for the depositions because I wanted to be prepared for anything. My hotel room became a sort of production center. One day GM's witness gave us all sorts of trouble. His name was Bill C. Bill C had replaced Ronald Elwell as GM's main testifying witness in the pickup truck fire cases. He testified for the corporation, and it was safe to say he knew everything there was to know about the pickup fire cases—at least until we came along. When we showed him the design drawing for the steel "Safety Impact" shield I discovered, he pretended not to understand what it was or what it depicted. He held the drawing this way and that and made sour little faces of feigned incomprehension. Since the deposition wasn't over, that night I went to the only store I could find in the neighborhood—a liquor store—and bought some red duct tape and a bottle of wine. Then I went back to my room, drank that wine, chopped up one of my banker's boxes, and used cardboard and duct tape to build a replica of the shield and support brackets. This was out-of-the-box autistic thinking at its finest—and literally "out-of-the-box," since I had cut up two boxes to create it. The next day we presented it to the engineer on camera. He couldn't help smiling and giving me a tiny nod. After a few minutes comparing my model to the design drawing he said "Well, I'm not sure the dimensions are completely accurate, but this does seem to reflect what is in the drawing."

Not satisfied with a cardboard model, back in Seattle I got in touch with Paul Josten, who worked at a Seattle forensic engineering firm. Paul had no engineering degree, but over the years his work convinced me that he was one of the smartest, most capable, and talented people at his firm. I had once seen a model he made for another case showing some giant manufacturing system at tiny scale. Miniature men climbed over miniature conveyor belts that would cause miniature death and destruction. It was a beautiful piece of work.

"Paul, if I brought you the engineering drawing, could you make us a full sized fuel tank shield?"

Of course he could! He found a used gas tank and support brackets at a junk yard, built a "frame rail" out of wood, and made a shield exactly to the specifications on the design drawing. It was a thing of beauty, with the fuel tank painted a fiery red, the shield a protective-looking blue, and the frame an innocuous black. I put it in my office instead of art. In days to come Paul would create several more such exhibits so that we could show a jury exactly what they were seeing in the photographs and design drawings.

I didn't want to do a full reveal of our new demonstrative exhibit to General Motors' defense team, so I used the GM approach, took a snapshot of the setup from close range, and then ran the picture through several generations of black and white photocopies. I thought I might fool someone, and it seemed to work decently well. The photograph now looked credibly crappy—like the ones they first gave us on the crash test reports. I wanted GM to worry that I had some back channel into their operations—that I'd somehow found some of those documents the "fire babies" tried to destroy.

We pulled it out on the next case while questioning the octogenarian fuel system engineer, George K. George K. was eighty something but sharp as a razor. He held up my counterfeit "old" document, squinted, made various faces and then dismissed the drawing.

"This isn't ours. This has ribbing, like in the drawing. For the test we just cobbled together a shield from scrap sheet metal. Did you fellows make this?"

He dropped the exhibit onto the table with distaste, but we didn't care. By showing them our exhibit, we also showed them how serious we were about getting ready for trial. In fact, I soon got to invite one of GM's attorneys to my suite of offices to look at the real exhibit.

"You've done all this," he asked, dumbfounded, and taking in row after row of numbered exhibits, demonstrative exhibits, and models.

"Yep," I answered. It was a nice moment.

On those early trips to Detroit we stayed at a hotel owned by General Motors. It was remarkably cheap—$49 a night, including a "happy hour" where bad beer and dank wine were served free of charge. The hotel was directly across the street from the General Motors Building, which is where we did some of our work, and down the block from the beautiful Fischer Building, where our court reporters' office was.

Every now and then, when Paul and I talked about dinner or some such, we heard strange things on the hotel phone—clicking sounds, squeaks, and once a gospel song. It was probably nothing but the crackle of an ancient phone system, but we decided to act as if the phones were bugged by beginning or ending each call with a bit of theater.

"Bill said he'd meet me later with the documents," I said, meaning GM witness Bill C.

Paul mumbled appreciatively, "Bill's a good man."

On the off chance they were dirty enough to listen, we wanted them to wonder about Bill.

The truth was simpler. We didn't have any inside connection. We didn't rely on a rogue engineer from inside General Motors. We relied on simple, hard work and, it turns out, the power of autism—the power of persistence, attention to detail, innovative methods, pattern recognition, and obsessive focus on an especially interesting story.

Doug's case settled a week or so before it was set to go to trial.

It settled after we had fleshed out what had previously been a somewhat murky story with new clarity. We found evidence to corroborate Ronald Elwell's testimony. We found photographs and design drawings for the "Safety Impact Shield." We showed how the trucks that "passed" GM's side impact testing each had some sort of structural improvement near the fuel tank that was not offered to consumers. We had an arsenal of carefully organized and devastating exhibits and videotaped testimony.

But happily, we weren't finished with General Motors. Before we were done with Doug's case, we found ourselves in a position to bring another GM truck fire case back from the dead.

It would be a peach.

28

Burnout?

As I write this I don't want to talk to any human being. I know that any condescension or misstep on their part could send me to an angry place—a place I don't want to go. At this moment I have an emotional hair trigger. It won't result in violence, but it could result in uncomfortably harsh tones. So I try to hunker down.

I think of Ishmael, from my favorite book:

> Whenever I find myself growing grim about my mouth; whenever it is damp, drizzly November in my soul; whenever I find myself involuntarily pausing before coffin warehouses, and bringing up the rear of every funeral I meet; and especially whenever my hypos get such an upper hand of me, that it requires a strong moral principle to prevent me from deliberately stepping into the street, and methodically knocking people's hats off—then I account it high time to get to sea as soon as I can. This is my substitute for pistol and ball. [10]

I cannot go to sea, so I try to slip undercover, or go to Italy, or Lake Tahoe, or for a long day of walking.

I've been here before, but only recently have I begun to suspect that I am experiencing the warning signs of autistic burnout—a time when the stresses of daily existence have built up to a point where I can hardly tolerate the world and most of the people in it. Most importantly, I cannot tolerate anything I perceive as disrespect.

I've begun to think the "blueness" that first sent me to a therapist was likely the beginnings of autistic burnout. I was not depressed in any normal sense. I could still do my job and enjoy most aspects of life, but there was an undercurrent of tension building, and it weighed heavily on me.

Today, however, I write from a place that is actually depressed, where the enjoyment of life is momentarily gone, and where friction with the living seems intolerable. I need to withdraw and restore myself. I need quiet, without conflict.

This is a new subject for me, but my understanding is that this sort of burnout can be much worse for other autistic people—especially those who mask at a high level, or who face sensory issues that I don't have, all off which is exhausting. I mask to some degree but not that much. I proceed through life pretty autistically, without bothering to smile when I don't feel it, without bothering to interact much when I don't want to, but other autistic people are forced to constantly mask and interact just to keep their jobs and to survive. Instead of faking it till they make it they're forced to fake it until they break.

My work is often stressful. The deadlines are unforgiving. The personalities on all sides are egotistical. The profession is adversarial, built on friction between opposing forces. We fight. We argue motions. We object. I often like it. I've often said it is the only place where I play hardball.

But I was incredibly lucky to learn my profession while working with Paul Whelan, who didn't care about any differences I presented, and who streamlined my job in important ways so that I could work in peace and quiet on what interested me. He also treated me with incredible respect.

I was also clever in my own right in how I organized my life. Without knowing I am autistic I knew I needed daily naps and frequent downtime. I knew my long walks were therapeutic. I knew I would do better by leaving a successful partnership and reducing my own workload.

If you work with an autistic person, and especially if you manage them, learn to recognize their strengths, their "weaknesses" (read "differences,") their working style, and their individual needs. Learn to recognize their stressors. Try to give them a break, or let them take one. Let them have quiet when they need it, and preferably a quiet place to work. Expect them to succeed, but don't expect them to do so by fitting into a neurotypical mold.

I know of course that this depressed irritability shall pass, and that I will find joy again.

But for now I'm hunkering down, doing my best to keep my distance from any and all irritants, and breathing.

29

Reopening Bob's Case

Doug's case was only the beginning of our work on GM pickup fire cases. On our first trip to the "repository" I found a legal complaint for another Chevrolet pickup case filed in Tacoma, Washington. Once home, I checked with the court and learned the case had been dismissed. We decided to contact the attorney. We tried phone calls, emails, and letters, but he ignored us. Eventually Paul and I decided to call the plaintiffs, whose names were Robert and Carol. We did it very carefully because ethics rules require that you only contact a represented party through their attorney.

Paul's office was a big corner one in an old downtown Seattle building. I parked myself on one of the chairs in front of the desk while Paul tapped in the phone number.

"Hello!" A friendly sounding woman answered. Paul explained who we were and asked if we were speaking with Carol.

"Yes, I'm Carol!" she told us. This was a chipper woman. Paul began to tell her why we were calling. "We represent a man burned in one of these trucks. We learned about your case and wanted to talk with your lawyer, but we haven't been able to reach him. We know the case was dismissed, and we want…"

"No!" Carol interrupted cheerfully. "It hasn't been dismissed. It's still going!"

Paul and I made faces across the desk. He explained that we had seen an order of dismissal. It appeared their case was done. We assumed there had been a settlement.

"Nope!" said Carol. "We haven't settled." said Carol.

"That's very odd," Paul told her. How long since you've spoken with your lawyer?"

It had been a while. We suggested she go talk to him. Carol said she would call the attorney and ask him to get in touch with us.

The lawyer never called us.

Within a day or two Carol called back and told us the attorney was nowhere to be found. "We went to his office. It looks like he's closed up shop. He's not there."

It turned out she was right—the lawyer had closed up shop and skipped town. And we were right that he had dismissed the case without their knowledge—a cardinal sin for any lawyer.

Starting that day Bob and Carol became our new exploding truck clients—and we hadn't even settled Doug's case yet.

Bob was a logger. He was in a crash on a road to the coast. Smoke from the fire could be seen for miles.

Bob was burned mainly on his arms. This mattered because Bob was a lumberjack, and those arms were his living. On the other hand, as a lumberjack, he was also a tough guy. He got back to work very quickly—which meant his case would not be as big financially as Doug's.

We didn't care. If we could revive Bob and Carol's case, it would keep us in the game—a game we enjoyed, played well, and that was growing more exciting every day.

After the $105 million verdict in the *Moseley* case in Georgia, the pickup fire cases had caught fire themselves. Before *Moseley*, just about every case settled quietly. We knew of only one exception, the *Adams-Esparza* case that San Francisco attorney Joe McCray tried to a multi-million dollar verdict in the early 1980s. I had met McCray at a dinner hosted by *Moseley* attorney Jim Butler in Atlanta and we became buddies over expensive scotch and wine. His verdict was all the more remarkable because McCray had been forced to try his case in near darkness, before Butler's firm subpoenaed GM turncoat Ronald Elwell, and before I and others started finding the documents and evidence that corroborated Ronald Elwell's testimony. Protective orders and quick, cheap dismissals with attorneys like Bob and Carol's incompetent, fly-by-night, and soon-to-be-disbarred prior attorney had kept the trucks a secret for a decade or more, but now big cases were erupting everywhere that a pickup truck burned, and the deeply held secrets of General Motors were being forced out through motions to compel, motions for sanctions, and trials.

We were having so much fun on Doug's case we would have worked on Bob and Carol's case for free, but it turned out we didn't have to.

By the time we met them, I had embarked on my secret campaign to become a lawyer. In most states you have to attend law school to take the bar exam, but I had two young kids and there was no way I would have considered spending money to go to law school. But in Washington there is a way to avoid that. The state bar association's *Rule 6* program allows full time legal workers with a bachelor's degree to enroll in a four year course of study that, if completed, allows them to take the bar exam. For years people had been telling me I ought to do it—and at some point before we got Bob and Carol's case I finally enrolled. I spent the next four years working four long days at the office and using Wednesdays to read law books at coffee shops and libraries around town.

One day I told an attorney at work, Bill Rutzick, about how Bob and Carol's case had been dismissed without their knowledge and how their attorney had skipped town as soon as we started looking for him. Bill was the resident genius at our firm. He tried asbestos cases, but also excelled at legal research and briefing. His "office" was whichever room he occupied for a particular period of months. Wherever that was, books and photocopied case reports piled up on the table, chairs, and on the floor in mounds that were often more than a foot tall. Bill was forever lost in thought, but would always stop to offer thoughts on a case if you asked him to.

He told me about Federal Rule of Civil Procedure 60(b)(6).

Bill was the exact right person to consult. He was probably the only person in Seattle who would have been able to point me to Rule 60(b)(6). Rule 60 is called "Relief from a Judgment or Order." Part (b) describes various reasons for relieving a party of a final order or judgment. Most of the reasons are pretty specific, but Rule 60(b)(6) is the "Professor and Mary Ann" of the rule 60(b)—a kind of catch all afterthought that allows an order to be vacated for "any other reason that justifies relief." Bill told me he'd never seen it used but thought it might be a good place to start.

Would he help?

Bill, who was busy enough already, just laughed. "No thank you."

Paul was on vacation, so I wrote a brief—a really good one that used all of my new skills as a legal researcher and legal writer. We filed it on June 23, 1994, sixteen days after dismissing Doug's case, and lo! Within a few weeks we received an order from the Court asking for additional briefing on why the Order of Dismissal should or should not be vacated.

After that, Bill joined the team.

That fall we put together a mini-trial on the prior attorney's dismissal of the case. His former legal secretary testified that her boss stopped opening mail weeks or months before abandoning his office and described piles of unopened mail and unread legal documents tipping over and falling to the floor. Problems with executive function, perhaps? No wonder he never answered us! The attorney's wife had been ducking service of a subpoena, so I carried my months old baby, Gemma, to the jewelry counter where she worked and served her myself. (Autistic innovation. She never suspected the geeky man with a baby would drop a subpoena on her.) GM sent up its toughest and best attorney, Mr. Evil himself, but it did no good. The judge, a longtime veteran of the Federal District Court and a one time defense attorney for big corporations, vacated his own order of dismissal. He told us he'd never done it before.

Which brought me one step closer to figuring out how that peach of a drawing—the "probable easy fix"—fit within the sordid history of the exploding truck.

30

Bob's Case

My sister Ann works with me. She and I often refer to our best cases as works of art. They are often huge and complex works of art—Hieronymus Bosch paintings come to life.

Bob and Carol's case, on the other hand, was a small masterpiece. A relatively minor case that had been dismissed unfairly, it became a thorn in GM's side, and an opportunity for us to dig up and expose some of the company's best kept secrets.

It began, for me, with the "peach."

For a couple of years now I'd become very familiar with certain obviously relevant and seemingly related documents produced by GM in our cases. These included simple line drawings of various fuel tank shields, fuel tank liners, and fixes and typed documents describing the pros and cons and pricing of the different proposals. They were often produced separately, standing alone, but all of them looked similar—simple, sparse documents with one subject per page. Several had dates in 1982, and a lot of them showed up scattered about in crash test files from around that time.

They looked like overhead projector slides—part of a presentation.

One described something called "Steel Shield (Mair Design)," a two-piece steel shield that protected the side and top of the fuel tank. That document identified one of the "disadvantages" of the Mair shield as "High Weight."

We all had a good idea whose shield it was and what "Mair" meant. Alex Mair was one of the top engineers at Chevrolet in the 1970s and 1980s. Mair's special affinity was evidently for trucks. One former engineer I talked to on the phone—we'll call him "Thomas" in this book—told me that Mair was an admirer of Earl Stepp, the Chief Engineer of the exploding pickup.

In the course of Bob and Carol's case, I would meet Mair—a dapper, proud, white-haired man who stared at me hatefully.

I suspect the reason Mr. Mair didn't like me was that I discovered his secret.

My first discovery occurred while working on Doug's case. I was in my office looking at stray shielding documents, and in particular the one that described the "Steel Shield (Mair Design)," when suddenly it hit me.

"Ale!"

"A probable easy fix."

"Ale" was "Alex," with the final letter chopped off by a photocopier.

The "peach" I had seen at the very beginning of Doug's case was a napkin sketch of the "Steel Shield (Mair Design)." During Doug's case we asked the fuel tank engineer, George K., if Mair had drawn the peach. He didn't know, but he didn't deny it was Mair's work.

In Bob and Carol's case we intended to ask the man himself, and as I began to assemble exhibits for his deposition, I recalled that in our files we had a declaration signed by Alex Mair in another case. I found it and compared the letters "Ale" on the sketch to the signature "Alex" on the declaration. There was no doubt whatsoever about that big, slanted-oval "A."

"Ale" was Alex Mair. The man must have gone to Catholic school. He had great penmanship.

This was significant. The quick, loose sketch of concentric circles that had reminded me of my sister's painting of a peach was a sketch from Chevrolet's Director of Engineering! General Motors management always denied knowledge of any defect in the truck, and to the extent there was one, it was considered an engineering concern.

But Mair was one of management's top engineers. His sketch was an important admission by management that the truck was defective, required a "fix," and that the fix was easy.

But it got better. References to a "Mair Shield" showed up in some of the files that documented a series of twenty-two fifty mph crash tests run by Chevrolet in the early 1980s—the tests Ronald Elwell had testified about to great effect in the *Moseley* case. Better yet, the Mair *sketch* showed up in some of the files, along with a series of line drawings of shields that appeared to show the evolution of Mair's sketched design of a heavy, two-piece steel shield into a simple, plastic shield, and ultimately into a molded plastic "bathtub" shield that was finally added to the pickup in 1984.

So it looked like Mair's easy "fix" evolved to become part of the design, and part of the product sold to customers.

(Spoiler alert: the version of Mair's fix that ultimately made it onto the truck may have been "easy" but didn't appear to "fix" much. Instead of protecting the fuel tanks in a meaningful way, engineers told us the wrap around plastic shield used on 1984-1987 GM pickups had the ability to carry fuel spilled in a crash from the point of impact to the point of rest, allowing for a bigger fire where the truck ultimately stopped moving.)

And then more.

As I prepared for Mair's deposition in Bob and Carol's case, I had another autistic moment when connections between various, far-flung documents and facts suddenly revealed themselves to me. I had begun to suspect that many of the overhead projector sheets describing potential shields and fuel tank liners, including the Mair shield, were prepared for an event. Then I saw it: a modest look-ing handwritten document signed by fuel tank engineer George K. with the caption AVOID VERBAL ORDERS and the subject line "CEC Show & Tell (management inspection)." The handwriting said "Move the following trucks into the CEC Auditorium on February 18, 1982." Then a list of numbers and letters.

And suddenly everything fell instantly into place and made sense!

The CEC was the Chevrolet Engineering Center. The numbers listed corresponded to pickup trucks that had been tested in the 50 mph side-impact crash tests—the test files where the "probable easy fix" sketch showed up. We had photographs of all the trucks identified in the "AVOID VERBAL ORDERS" memo. They were all smashed in the side with their fuel tanks crushed, burst open, and dangling. Tanks broken like watermelons, Ronald Elwell had said. So it turned out that the "Show & Tell" of crash-tested trucks was a gory presentation of badly damaged truck cadavers staged to force management to approve a change in design.

And suddenly another gear turned, and I knew exactly who the "Show & Tell" was for. One of the overhead projector documents made it clear. Under the title "Fuel System Integrity" it said,

Increase in Litigation

Executive Committee Request

Improvement potential

Most of us had "show and tell" in kindergarten. This was a "Show & Tell (management inspection)" of crash-tested trucks for the Executive Committee of the Board of Directors of General Motors.

Former GM engineer Ronald Elwell had once spoken about just such an undertaking. I forget where I saw it, or his exact wording, but it was essentially, "They dragged these brutalized trucks in front of management" to show them what the problem was.

And here they were. We could use the photographs from the test reports to stage the same "Show & Tell" for the jury.

I knew that in our huge collection of GM documents we had a number of highly redacted minutes of the Executive Committee—basically nothing but the names of the attendees and the dates and times of their meetings. I pulled them out.

And there it was—a set of mostly blank minutes from the Executive Committee with the same date as the "Show & Tell"—February

18, 1982. The only difference—the CEC show was in the morning, and the Executive Committee meeting was in the afternoon, meaning that the organizers scheduled time for board members to attend the "Show & Tell (management inspection)" before their meeting at headquarters a few miles away.

We immediately began an all out effort to learn more. We wrote to GM's attorneys. We did formal document requests for the minutes of the Executive Committee. We noted up the depositions of Alex Mair and other top executives. We began a search for former Executive Committee members from 1982. And we served a notice of deposition pursuant to Rule 30(b)(6) asking for information about a show of crash tested trucks at the CEC auditorium on February 18, 1982.

Rule 30(b)(6) requires an organization to prepare someone to testify on behalf of the organization about the organization's knowledge on subjects identified in the notice. Used right it's a very powerful tool. The person can't say "I don't know." The person has to be prepared to testify about what the company knows, or should know.

Just for fun, I returned to the classified section of the little shopping newspaper that I'd seen at various GM facilities and had used to locate Toby C. My new ad was simple and sweet:

> CEC Show & Tell of Crash Tested Trucks. February
> 18, 1982. Who Was There? $100 for Information.
> Call Peter or Paul.

I put in our office phone number. We hoped someone would respond, but we really didn't care—the secondary purpose was to psych out GM, make them wonder what we knew, and keep their witnesses honest. It would look bad to deny you attended a meeting if a chauffeur later testified that he'd taken you there.

The publication date for my ad was before the day we'd be arriving for the CR 30(b)6 deposition on the subject of the "Show & Tell." I was at the office and got a mysterious call.

"Are you Peter?"

"I am," I said. At least this time the mystery caller got my first name right. The next mystery caller would call me "Jack."

"Did you publish an ad?" the caller asked me.

I said "yes" and the caller hung up without another word. The call had to be from GM's legal department. I figured our message got through.

Once again we were staying at the old hotel across the street from the General Motors Building. The morning after we arrived I walked throughout the complex of General Motors buildings looking for my classified ad. The papers were usually distributed free of charge from small, open boxes in different lobbies and corridors. Usually there were a couple dozen papers in every box. This time every box was empty.

My ad made someone nervous enough to grab and toss every copy of the newspaper, advertisers be damned. (I would later get a message from the newspaper telling me my ads were no longer welcome and would not be published.)

The weirdness continued.

That night I had business at the front desk. While waiting, I heard one of the hotel desk clerks make a call to the younger of the two GM lawyers on our case. "Mr. S., your pizzas are here." I knew Mr. S. He was Mr. Evil's bland sidekick.

The clerk actually used a number when describing the pizzas, and it was a large number, like six or seven—way too many pizzas for one skinny lawyer, and there was almost no way that Mr. Evil was eating anything as cheap and simple as pizza. I figured it was another clue that we had them in a tizzy about the "Show & Tell." This guy was working with a whole team.

Then, in my room, the final clue. I get a phone call. Let's pretend the caller asked for Jack.

"Jack?"

"No, sorry. You must have the wrong room."

"Jack O'Neil?"

This time I laughed. "Sorry, not me!"

I hung up the phone and smiled. I knew of a Jack O'Neil. Jack O'Neil was rumored to have been one of the "fire babies," the young lawyers who purportedly collected and destroyed sensitive documents relating to the pickups.

Was there a "fire baby" reunion taking place somewhere in the same hotel—a reunion involving a whole bunch of freshly delivered pizza? A reunion organized to figure out just how much we knew about the "CEC Show & Tell?" Did one of the "fire babies" ask for Mr. O'Neil's room and get the wrong Mr. O'Neil?

Whatever, that night or the next morning we were told that we had travelled in vain. GM's attorneys told Paul Whelan the company would not produce a witness at the scheduled Rule 30(b)(6) deposition. This was an incredible violation of both courtesy and the court rules. It would mean sanctions for GM or its attorneys.

These were incredible and sometimes frightening times for me. I was usually the person who had selected the witnesses and exhibits, and who scripted the depositions. I was constantly worried I had got something wrong. Although I thought Little Priest was long gone, on my trips to Detroit I looked for comfort in the Gideon bibles in the hotels and motels we frequented and learned the value of the psalms, which were often about wretched true believers looking for protection from their enemies. "Keep me from the trap that they have laid for me and from the snares of evildoers!" Or, "Arise, O Lord! Deliver me, O my God! For thou dost smite all my enemies on the cheek, thou dost break the teeth of the wicked."

Good stuff! Some doubt the power of prayer, but these psalms worked to calm me every time.

I had good reason to be paranoid. I never ate breakfast at the hotel. It cost too much for my conscience. Instead, I ran to a nearby coffee stand for a good bagel and some bad coffee. But one morning

I wandered into the restaurant looking for Paul and startled the Chairman of General Motors. I knew what he looked like because I had done my autistic research. The surprising thing was that he seemed to know what I looked like, too.

I turned the corner and saw him, ten feet away. He saw me, too, and practically spit out his coffee.

This is not a man who should have known I existed, but he appeared to, and appeared to be worried, too.

He was sitting with a tall guy I would later describe as a "goon." At a convention I asked some attorneys who the goon might be. They told me my description fit GM's security chief. The conclusion I drew was that GM security was following Paul and me around Detroit and taking pictures of us. The Chairman was probably startled by my sudden appearance because of the clandestine photographs of me and Paul Whelan that were spread over his breakfast table.

Good.

In addition to publishing ads, I used to call anyone at GM I could think of. I once called Roger Smith, a former chairman, the guy Michael Moore said was impossible to talk to in the film *Roger and Me*. Smith wasn't impossible to talk to. I called him, and he called me right back.

His number was listed in the white pages. I called. A woman answered. I told her exactly who I was and left a carefully scripted message that I'd written down in advance so that it was foolproof. I didn't want to be accused of wrongdoing.

I told her I was a paralegal from Seattle working on a case involving a Washington State man who was burned in a Chevrolet pickup truck, and that I had some questions for Mr. Smith.

Within minutes, Mr. Smith returned my call. I repeated my script. I asked if he had attended the CEC Show & Tell.

I didn't get any information, but I had fun, and the message got through to the General Counsel's office. I just wanted them to know we were working hard, creatively, and all the time.

(One of GM's attorneys later wrote me saying he looked forward to the day he could hold me accountable to the civil rules. He never tried, and wouldn't have gotten a lot of traction or satisfaction from the effort—but we held him and GM's other attorneys accountable at every opportunity, of which there were many.)

In addition to Smith, I called engineers and middle managers. I still have a notebook of addresses, phone numbers and my scribbled notes. Most weren't terribly helpful. One, however, was a mother-lode of information. This is the one I'm calling "Thomas." His job was to work on body parts, not fuel tanks. With our new, sharper photographs I began to see a variety of body parts and reinforcements near the fuel tanks on the crash-test vehicles that never made it onto the trucks sold to consumers—bits of metal designed to strengthen parts of the bed near the fuel tank or to blunt sharp edges to prevent the bed from piercing the tank like a can opener as had happened in earlier crash-tests. With my new understanding of the GM numbering system I could track down the Engineering Design Orders and notes, and we were able to force GM to produce the design drawings—and then get Paul Josten to build them for us.

The first time I called him, Thomas regaled me with stories but also told me he had mental health issues and warned me that sometimes he'd be much less coherent. That day his memory for detail was remarkable and lucid. He dropped names like DeLorean, Stepp, and Mair. He told me that Mair and Stepp, the truck's chief engineer, drove to work together and that Mair was enthralled by Stepp's university education in engineering. He recalled Stepp being uncomfortable with the old in-cab fuel tank and asking if he could design a "pocket" for a fuel tank outside and behind the cab. (We'd seen blurred photos of just such a prototype.) He remembered that GM purchased and disassembled International Harvester pickups to learn how the much smaller truck company designed and protected its own side-mounted fuel tanks. He said he thought maybe the location was okay if International Harvester "got away with it." He said that GM's own side-saddle tank design was a last minute choice after years of failed efforts to put the tank elsewhere. (I was able to corroborate this statement in the draftsmen's notes.) He blamed the side-mounted tank design on John DeLorean's "40-gallon goal." In talking about DeLorean's power at Chevrolet he said, "Even Alex Mair had to listen to him." He described DeLorean's idea of making the back of the cab into the fuel tank—an idea he considered stupid, expensive and impractical, but one he had to investigate because "DeLorean was the boss."

The only thing Thomas didn't remember was his own work—the body reinforcements that bore his name. It was as if he had to deny any connection to a design he believed was both stupid and dangerous.

Talking to Thomas that day was a like a gift from God. It was a guided, dreamlike tour of my own discoveries. The people, events and things I had obsessed about for years were suddenly real, described to me by someone who knew them and was "in the room where it happened." I asked if I could visit the next time I was in Detroit. Thomas said "sure." And at some point in the next few months I proved that everything he told us was true. I found a presentation showing the back of cab as gas tank. I followed scribbled fuel system design notes from the inception of work to the final design that showed repeated efforts to put the fuel tanks between the frame rails and behind the cab but that were abandoned in the final months for hastily drawn outside the cab fuel tanks—all for the elusive "40 gallon goal."

Alas, on our next trip to Detroit, Paul and I would learn that Thomas was also right about his own difficulties with mental health.

31

A Basement in Pontiac

The next time we go to Detroit we head to the city of Pontiac, where Thomas lives. Detroit is in sad shape in the mid-1990s, burned up, torn down, mostly empty lots with the occasional solitary home or small business, liquor stores, and storefront churches. Pontiac, though not burned down, seems even sadder, and every turn we take it gets bleaker—a town down on its luck. I have tried to stay in touch with Thomas. He has agreed to testify in one of our cases, but I'm worried. The last time I called he was having a hard time. He talked about a ray that General Motors had focused on his brain. Paul and I have worked all day. We are tired and hungry. We grow increasingly giddy as we approach his home.

I invent a headline.

Attorney and Paralegal Found Dead in Pontiac Basement.

We both laugh. I park the car in front of a poorly maintained home on what was obviously a once nice street of modest homes.

We knock at the door. Paul steps back.

Thomas answers, dressed in a t-shirt and boxer shorts. He could be my dad unsteadily opening the door while I fold newspapers.

"Hi, Thomas. I'm Peter O'Neil. I called earlier. And this is Paul. Is this still a good time to talk for a moment?"

Thomas examines us briefly through heavily lidded eyes.

"Follow me," he says.

He turns and shuffles across the room towards the kitchen.

I follow obediently, but this is not the girl with the wink and smile. My heart is suddenly pounding, and I have no expectation of a kiss. I'm expecting something more like a hammer, to the cranium.

Thomas opens a door leading into darkness.

"Follow me," he says, again.

I see stairs dropping precipitously.

I follow slowly downstairs towards the basement.

Paul stays in the kitchen. I give him a desperate look. He shrugs, smiles and shakes his head "no." I'm annoyed but recognize it might be useful to have someone there to call 911.

Still not a word from Thomas as we shuffle into the basement. I am basically blinded by fear. My joke has come true, except that the headline will be "Paralegal Dies in Pontiac Basement. Attorney Escapes Grizzly Death, Calls Authorities."

Thomas shuffles towards a flimsy gingham curtain on the far side of the basement. I can hardly breath. I expect the curtain to be hiding the bones and drying flesh of the last person curious enough to track Thomas down.

"Look!" he says, grabbing the cloth and flinging it aside. My terror peaks, then subsides immediately.

It's a toilet.

"My son installed it," he tells me, tonelessly.

After exclamations and compliments we return to the kitchen. The interview doesn't last five minutes. We get no information. I tell Thomas we have to go, but that we'll be in touch.

I am in the driver's seat, and we are slowly moving away when the tension finally releases. I begin shuddering with laughter. Snot and tears pour out of me. Paul is laughing too. I struggle to get out words.

"You made me go down alone!"

"I didn't want to die," he says.

I pull over down the block until I have stopped laughing and am calm enough to drive back to Detroit for some stiff drinks and dinner.

32

More Trucks

B ob and Carol's case was a whirlwind of activity. Paul brought in his partner Michael Withey to help, and the three of us traveled around the country taking depositions. Mike and I went to Petoskey in the far north of lower Michigan to question former General Motors chairman Howard Kehrl. The deposition ended abruptly after Mike asked Kehrl, white haired, retired, and dressed exuberantly in a brightly colored Hawaiian shirt, to explain why "crush space" is important to automotive design. In response, Kehrl compared the GM pickup's gas tank to the can of pop he was holding.

"If I take this can and squeeze it, pop comes out, right?"

The whole room was suddenly electrified. Even though he was holding a Pepsi, and not a Coke, everyone understood that Kehrl's analogy was *the real thing*. Before GM's attorneys could even squeak Mike asked Kehrl to elaborate.

"I just showed you. Squeeze it like this and out comes the pop."

Or gasoline, as the case may be.

"All right. So you want to prevent fuel leaks after a collision."

"That's right. It's the whole game."

Yep. And game over, from our point of view!

Deposition over, too, at least for now. The evilest man alive and his Washington, D.C. compadre stopped the deposition to argue for ten minutes, then called a halt to the proceedings. Later that afternoon we all squeezed into a tiny propeller plane for an uptight flight back to Detroit. Mike worked on a motion to compel and for sanctions, Mr. Evil drank something stiffer than Pepsi, and I just enjoyed myself gazing at the green farmland below with a beatific and victorious smile. We ultimately won Mike's motion, and Kehrl was ordered to finish the deposition at GM's expense, this time in Southern California. He wore the same Hawaiian shirt.

Mike and I also flew to Florida, to a fancy beach community on the east coast to take the deposition of another former chairman. The trip was memorable chiefly for the bright red cardinal I saw the morning of the deposition—a first for me—and the beautiful scallop shells that littered the beach.

Paul and I won a couple of motions relating to the CEC "Show & Tell (management inspection)" and the Executive Committee minutes. GM's lawyers claimed they couldn't find any information about the show other that what they had already produced. The judge was not amused. "I bet if I were the president of General Motors, I could find out who was there in ten minutes," he told them. Then he told GM's out of town attorneys to read Washington's most important case on discovery sanctions—the fines and punishments available to the court to discourage discovery abuse.

We took the deposition of Alex Mair. When it came time for the sketch I call the "peach," he admitted that the words "a probable, easy fix" were in his handwriting and included his signature. He first said it must have been done in 1972, but then admitted he didn't know when it was drawn. When asked about the sketch itself he singled me out for an extremely dirty look.

"I make better drawings than that" he testified.

I'm sure he does—but it doesn't mean he didn't make this one. Besides—the drawing has a certain *je ne sais quoi*. It was done by a practiced hand.

With all the typed documents describing a "Mair Shield" from the late winter and early spring of 1982, I was convinced that the "probable easy fix" was drawn on a napkin or scrap of paper around the time of the CEC "Show & Tell (management inspection)" and that it evolved from a heavy steel shield to a lightweight plastic "bathtub" around the tank as it proceeded into production, eliminating the disadvantage of "High Weight" that was mentioned on the "Mair Shield" documents. It didn't seem like a coincidence that both the napkin sketch and the other line drawings of similar shields were in files relating to the 1980s crash tests. The lightweight plastic shield was used during the final three years of production. It seemed to help with crash tests but didn't help much in the real world. At any rate, the credibility of Mair's testimony would be for the jury to decide.

But the case never got to the jury. In August 1995 we filed a lengthy motion for sanctions. The day before that motion was to be decided, I heard Paul's name over the intercom. GM was calling. Paul was paged several times that day, with increasing frequency, and before the motion for sanctions was decided, the case settled.

We were not done, though.

Before the case settled, I travelled to a convention in Atlanta. The convention focused on automotive defects. As I entered the dark hall, I was pleased to hear the lush southern drawl of Jim Butler, the Georgia lawyer who won the *Moseley* case. And as I found a seat, I was surprised to hear Jim say my name.

"Is Peter O'Neil here?"

I meekly stood and listened while Jim Butler sang my praises and my growing knowledge of the GM truck story. At the next break I was surrounded by attorneys and paralegals with similar cases. One of the last to greet me was an Oregon lawyer named Larry Baron. Larry said he had a case he wanted to talk about and asked if we could get together before the conference ended. We agreed we'd meet the next day.

That night I was wined and dined by the Butler firm along with several burning truck VIPs—among them Joe McCray, the San Francisco lawyer who had tried and won the first big case involving the pickups in the early 1980s. I sat next to Joe and drank wine while he drank whiskey or gin and we swapped knowledge about the trucks. It was a heady new experience for me.

Larry Baron and I met up the next evening at a bar near the convention hotel. This time I was buying. Larry told me about his case and the short-sighted partners at the firm where he then worked. Larry's case involved Anne, an Oregon grandma who was driving her two grandkids in a Buick sedan, when a GM truck ran a stop sign and pulled onto the highway in front of her. Anne's car hit the side of the truck and was sprayed with gasoline. There was, of course, a fire. The driver of the truck was fine, but Larry's client, Anne, was trapped with her grandchildren inside the Buick as flames grew around them. Some Latino farmworkers stopped and reached through the flames to cut the seatbelts and pull Anne and her grandson out of the fire, but they couldn't save Anne's granddaughter.

Larry's predicament was that Oregon had a statute that made it impossible to sue for a product as old as the Chevy truck—but Larry was determined to change that law. He asked the partners at his firm to support his effort. Their inane response: "not one dime." Someone actually put that in writing in a case that would settle for many, many, many, big, fat dimes.

I told Larry he should bring the case to Paul Whelan.

"I've heard a lot about Peter O'Neil," Larry told me, "but I've never heard of Paul Whelan. Why should I bring the case to Paul Whelan?" Larry was from Oregon by way of Detroit. If he had been a Washington lawyer, he would have known about Paul.

"Because Paul Whelan is a really good lawyer," I told him. "And because Paul lets me do what I do."

We arranged for Larry to visit Paul the following week. Paul and Larry instantly became best of friends, and when Larry successfully lobbied to change the statute of repose in Oregon to specifically exclude pickup trucks with side-mounted fuel tanks, he started his own law firm, and we filed Anne's case. To make good matters even better, Joe McCray, who owned a ranch in Oregon, was retained to represent the estate of Anne's granddaughter.

If Bob's and Carol's case was my own work of art, Anne's case became an extraordinary group effort, in which Paul, Mike, Larry, and I all contributed.

One of my favorite times was a brief and hilarious faxed flirtation with John DeLorean. It was my idea. I had put together the history of the truck, but I couldn't testify, and I wanted someone who could credibly tell the whole story.

I had done a ton of research on DeLorean, reading several books, talking to several former engineers, and I had decided that the entire side-mounted tank business was his fault. Maybe he could redeem himself by confessing! The stories told by engineers were funny and graphic. One described DeLorean with his feet up on a desk and mocked DeLorean's misguided idea of turning the sheet metal of the back of the cab into the back side of the gas tank itself—in other words, adding a giant blister of gasoline to the passenger compartment of the truck. Great idea, John! More than one of the engineers I spoke with described DeLorean's obsession with getting 40 gallons of gas onto the truck.

In his book, DeLorean boasted of the Planning Committee's work on the pickup truck. If we could get him to testify that the design was a mess, it would be powerful. I found his address and put together a letter trying to lure DeLorean into testifying. I wrote it for Paul's signature and mailed it.

And he called us! Holy Roger Smith, Batman!

Remarkably I have no memory of this event, only notes. Maybe he simply left a message? Maybe he spoke with Paul? At any rate, we corralled several other lawyers, including Butler and McCray, to fine tune our correspondence, still trying to lure him into helping us. We sent our response on December 4, via Federal Express. On December 7, a day that in this instance shall live for me in hilarity, we received his faxed reply.

Dear Mr. Whelan;

I have reviewed the materials you sent me. I do recall this development program rather vividly.

*I would be pleased to meet with you and provide whatever informa-
tion I can on an anonymous basis. You have missed the most important
single person in this matter.*

*My regular consulting fee is $50,000 per day with a two day mini-
mum, $100,000. I have just completed a major project for the Chinese
Government and would be available in either New York or here over
the next several weeks. I should point out that I was recently contacted
by another organization in the same matter. I will only work for a
single client in a given area.*

Sincerely,

John Z. DeLorean

Remember, those were mid-1990s dollars. We laughed at his proposal, and none of us believed a word that he wrote, but for a month
we exchanged faxed letters worthy of the Donald Trump-Kim
Jong-un love affair. Ultimately, we decided that he was a scammer
and dropped the whole thing—except that we made a valiant effort
to serve him with a subpoena to testify. DeLorean was a cagey bas-
tard and experienced with the law, so we were never able to get him
served.

I would try twice more to find my star witness. Once we hired
a famous automotive engineer to become our historian. I gave him
an elaborately organized set of documents and a scripted dialogue
worthy of Socrates or Plato. All he had to do was learn it. Instead,
he got into the sport of what he called going "*mano a mano*" with
the Evilest Man Alive. In the hand to hand combat that followed,
evil won. The deposition was a complete waste of time and money.
Then I had the brilliant idea of giving Ronald Elwell his documents
back. Elwell had testified magnificently in the *Moseley* case, but he
wasn't able to back up his testimony with corroborating documents,
all of which were taken from him by General Motors. But Elwell
could be subpoenaed to testify. I wrote a script for Paul, organized
about 100 exhibits, and subpoenaed Elwell. Some retired judge was
wheeled in to mediate any disputes that arose during the deposition.
At first Elwell fought and argued, and then he realized that I had

figured out the entire story and backed it up with documents. With my script all he had to say was "yes" or "no" to every question. Except for the old judge, who was more full of himself than a stuffed pizza, and who constantly interrupted with the meaningless phrase "be that as it may," the deposition went gloriously. Elwell sidled up to me during a break to tell me "You've really massaged these documents!" Whatever that meant, (or should I say "be that as it may,") it made me nervous to have him near me because he was under various protective orders and wasn't allowed to speak to me about anything related to GM. I reminded him of that and walked away.

Anyway, I felt proud. We had given Elwell back the documents that GM had taken away from him—documents that corroborated his testimony. But my happiness evaporated as soon as Mr. Evil began his own examination. He had been staring at Elwell with a devilish grin throughout the deposition, obviously trying to get under his skin. Now he pulled out some sort of document Elwell had signed years ago. Who knows what it was about, but Elwell denied vociferously and stupidly that it was his signature. This might have been just a few minutes of testimony, but it seemed like hours, and Elwell suddenly seemed like an incredible (as in not-to-be-believed) mistake. We never even tried to use the deposition.

John DeLorean brought us to a fellow named Robert Lund. A memo I wrote shortly after the DeLorean exchange quoted De-Lorean's book to call Lund "the general sales manager I wanted."[11] My memo went on to describe Lund's rise to power at Chevrolet, where he served as General Manager until February 1982—the month of the "Show & Tell" of crash-tested Chevrolet trucks. I put together a deposition script that was organized like a sonata, in three movements, all of which took place under Lund's watch. The first part of the deposition was to cover testing of the truck and GM's knowledge of the hazard it presented; the second part would force Lund to deal with police reports of fuel fed truck fires that General Motors had received during his tenure; and the third part would be lawsuits—the "Increase in Litigation" that led to the CEC "Show & Tell (management inspection)."

In the deposition Lund initially agreed he had "ultimate responsibility" for safety related issues at Chevrolet while he was at the top. He then testified that no one ever told him that the GM pickup leaked in four government-mandated side impact crash tests run during his tenure. He testified that no one told him about the dozens of truck fires that were reported to GM during this period. As the underarms of the young GM lawyer's shirt became drenched in very visible sweat, we confronted Lund with those reports and asked him to read one aloud.

"It says something about 'arms outstretched. The body was burned beyond recognition. The medical examiner Joe Lieb arri ved.'"

He then paused, and added his own commentary:

"But, obviously, selling in excess of three million cars and trucks a year, I can't begin to read any of the accident reports."

It was pathetic testimony from the general sales manager that John DeLorean wanted. A jury could decide which was more important to Lund and his company— safety or sales.

Anne's case would settle during its third mediation. Anne sat with a rosary, quietly praying throughout the final day of mediation. Her face was badly scarred by fire. She had lost her leg and parts of her ears. She had lost her granddaughter.

She had not, however, lost her sense of humor.

At the end of a long, hard day, she reluctantly agreed to a settlement, but added one condition. All day we had heard about General Motors' bean counter and his painfully obtuse interactions with the mediator. Anne began speaking quietly.

"I'll agree to settle, but on the condition that awful man meets me on the courthouse steps, bends down, and gives me a big, wet kiss—not on the right cheek, not on the left—but right in the middle of my big, fat ass!"

Hours of tension disappeared into laughter and the mediator went into the other room to close the deal.

Anyway, we already had two more truck cases—both in Southern California.

We were on a roll.

33

I Become a Lawyer

I did my first closing argument at the age of forty-three. The trial involved a young man who was badly burned when the old dump truck he was driving tipped over, spilled fuel, and burned.

We had a good product liability case against the truck manufacturer, but it was complicated by lots of potentially confusing issues. Among other things, the accident happened the first time our client drove the truck, and the defense argued that he had contributed to his own harm by agreeing to drive without formal training.

So at some point in the closing argument, I said, "You've watched me learn a lot on this job. That's the way we do it here—people learn by doing stuff."

What the jury didn't know (and what I longed to tell them) was that I started the case as a paralegal. I learned to be a lawyer on the job, spending my days working on big product liability cases and my nights and weekends struggling with the rule against perpetuities, the *Palsgraf* case, and *Marbury v. Madison*. I did this as a participant in a Washington State Bar Association program that allows full time legal workers to study for the bar exam without going to law school. When I began the program, I was the primary wage earner in my family. I had a wife, two kids, and a mortgage. I was not inclined to go into debt to study law. (I saved the going-into-debt part for later, after I became partner.) The Law Clerk Program allowed me to keep a job that I liked and to earn a good living while learning the law.

Washington is one of about half a dozen states that still offer people an opportunity to take the bar exam without going to law school. The program is a highly structured, four year course of study that covers every subject on Washington's bar exam, from torts and contracts, to criminal law and community property. You study constitutional law. You study business law. You study real property, wills and trusts, and administrative law. It's grueling, and a little relentless, but it works.

I passed the bar exam four months before trial.

Within a month I took my first deposition. The witness was a nationally renowned accident reconstruction engineer. We had met several times during my years as a legal assistant, and he always seemed to like me, but I felt completely out of place questioning him as a lawyer. During the first few questions my voice warbled like one of those old musical saws they played on the *Little Rascals* movies.

That's why I knew how our client felt when his boss ordered him to drive the old dump truck for the first time. As we headed into trial I kept having to jump into the driver's seat again and again.

I became increasingly comfortable doing depositions, but there were always new learning experiences. A day before trial, during motions, Paul Whelan dug an elbow into my side at counsel table. The defendant's lawyer was arguing a motion to exclude a number of documents that were important to our case. I had written the responsive brief, but my plan was to sit quietly and watch Whelan argue the motion in court.

Whelan had other ideas.

"Get up!" he whispered.

I felt like a little bird being pushed out of the nest. I flapped as hard as I could and argued the motion, though I did it quite autistically. While the Ford attorney was making his argument I started walking in circles behind my podium while listening intently and organizing my response. "Stop walking!" Whelan hissed at me. I hadn't even noticed what I was doing. I stopped walking and won the argument, but hardly noticed. After the judge said I had won, I kept arguing my case.

"Stop!" Whelan whispered, loudly. I stopped.

As I argued and won other motions that day I stopped feeling like a hatchling and began to feel like a magnificent, soaring eagle.

But I didn't fly quite so high throughout the trial.

I did fine on my part of the opening statement, even after Ford's attorneys objected to all of my proposed exhibits. They thought they had me rattled, but I knew the facts of the case better than anyone. We had not objected to most of Ford's proposed exhibits, so I walked over to their desk, pulled out several large photographs from their pile, and made my argument.

But then the jury saw me put on my first witness, and it wasn't pretty.

The defense attorney objected to virtually every question I asked. I could tell he enjoyed himself. The judge sustained every objection. I didn't have a clue. I'd hear the objection, rephrase the question, and get the exact same result.

"Sustained!"

It probably lasted a minute and a half. Like a truck rolling to its side it felt like an eternity.

I looked back to the plaintiff's table. Whelan shrugged.

"No further questions!"

The truth is I never had any particular ambition to practice law. I started down the path by accident after returning from a three year stint in the Peace Corps. I was a newlywed. I had a new, albeit small, mortgage.

My brother was a Seattle lawyer. He gave me a two week project at his firm handling some administrative chores. Ten years later someone delivered a bunch of roses to mark my 10th anniversary with the company. That's when I decided I had to do something.

By then I was one of the more senior paralegals. I'd become something of a quiet rumor working with Whelan on the truck fires and other big product cases. I had an instinct for finding needles in the hay and enjoyed sticking those needles into the sides of corporations that I thought were hurting people needlessly.

The one thing that I never entirely enjoyed was telling people what I did for a living. When you tell people you are a legal assistant or paralegal, they assume you spend your days setting up appointments or doing mundane research. The truth is I got to use and develop an exciting variety of skills. I wrote. I researched. I interviewed clients and witnesses. I located people. I made my own demonstrative exhibits. I did investigations. I organized stuff. I helped with document productions. I traveled. I took videos and photographs. (I once saw one of my videos on the local news. I was mortified to see the disclaimer "amateur footage" superimposed on my work.) I kicked around at accident scenes hunting for evidence. I inspected crashed cars and trucks. I talked with experts. I wrote scripts for depositions. I wrote interrogatories, requests for production, and motions to compel. I flirted with John DeLorean. I angered Alex Mair. I phoned Roger Smith. I descended fearfully but bravely into Thomas's Pontiac, Michigan basement. I did all sorts of things—but when I told someone what I did for a living they always sort of looked bored and said, "so you do research for the attorneys?"

Then I had kids. When I applied to participate in the program, I wrote the following:

> Daughters can be powerful motivators. My second was born a few days ago. She weighs eight pounds something. Of course I want to feed her and clothe her and help send her to college. I want to be there for her as much as possible. And I want my daughters to know they can achieve their goals.

And I knew I could be a sharper thorn in the side of those corporations if I became a lawyer.

I would study law the old fashioned way. I would join Lincoln, Marshall, and Oliver Wendell Holmes as a home schooled lawyer. It didn't matter if I passed or failed. It didn't matter if I ever worked as a lawyer. It was enough that I somehow make sense of what I'd been doing all those years as a paralegal.

That's what I thought at the time, anyway.

When I went to Whelan and asked if he would tutor me I had an unfair advantage. I knew he'd say yes. We had worked together a long time and he had let me take a major role in many of our cases. A sort of pained but resigned expression passed over his face. He probably had a notion how much time and work he would have to put into the project.

Every month for four years he or an "assistant tutor" would have to prepare a course outline, talk with me about the law, and then write and grade an exam. Although the program provides some of the structure and a few guidelines, preparation of the courses and examinations and grading of the work are the responsibility of the tutor. In other words, it's a huge commitment.

Paul was lucky in one respect. For much of the time I was studying I was at a large plaintiff firm. At least seven different lawyers there offered to help me with courses, and it was a pretty impressive faculty. Whelan taught me torts and evidence. I had a private course in constitutional law from Leonard Schroeter. Bill Rutzick taught me civil procedure. Former King County Prosecutor Becky Roe taught me criminal law. A future judge named Doug McBroom was nice enough to try to teach me the Uniform Commercial Code. Lord help me if I ever need that particular bit of legal knowledge. Neither of us could figure it out.

Friends and family also chipped in. Rosemarie Warren LeMoine taught me family law, and my brother Paul, in New York, took on the courses that no one in our circle of personal injury attorneys knew what to do with, like tax law and corporations.

But for the most part it was Whelan, and he took the job seriously. He gave me lists of cases and statutes to read. He grabbed opportunities to talk on case-related drives to Portland and Bend, Oregon. Examination questions were handled in great secrecy and handed to me in sealed envelopes like Academy Award results.

My study halls were city buses, exercise bikes, and coffee houses. (The problem with coffee houses is that my mind will follow good music and cause me to lose track of my reading.) Most Wednesdays I went to the University District. I'd begin with a few stiff coffees at a noisy coffee house, then hit the law library for as long as I could stand it. I tended to study on the go, moving from spot to spot to ease the monotony.

All the while the rest of my life kept moving. My younger daughter, Gemma, didn't get to see me as much as my first daughter Jade had, at least during the first two years of my program. I had to disappear a couple of evenings a week to read.

I was never at ease. I had trouble judging my own progress. I occasionally envied traditional students who could see how their grades stacked up against others. My tutors gave me good marks, but I didn't quite believe the evaluations because they were made by friends and coworkers who had no curve to grade me on. I was always top of my class and bottom at the same time. Looking back, I think that the ambiguity helped. It forced me to work harder, just in case.

Although it sounds funny, I think in a strange way it helped not to have a regular professor. No one spoon fed me anything. I often spent hours struggling to understand a concept, and then read dozens of cases to make sure I had really understood. Bill Rutzick told me at the start of the course to read 10 or 15 cases a week. I took it to heart and destroyed a small forest making photocopies. When I finally *did* have real professors, at the bar review course, I knew the struggle had paid off and that I'd actually worked my way to some sort of an understanding.

I remained vaguely paranoid throughout. I kept expecting a letter from the Bar Association telling me that I had got it completely wrong, that my work was not even in the ballpark, and that I had no chance of passing the bar exam. But instead, silence.

In the meantime I was taking a growing role on our cases. I gained a new feel for legal research, a subject that had always seemed a little frightening to me. I wrote a motion for certification to the Washington State Supreme Court. It was denied. I wrote most of the opening brief that raised Bob and Carol's case from the dead. That same case ended the day before a major sanctions hearing for which I wrote most of the briefs. We did some great discovery during the years that I was studying, and I played a major role in that.

I tried to keep my own expectations low, but it wasn't easy. For six weeks prior to the bar exam I stopped working to concentrate on the bar review course. My then wife took the kids on an extended visit with her parents in Togo. I lived a monkish life of study, exercise and extremely drab cafeteria food. I abstained from alcohol for months. I administered almost a hundred practice tests to myself, writing each response in longhand and timing the response.

When it came time for the exam, I got myself a hotel room near the test site, spent the afternoon studying, then went for a long jog. I went to bed early.

And I lay there, never sleeping a wink, an insomniac for the first time in my life.

I had thought I was less than fully invested in the process. I had pretended that was my secret weapon. I would pass because I did not care. I had not spent a dime on law school. It didn't matter if I passed or failed.

As my oldest daughter used to say: "Yeah, right."

My handwriting that first day looked like a three-year-old's, except vaguely psychotic, with dark, shaky lettering. I lived through the day on shots of espresso. I was so exhausted that night that I actually did sleep. After the first twenty-four hours of caffeine and exhaustion, the second day of the exam felt like a vacation.

It was raining in October when the results were due. Our mailman parked at the corner and started on the other side of the street. I watched him go from house to house. I had absolutely no notion what the results would say. I heard our mailbox bang shut. I grabbed the envelope and sat down.

I told myself it didn't matter if I passed or failed.

Yeah, right.

34

My Friends the Engineers

Though I have always had trouble making and keeping friends, there is one group of people that almost always seems to like working with me.

Engineers.

Armed only with a bachelor's degree in English and few math skills, I nonetheless sort of understand their language.

I've already mentioned Peter F. We met in fifth grade in Sacramento, and for several years we were nearly inseparable. One of our early games was building a large, very detailed cardboard cockpit (an idea we stole from my brother Danny) that we used for imaginary trips into outer space. Peter taught me about telescopes. He had a wonderful machine in his bedroom that created miniature bolts of lightning. He and I built a lie detector complete with toggle switches, a whirring motor and a paper tape "readout" with a frantically waving "liar" line that we used to trick Stevo, who could be counted on to not tell the truth. I found Peter again while searching for long lost GM engineers at the Seattle Public Library. It turned out he, too, had moved to Washington State and lived across the lake from me in Bellevue. And it turned out he had become the engineer he was always meant to be.

When I started working on automotive product liability cases I had to learn to speak engineering fast. It was easy, even though I couldn't do the math, because I got to work with and against a lot of great engineers, many of them former car and truck designers. I liked them all, and they seemed to like working with me.

Even the ones who worked against me.

My very first deposition, as a newbie lawyer forty-three years of age, was of a grizzled but friendly engineer we'll call John. *Doctor* John. He had a Ph.D.

Dr. John is the sort of expert you like to have on the other side. He always did his best to help the lawyers that hired him, but in the end, he told the truth.

He had a western flair—cowboy boots and a sort of a drawl, and he was almost always smiling. We first met when I was a legal assistant, and I appreciated that instead of treating me like a sidekick, he learned and remembered my name. Once, when General Motors' attorneys had me served with a subpoena at a truck inspection in Southern California, Dr. John said, loudly enough for the GM lawyers, to hear that I had his permission to punch them.

It was a joke, and I didn't, but I was grateful.

But despite his easy charm, I was properly terrified the first time I had to sit in front of him and ask questions in front of two other attorneys and a court reporter.

I began with a wavering voice—always a sign I'm afraid—but quickly settled down. I had put together a script of every question I intended to ask, and the first ones were easy for him and for me—name, occupation, and some questions about his file. I had written dozens of such scripts for Paul Whelan, and now I did it for myself without knowing how utterly autistic it was to plan out every word of a difficult conversation.

I had done lots of preparation. Our case involved an ancient, 1967 Ford dump truck that had crashed onto its side, spilled fuel, and burned. I had learned about other, similar cases Dr. John worked on, and I quickly started getting "admissions"—things that helped our case that he had to admit were true. One of the defenses was that the dump truck was too old to be on the streets, but Dr. John admitted he owned and drove two older pickups and testified they were still safe. We were arguing the gas cap got twisted off by the road surface after the dump truck tipped to its side and slid down the road. I asked Dr. John if he had ever testified that the same thing had happened in a case involving a similar truck.

"I think you know the answer to that is yes," he testified with a grin.

He also admitted that in another case he testified that a Ford in-cab gas tank like ours had failed in a frontal collision, spilling gas inside the truck cab.

The truth was that he seemed to enjoy the deposition, treating it like a friendly game of chess. He even seemed to enjoy that I was scoring points.

A very experienced attorney, Murray Kleist, went with me to the deposition. As we walked back to our office afterwards, he congratulated me and walked me through various points I had scored. I was on cloud nine. As a brand new attorney, I hadn't been sure I could do the job. Turned out, I could. But the universe sent a dash of humility to cool me off. Two pretty teenage girls suddenly jumped towards me screaming, "It's you! You're him! You're him!"

And then the final cruelty: "You're Kenneth Starr!"

I don't know which is worse—that they were pranking me so cruelly, or that they actually thought I was Kenneth Starr. I pushed on and tried my best to return to the joy I had been feeling after my first deposition.

I had begun that case as a legal assistant. I ended it doing opening statement and closing argument at trial. In between I got a lot of practice with lawyering and engineers.

One hot shot engineering expert for the defense was in Chicago. Whelan and I had first gone to Detroit where I did a corporate representative deposition of Ford, and then to Chicago where Paul was going to depose the expert engineer. It was almost Christmas, and Chicago was cold, windy, and beautifully lit for the holiday. Paul wanted to get home to his wife and kids but we were supposed to spend the entire weekend there before our Monday morning deposition.

I told Paul to go home. I had prepared the script for the deposition, anyway—why not take it? I still appreciate that, even though it would only be my third deposition, Paul left and let me handle it.

I got to the location where the deposition would take place on Monday morning and found the Seattle attorney who defended parts of the case waiting with his engineer. When they realized the newbie forty-three-year-old lawyer was going to take the deposition, they became almost giddy and tried to insult me. As we waited for the court reporter the attorney and witness made jokes about "male secretaries" and tittered like schoolboys. I did a good enough deposition, and the expert stopped laughing.

Later the same engineering expert came to trial. He was preceded by a glorious, very costly, and nearly meaningless "experiment" that used a giant hammer to smack the gas cap of a truck like the one in our case. (It's instructive to know that automotive defendants will spend almost any amount of money to crush in court the people they have injured with their defective designs.) The "experiment" was a junk science farce. It looked cool but proved nothing. I filed a motion I called "Motion in Limine to Strike Hammer." The title caught the judge's attention.

"I like this hammer," he told us, grinning. "Three hundred fifty pounds it says on it? Three hundred ten? What is it? A big chunk of lead?"

"Well, your honor, we don't know what it is," I responded, and explained that we had been surprised with it after the expert's deposition and just prior to trial. I asked that it be kept out of the trial until I had a chance to depose the expert again. The judge agreed.

I took the expert's second deposition the night before he was scheduled to testify. The next day Paul Whelan gave a scathing description of the hammer experiment to the judge. Sensing defeat, so did Ford's lawyer, who suddenly admitted this incredibly expensive bit of junk science was no longer an experiment, it was a now a simple demonstrative exhibit.

The judge's ruling was swift.

"It proves nothing. You can prove what you just stated with a straight edge."

The hammer was gone. Score one for male secretaries.

But our guest from Illinois had other surprises. At the deposition he revealed yet another expensive exhibit—a detailed model of the accident vehicle. He described it in glowing, science-like terms. He had created it from detailed scans of the actual dump truck in our case.

The problem: the scans he used to create the model weren't accurate, so neither was the model. At the deposition I pointed out that his seventy-five thousand dollar model, which I was seeing for the first time, didn't include a dent in the door that was critical to our theory of the case. The expert admitted this was true. He couldn't explain it—but it meant that his fancy little dump truck became a garbage truck.

Poof—another exhibit eliminated from the case. The expensive but inaccurate model was never seen again.

This expert was the only witness I cross examined live at that trial. I did okay. I asked if he had looked at any other real crashes involving the design. No. I asked if he had looked at any of Ford's own crash testing of the design. No.

Our case was tried in federal court in Tacoma. A lot of this expert's testimony focused on the rigidity of the dump truck's steel frame. We claimed the frame twisted as the truck tipped and allowed the cab to slap the road surface. Ford's expert claimed the frame couldn't possibly twist the way our engineers said it did—that the steel frame was too big and strong to bend or twist.

So, I began to ask about a bridge every Washington resident knows. Weirdly, I only had to say the words, "Do you know..." when he burst forth with the answer.

"The Tacoma Narrows?" he interrupted, with a giant, unhappy smile. "Yes, every engineer knows that one!"

Yep. So does every member of the jury. They drive over it often, and they've all seen the movie of it twisting in the wind, like you.

"Okay," I said. "And that bridge was made out of big steel, and I just remember movies of the steel and concrete bending and twisting..."

"Right!"

The male secretary now had a trained pet! One who barked on command!

When we were done and I was packing up my gear he sidled up to me with a smile.

"So really—what school?"

"What do you mean?" I asked.

"What engineering school did you attend?" he asked, grinning.

"My only degree is in English Literature," I told him.

Today I might add, "with an emphasis in Autistic Studies."

At my next trial I had a similar experience. It was a case against Hyundai for a weak front passenger seat that collapsed and allowed our seat-belted client, Jesse Magana, to slip backwards out of the seat and smash through the back window and into the dirt near the road. Jesse was instantly paralyzed.

Everything about that case was complicated and crazy—except Jesse.

Jesse was the front seat passenger in a tiny rental car driven by a goofy kid he hardly knew. They had met fishing and the kid told Jesse that his car had broken down. Jesse—a man who spent his life helping people—offered to help the kid fix the engine. (Jesse's willingness to help others came out during trial as a small parade of witnesses described his volunteer activities.)

Jesse and the goofy kid pulled the engine, removed the manifold, and then had to run to the auto parts store for a new gasket. Jesse sat up front and wore his seatbelt. The kid drove. The kid's wife sat in the back without a seatbelt.

They were driving down a narrow county road when the kid got scared by an oncoming truck, jerked the wheel, and lost control. The car slid sideways, tripped, and slid on the driver's side into a tree, which put a big, tree-shaped dent across the hood.

The car then spun around the tree and returned to its wheels. The centripetal force from spinning around the tree was such that Jesse's seat back collapsed, and he flew backwards through the car, smashing through the back window glass and bending the hatch. He landed fifty feet from the car and was never able to walk again.

Hyundai's attorneys had one good line. They called the crash *Mr. Toad's Wild Ride*.

But the ride got even wilder when, for reasons unknown, the driver told the police, and then Hyundai, that Jesse was in the back seat, and that the driver's wife, who was pregnant, had been the front seat passenger.

It was a preposterous lie. The pregnant wife was found pinned beneath the collapsed front seat back with a fractured femur.

Even more preposterous, Hyundai ran with it, and Hyundai's expert on occupant motion made physics defying charts to show all of this happening. In the expert's charts, the unbelted back seat passenger rose a foot or so above the seat as the car spun around the tree.

Amusingly the driver's own expert, a professor from the University of Oregon, testified that the driver was wrong—that Jesse had been up front and the driver's wife in the back.

And so did the first responders.

And so did Jesse.

And so did our experts.

And eventually, the driver, Ricky, more or less said it, too. In a second deposition immediately before trial, he admitted he really didn't know where Jesse had been sitting. His wife said pretty much the same thing.

Jesse was injured in a 1996 Hyundai Accent. It was tiny, but you couldn't necessarily tell that from photographs. I wanted the jurors to see how small it was because then Jesse's short flight backwards through the rear window would make more sense to them. Near the end of our part of the trial I happened to see an identical model near the courthouse. I flagged it down and told the teenaged owner I'd pay him $50 to show up with his car the next Monday. I would have to ask the Judge if the jury could walk outside and see it.

In the meantime, Hyundai unveiled its own "Big Hammer." It was an expensive, last minute, pseudo-scientific "sled test" that used part of the body and passenger compartment of a Hyundai Accent that was exactly like the one in our case, but from a different model year. The sled test had all sorts of problems in terms of admissibility at trial because, though it looked scientific, it wasn't anything like our crash. In our crash the car rotated 90 degrees, tipped to its side, and then struck a tree that sent the car into a fast spin. The airbags fired, pushing Jesse backward, and centripetal force did the rest, throwing Jesse rearward hard enough to break the seat. The seat collapsed onto the driver's wife, breaking her femur and pinning her, and Jesse slid backwards through his seat belt and shoulder harness, across the wife's face, and out the back hatch, which was broken in the process. It was a miracle Jesse survived at all.

But in Hyundai's silly "test," a portion of the passenger compartment of a car, with no roof, slid forward a few feet on steel rails and the airbags were fired remotely. The airbags barely touched the crash test dummy in the front passenger compartment. There was no spinning, and no centripetal force. It looked like a theme park ride for very small children—and sort of a dull one. Instead of *Mr. Toad's Wild Ride*, it was *It's a Small World*.

Our case wasn't about airbags—it was about the weak seat back as part of a defective occupant restraint system. I felt pretty confident we would knock this fancy test out of the case as soon as I saw it, and if we didn't succeed in knocking it out, we would use it to our advantage by showing the jury all the ways in which it was different and irrelevant.

Friday was an off day for the jury, so we used it to talk with the judge about things like viewing the car I had flagged down outside the courthouse. I had subsequently learned the car was identical to the one in our case, but a different model year. (The car was produced from 1994 through 1998 with no changes.) Hyundai's counsel stood and objected sanctimoniously that we had the wrong model year. Whelan and I looked at each other with disbelief and joy. The judge disallowed the viewing on the basis of model year.

The next Monday Hyundai began its case. It was time for Hyundai's expert, a dapper and very expensive little man from Texas. I had filed a motion to exclude his sled test. Now I raised my objection, and there was a hearing.

You have to appreciate about how expensive these tests are to produce. The dapper little expert charged $850 dollars an hour for his time. His many assistants charged some fraction of that. To perform the test they bought a car, cut it apart it, painted it to look nice, rented a "sled" facility, rented crash test dummies, brought in technicians to run and record the test. I don't know what it cost, but it had to cost a lot.

So, we have a hearing, and the little man watches while I explain all the many reasons the test should not be allowed in front of the jury. I include the fact that the car used in the test was the wrong model year, just like the car we wanted the jury to walk past and look at the prior Friday—the one Hyundai had objected to.

The judge said fairness required the same ruling. The test was thrown out, and the expert's testimony was limited to very discrete areas relating to the airbag.

We had hardly mentioned the airbag in our case. There was no real need for expert testimony on the issue from Hyundai, but Hyundai's attorneys must have wanted to get some bang for the many, many bucks they'd paid this man. The jury was probably baffled. Why is this man here? He talked about abrasions the airbag might cause. It was pointless.

When he was asked to show the jury an airbag assembly, he asked a young woman who was part of the defense team to hold it and carry it around, evidently because he didn't want to get his own very expensive suit dirty but wasn't worried about her less expensive one. There was something bizarre about the whole thing.

Hyundai's counsel pushed the testimony right up to the end of the court day. I was worried we'd adjourn, because I had a plan to dispense with the expert expeditiously. When Hyundai finished, the judge asked if we should come back the next day for cross examination. I stood and said, "Your Honor, if we can stay a few more minutes, I think we can finish today."

She agreed and told the jury we might run late. I knew we wouldn't. Since he'd done nothing to hurt us, my questioning would be brief.

"I believe we've met before; is that correct?" I asked.

"Yes, sir."

"And you've done a fair amount of work looking at the car before, and again here at trial?" (I didn't mention the tests he'd done. That might open the door to admitting it into evidence.)

"Yes." He was smiling. It was flattering testimony. It suggested he was a hard worker, and thorough. He had not arrived at his opinions without considerable thought and effort.

"And you've looked at the documents?"

"Yes."

Now came the part I relished. Every time one of our experts testified Hyundai's lawyer made a point of asking how much they charged per hour. It was always something in the low hundreds of dollars. So, I smiled.

"We've got a sad tradition where the first lawyer gets up and asks questions and then the second lawyer gets up and says 'What's your hourly fee?'"

"And the answer is $850 an hour" he said with a strained smile.

This was Clark County, Washington in 2002. You could easily seat a jury of twelve Clark County working people where not one juror made $850 in a *week*.

"I have no further questions. Thanks."

And Mr. Dapper was on his way back to Houston.

But my favorite engineer on Jesse's case was my friend Larry Tompkins. Larry had a speech issue that sometimes made it hard for him to tell a story, but as he testified in front of a jury, Larry surprised me with his engaging manner, describing his career as a design engineer with Chrysler and Toyota and the fun he had as a race car driver. The jury seemed to love him. Like his counterpart, the same Dr. John I'd battled in my first ever deposition who was now testifying for Hyundai, Larry was among the last of the old school accident reconstruction engineers—people who used pencil, paper, a slide rule, and measurements done with tapes and rulers to reconstruct every aspect of a crash. On this case, as usual, the two more or less agreed. They came up with reconstructions of the crash that were nearly identical.

During Jesse's trial I suddenly understood, though in a somewhat incoherent way, why Hyundai's biomechanics expert was so wrong. He had created storyboards that showed the back seat occupant rising a foot or more off the seat as the car spun around the tree. An expert on our side had laughed about that, saying it defied physics, but I had so many things to worry about during our part of the trial that the physics weren't clear to me. But now, the night before my old friend Dr. John was scheduled to testify, I began to understand the physics in some still incoherent and inexpressible way. I remembered a moment from my sister Maggie's physics class at U.C. Berkeley that I had visited when I was twelve-years-old. The professor had sat on an old, wooden swivel chair and spun himself on stage. As he pulled his arms and legs closer to his body, the chair spun faster. He told us the phenomenon was called "angular momentum," and was the same law of physics that Olympic skaters used during their spins. I called Larry late at night to hash it out. Was the car moving faster after it hit the tree? Was angular momentum involved? I described my visit to Maggie's physics class thirty years earlier. Larry laughed and patiently walked me through the science and the math. I was wrong about the physics but correct about the result—the back end of the car moved faster as it spun around the tree than it had been moving at the time of the collision. Larry even worked out an equation for me to use with Dr. John while he was on the stand. I can't do math, so I put the answer on a piece of paper and put it in the pocket of the shirt I would wear to court the next morning.

That same night, after dinner, I ordered some giant photocopies from a copy service and raced across town to a discount store to buy foam board, glue sticks, and various office supplies. Back at the hotel I carefully cut, glued, and drilled. I soon had a demonstrative exhibit that looked just like the goofy one from Hyundai's expert that showed the backseat occupant flying up off the back seat towards the ceiling of the car, except that mine had a difference—the car was on a separate piece of foam board and was attached in such a way that it could actually rotate around the tree, just like in the accident.

When I got to court the next morning, I set it up and hid it with another foam board. You couldn't see from a distance that my new version of the Hyundai expert's exhibit had a part that swiveled. That morning, in court, I walked Dr. John through the crash. I asked him to do the calculation Larry had provided me, and when he hesitated, I merely had to reach towards my pocket for the response for him to blurt out the answer; he knew me and knew I'd have it. Then we began to discuss the other Hyundai expert's opinion that the backseat passenger (who they claimed was Jesse) rose off the seat when the car's hood struck the big tree. Dr. John agreed that the car was sliding on its side at a certain speed. He agreed that when the hood of the car hit the tree the occupants would want to keep moving at the same speed the car had been going.

And then the zinger—and this is where I began to pivot the car around the tree like a clock dial. Dr. John responded with a big grin.

I asked Dr. John if the back end of the car would have to move a longer distance than the front end as the car rotated around the tree. He agreed that it would. And did that mean the back of the car would have to move *faster* than the front of the car because it had farther to go. He agreed that it would. I think he actually enjoyed this.

And would the back of the car, including the back seat, actually move faster than the unbelted occupant of that seat?

Yes, Dr. John agreed, it would.

And would the back of the car move faster than the car had been going at the time it hit the tree.

Yes, it would.

And would the back seat occupant be kept in his or her seat because that seat was moving faster than she was?

Yes.

In other words, the other Hyundai expert's opinion was completely wrong. He had testified that the occupant of that seat would fly up towards the ceiling, but in fact the seat would stay with that person—in fact, move faster—and the person would remain snugly within it, despite not wearing a seatbelt, as the seat back in front of her collapsed onto her femur, and my client, Jesse, flew backwards over her and out the back hatch.

It was a small Perry Mason moment, and one Dr. John seemed to enjoy.

Larry Tompkins and I would continue to work together here and there on other cases, and we saw each other now and then in real life. Once he and his wife invited Rebecca and me to join them at a Seattle Mariners game. He often turned me on to good bar-b-que places. Any chat on the phone with Larry became at least 30 minutes longer as Larry thought of new stories that he wanted to tell me or

Ann. When I had a case involving a runaway mobility scooter—the sort of thing you see the elderly and disabled using—Larry laughed and agreed to put his six-foot-four-inch frame on a disabled scooter and roll it down the soap box derby hill in Salem, Oregon. (We never managed to do it, but it's still a vision I enjoy.)

One day I got an email with the subject line "Notice of Impending Death."

Pure Larry Tompkins.

A year before this I had to drive to a hospital in Vancouver, Washington to say goodbye to my client and friend, Jesse Magana, who was fatally stricken by a sudden infection. Now I had to go to the same hospital to say goodbye to Larry. Both visits were among the harder things I have ever done. The visit with Larry was particularly hard because his mind and spirit were as sharp as ever, but his blood system was failing, and he had received his last transfusion.

It's hard when you can't say "see you later" as you leave old friends for the last time.

35

Special Interest, Special Focus

After the GM truck cases the same phenomenon took over whenever I got a new case. For a period of years, I would fixate on Ford pickups with in-cab fuel tanks. Then Hyundai Accents. Then John Deere Tractors. For shorter times it might be child resistant bottle caps used on drain cleaner, or heating pads, or temporary concrete barriers, or tires. Once it was a badly designed gum machine.

My kids were as involved as me. Jade and Gemma would hold onto their seats as I screeched off the road at the sight of a farm tractor, but then they got to sit in the old tractor for a minute while I talked to the farmer and took pictures of the rollover protection system. Rafferty snapped pictures of the concrete barriers temporarily dividing the interstate while I drove and shouted instructions.

For a period of three or four years Paul Whelan and I had three tragic cases where kids fell from the upper floors of apartment buildings. It turned out to be a seasonal phenomenon that repeats itself whenever weather gets hot. We treated the cases as product liability cases, but brought in a host of other defendants including big property management companies.

For several years I stared at windows on new construction as I drove past, but by the time we filed our second or third case, I could relax a little because my sister Ann had started working with us and was able to absorb a lot of the obsession. She seemed custom made for it.

Ann and I were born two years apart in the mid 1950s, and maybe not for the first time. An infamous family Ouija Board session told us that Ann and I had previous lives in rural England where we were purportedly born a few years apart in the 1230s. Were we brother and sister then, too, we asked?

"NOW AND FOREVER," the board responded.

Ann began working with us on Ford Explorer rollover cases. After we won a motion to compel the production of "other incident" documents, Ford took revenge by delivering more than 30 bankers boxes of police reports, photographs and legal complaints relating to thousands of Ford Explorers that had rolled over. They didn't anticipate Ann. She went through every page, organized them, scanned them, and created an enormous database of thousands of rollover incidents from which our experts were able to pick the very best for use as evidence at trial.

Once we had a case involving two young baseball players killed when a defectively manufactured tire split apart on the highway. Their truck rolled over at freeway speed, killing them both. One of the young men was a number one draft pick. His case was easy, but he wasn't our client. Our client was a 38th round pick.

We knew that lots of late round draft picks made it into the major leagues, including stars like Mike Piazza, who was drafted in the 62nd round. But what Ann did was beautiful—she collected the baseball cards of all these improbable major leaguers and put together a notebook of them for our experts and as an exhibit for trial.

Persistence. Attention to detail. Now and forever.

On the window cases Ann's persistence and attention to detail went full steam ahead, and she added another autistic trait: outside the box thinking.

Long before I knew about autistic attributes, I organized a seminar for paralegals called "Thinking Outside the Cubicle." The idea was to get paralegals and other legal professionals to stretch their creative wings a bit. I taught them to think like an autistic person!

But Ann was a natural.

During the final window case, our property management defendant denied ever having another case like ours—i.e., one where a curious toddler climbed out an easily accessible upper floor sliding window and fell to the hard concrete below.

The problem was, they'd managed the property at an earlier case of ours!

But as we were preparing for mediation, I told Ann to keep looking—to use online search engines to find another incident involving a child at a property managed by the same company. She worked on it for days, and as she did so she learned that to get new results, she simply had to keep changing the wording of the search, and so she kept typing different combinations.

"Child falls from window."

"Toddler falls from window."

"Child injured in window fall."

"Child tumbles to death from window."

The more combinations she tried, the more incidents she found—but none of the stories mentioned our management company. I told her to keep working.

I was across the state on another case driving homeward. Ann kept phoning.

"I feel like I'm getting close!"

"Keep looking!"

Our mediation was the next day. If we caught this company lying a second time, they'd be in trouble. One of my special talents has been to hold companies responsible to the rules of discovery. When they lie, I catch them.

Or Ann does.

Halfway home she called, barely able to control herself. "I found one! I found one!"

It was a property in Florida managed by the same company—and a child fell from the window. It was big news in Florida at the time.

Our case settled the next day for twice what it might have otherwise.

And it wasn't the last time Ann's work had this result.

These days I can think about birds and books because Ann can't stop thinking about our cases. A few years ago, it was on our case involving a so-called "mobility scooter," one of those four wheel motorized devices they advertise for the disabled and elderly.

Our client was the remarkable Lea Black—a middle-aged, former president of an aeronautics company who suffered a stroke on a business trip to London. In her disability retirement she made a habit of helping homeless people on the streets near the downtown Seattle assisted-living center where she lived, and often used her mobility scooter to visit them. One day Lea was out delivering free socks to her homeless friends when her scooter started making a funny noise. Then, all of a sudden, the scooter started rolling, faster and faster, down a steep hill towards a major cross street. Passersby estimated the scooter (which had a top speed of six or seven miles-per-hour when it was working properly) reached thirty mph before hitting a passing car, tearing off its bumper, and leaving a big dent in the rear fender. Lea flew through the air, hit the pavement, and broke twenty-two bones. Worse, in an effort to slow the speeding scooter, she dragged her foot Flintstones style, and scraped off the front of her shoe and four of her toes. When the EMT asked if she wanted him to send the toes to the hospital with her, Lea said, "No, thanks. I follow the five second rule."

That's Lea.

Her case was remarkable. Once again, the corporation was a shameless liar. (They seemed to take *pride* in it.) They got in trouble with the court, and the court issued an order requiring them to produce any incident of alleged "freewheeling" or "brake failure."

Those were my words—they came directly from our request for production.

The company lied so often they got in more and more trouble, and eventually we began to think about filing a motion for sanctions. In fact, I had it mostly written, but I wasn't sure we had enough to get a big sanction, so it just sat there.

Then one day Ann calls. It was just like before.

"You won't believe it!"

This time no one told her to keep looking for other incidents, but she did, on her own, whenever she had extra time. And this time Ann found a U.S. District Court case in San Francisco, filed just after Lea's case, with a complaint that used the words "freewheeling" "brakes" and "failed" about a dozen times. The case went all the way to the Ninth Circuit Court of Appeals.

This case had been filed right around the time that we served our requests for production. The company fought it for more than a year, but never told us about it, even after the court ordered them to produce all such cases.

This was not simply an omission, it was an outright lie.

Worse, a month after the court issued its order requiring the company to identify all such cases, the woman died, and we lost any chance to take her deposition.

We called the lawyers for the lying company and told them the news. Within hours they produced more than 100 pages of documents about the case, but it was too little, too late.

We filed our motion. The judge demanded an in-person hearing and ordered various members of the company's legal staff to travel thousands of miles to Seattle to testify. That's the power of a federal court judge. We had a one day mini-trial. We laid out all the evidence, but we focused on Ann's discovery—the woman whose case the scooter company had kept secret despite a federal court order.

At the end, the magistrate's voice began quietly and built to a low rumble of anger. In 30 years, he said, he had never seen anything like it outside the movies.

He said he was granting our motion for sanctions, and he told the defendant that while he wrote his order, they should do whatever they could to settle the case.

And a few days later, it was done. The case settled, thanks to Ann. Her persistence. Her focus. Her attention to detail.

And her special interest in getting justice for her clients.

36

Working Outside the Box

Almost everything I've read on the positive traits of autistic people mentions our ability to approach and solve problems in new
and innovative ways. We think outside the box—or at least outside
the neurotypical box. We not only invented the wheel, we reinvent
it, every time, as needed. That's why such a large percentage of
musicians, artists, scientists, and engineers are autistic or otherwise
neurodivergent. Our brains work differently, so we think differently
and see things from a different perspective.

I've given several examples of innovative work from my own career
already. I did most of it for the sheer fun of it. How many personal
injury paralegals take it upon themselves to correspond with figures
like John DeLorean or call former General Motors Chairman Roger
Smith at home? How many taunt a corporation with personal ads
offering cash rewards for witnesses? In the mid-1990s, how many
people thought to use emerging imaging technology to colorize
photographs and design drawings to make harder-to-see elements
like gas tanks and fuel tank shields more visible to non-experts? How
many people would have decided to build a model fuel tank shield
in their hotel room from cardboard and duct tape for use the next
day in a videotaped deposition? How many new attorneys have built
funny exhibits with moving parts to trap unsuspecting experts into
admissions in a deposition or at trial?

Throughout my career I've kept myself entertained, and my opponents off-balance, by attacking problems in unusual ways.

In one early case, a man tampered with an over-the-counter drug by putting cyanide in several packages and sneaking the tampered packages back into stores. He then poisoned his own wife, and spent days calling the company and its representatives, telling them there could be other tampered packages on the shelves. He evidently wanted to sue the company for big bucks at the expense of his wife.

His wife didn't die. My guess is that the man deliberately put only enough cyanide in the capsule he gave his wife to make her ill, but he put enough in the other packages to kill anyone who took one of the capsules. Our client's husband and another man took those capsules and died minutes later.

Our case against the pharmaceutical company was for its negligently slow response to an obvious crisis. (Not only did the murderer call, so did his wife's doctor.) After being notified the woman fell sick with cyanide poisoning immediately after taking their product, the company hemmed, hawed, and dithered for more than a week before having the product pulled from shelves. Two people died in the interim, including our client's husband.

Part of the company's reasoning was that they had made the product "tamper proof" by using a blue "safety seal" to glue together the two halves of the gelatin capsule.

One problem with that theory: the "safety seal" didn't work. And anyway, the murderer wasn't sophisticated. He simply replaced one of the capsules in each package with a new, unsealed capsule full of cyanide.

But I knew the "safety seal" was nonsense. I'd proven it to myself, and I wanted to show the defendant company.

During a deposition of the manufacturer's foremost advocate of the "safety seal," I held a capsule under the table, cracked apart the so-called "safety seal" by squeezing the capsule gently with my thumbnail, separated the two halves of the capsule, wrote and dated a tiny note, inserted the note into the capsule among the beads of medicine, and closed the capsule again so that the "safety seal" appeared to remain perfectly intact and the note was barely visible. I did this all under the noses of the defense attorneys and the company's witness. I showed it to Whelan during the deposition, but this time he was not ready to go quite as far outside-the-box as me. Since he decided not to use it as an exhibit, I still have the remnants of the capsule on my nightstand thirty years later.

In a case involving a dangerously powerful airbag I worried that the manufacturer would rightfully criticize our client for letting her child sit in the front without a seatbelt. The mom was only driving her son a few blocks to school, but it proved to be the biggest mistake of her life—the boy slid into the airbag and was killed when it fired in a crash that barely dented the car.

We were suing because of the crude sensor, which allowed the bag to fire when it wasn't needed, and because the bag itself fired at too high a velocity for a low speed crash. As it happened, the case involved the earlier model of a car I owned. My newer version had a better airbag and a better airbag sensor. The improved airbag would not have deployed in this crash, and if it did fire, it would have fired at a gentler velocity.

But both the newer and older car included an odd and recklessly dangerous feature—a little jump seat between the front seat driver and passenger that would only fit a child and that only included a lap belt and no shoulder harness. A shoulder harness is what prevents a person from moving dangerously into the airbag.

Since my daughter Jade was the same size as the boy who died, I had her sit in the jump seat, buckle the lap belt, and then lean her head towards the driver and passenger airbags. Her head touched both airbag covers. Even if buckled, a child in this middle seat would have been badly injured or killed in the same crash. The photographs of Jade in such a vulnerable position and without the benefit of a shoulder harness didn't eliminate the fault of the mom in our case, but it helped to balance her fault with that of the manufacturer, and helped us resolve a very difficult case.

In a freeway construction case, we argued that the temporary concrete barriers used to divide traffic on the interstate during construction were not properly anchored. In theory, they were linked together with steel pins, but when a truck knocked several of them across two lanes of oncoming traffic, injuring our client, we noticed that the last remaining barrier didn't move an inch—evidence that it wasn't properly attached to its neighbor prior to the crash. To demonstrate the failure to a mediator I pulled out my children's 30-year-old set of wooden blocks, put eyelet hooks in both ends of several rectangular ones, and used wooden matchsticks to link them together just like the concrete barriers were supposed to be linked. When I crashed a toy truck into the chain of red blocks, all of them moved. When I removed the matchstick that connected the last of the blocks to the chain and repeated the crash, all the blocks moved except the one unattached one—exactly what happened in our case. I would have performed the same demonstration at trial but didn't have to. The case settled.

In Lea Black's case of the "mobility scooter" that failed on a hill and sped up to 30 mph before crashing into a car, I tracked down reports of another such failure in Portsmouth, England, and was able to follow that victim's route on Google from the scooter store where he reported a funny noise (they ignored it) to the hill where his scooter failed and ultimately crashed. Like Lea, his scooter was clocked at 30 mph. The online mapping photos brought a consumer complaint to life during a video deposition.

We had a tractor rollover case in which our client's husband died of asphyxiation after being squeezed but not crushed underneath the tractor's roll-bar after the tractor tipped on a hill, making it impossible for him to breathe. Lots of people have sued tractor companies for not having a roll-bar, but we may be the only ones to have sued them (twice!) for a roll-bar that was defective in design. As the case progressed, our paralegal, Bonnie, found a patent of an earlier design of the same roll-bar but with an extended crossbar at the top that was designed to prevent the driver from being pinned or crushed by the roll-bar itself—exactly what happened in our case. Another assistant, Monica, found ads in an old agricultural magazine that showed exactly how the crossbar worked. The particular tractor company is so popular you can buy toy models of their tractors, and I found a scale model of our tractor with the older, better roll-bar at a nearby garden supply store. (Later in the case I would get testimony from the company's witness suggesting that the extended crossbar at the top of the roll bar, specifically designed to protect the driver, was removed as part of an across the board cost-reduction effort within the company.) At a deposition of the responding EMT, the company's attorney asked the firefighter to illustrate how our client was pinned beneath the roll-bar. When the firefighter said he wasn't a good artist, I pulled out the tractor model. No slouch, the company attorney pulled out a wooden artist's mannequin with moveable limbs—but the EMT struggled to recreate the scene because the mannequin was way too big for the model tractor. That's when I revealed "Pipe-Cleaner Man," a tiny figure I had made from pipe-cleaners and dressed in colored masking tape. I even fattened him up to the size of our client's deceased husband. The EMT bent him into exact position beneath the tractor roll-bar and we took a photo. Pipe-Cleaner Man still gets a chuckle out of the few of us who remember.

The list could go on and on. I bought used car seats from various model Hyundais and took them apart to prove to a judge they were all built the same way with the same defective part and should all be admissible as other incidents in our case. I bought a half dozen different "child resistant" bottle caps to figure out which were made properly, and which were dangerously defective knockoffs. I turned the contents of legal files into effective settlement films that demonstrated both liability and damages in seven or eight minutes.

By themselves none of my examples are particularly unique or special. Taken together, they show the value of hiring and accommodating people who see, think, and work differently.

Diversity, in all its forms, is a good thing.

37

Rebecca

I've credited various people, places, and things with "saving my life." My family was first, giving me acceptance, support, and playmates. Peach Tree High School was second, providing me a safe place to be me and renewing my interest in school. Africa was the third; the people there ignored most of my quirks and taught me some basic rules about sociability. I found friends there and a real girlfriend, who became my first wife. Paul Whelan gave me accidental accommodations and a surprisingly successful career.

My children give me love and purpose.

And then Rebecca.

At a moment when I was overwhelmed and nearly suffocating under the twin responsibilities of work and single-parenthood, Rebecca showed up in the guise of an unexpected email and offered new hope.

It had been the winter, spring, summer, fall, and another winter of my discontent. I was divorcing, with de facto full custody of Jade and Gemma, and it was not easy. When I went to trial against Hyundai, the girls' mother helped. Going to trial against Ford a year later, she refused, and I was forced to hire strangers to take care of them while I spent each week in Tacoma. A young waitress at the neighborhood pub came well recommended by a coworker of mine and did a fine job taking care of Jade and Gemma when she could, and somehow I found a second woman in the neighborhood to provide loving care after that.

Though I couldn't tell you their names, and though I haven't seen them since, I have to credit those two young women with saving my life, too.

But I was on life support at best, grumpy, stressed, and unhappy, and it was clear my law partners had discussed the "Peter problem." They all began looking for women to introduce me to. One invited me on a blind double date. It was fine, but there was no reason for a second date. Paul Whelan gave me the phone number of a Nordstrom sales associate he and his wife thought I might like. I met her for a walk, and it went well enough that we each tried several times to schedule a second get together. In the middle of all this Mike Withey tried to introduce me to his friend Rebecca. Although I had gamely tried the first two times, I told Mike, "No thanks."

And then the email, charmingly written—something about putting her courage in her ten fingers.

Rebecca suggested coffee. The idea of meeting somebody over coffee has always frightened me. All that eye contact, and caffeine adding jitters to an already tense situation. I knew I would prefer alcohol to loosen my conversation, but instead I suggested a walk. Long before I knew I was autistic I knew I didn't like eye contact. It makes me nervous. I stop thinking about the conversation and think only about the eyes. A walk removes that burden.

We agreed to meet at Discovery Park, a big, partly forested place along the coast in northwest Seattle.

I had done my autistic preparation and knew that I was meeting an actor. I found a picture of Rebecca online, doing a role in some Greek tragedy, looking beautiful and way too young for me.

We met at the park, a grassy, wooded outcrop into Puget Sound, and headed out on a trail. I was interested that Rebecca had spent a half year abroad in London, which reminded me of my time in Italy, and I was impressed how much she discussed her family. Family is important to me.

When it started to rain, we decided to go to a pub Rebecca knew. Now we were seated one across from the other, but I was remarkably comfortable. After a couple of hours and a couple of beers we crossed the intersection to a Thai restaurant she knew and sat at the bar to eat. It was a funny first date. At the restaurant we each talked about our failed first marriages, which in turn led to a big reveal—our first date was happening on what would have been the anniversary of Rebecca's first marriage.

And about six hours after we met, on a sidewalk outside the restaurant, we kissed each other on the cheek and said goodnight. I hurried on to attend some little gathering with friends and glowed over what had happened.

I had been completely comfortable for five or six hours on a first date.

Remarkable.

It didn't take long for the relationship to get serious. It also didn't take long for me to start my trial against Ford—a painful, four week affair that had caught the attention of lawyers across the country, the first serious trial of a Ford Explorer rollover. Much of our early romantic life occurred during that trial. I remember Rebecca showing up in court a couple of times. I remember Ford's primary attorney—quite the opposite of the evilest man alive—asking if I had a date on Valentine's Day. I was happy to say yes. I met Rebecca's dad for the first time on a Friday during trial, and once, on another mid-trial Friday or Saturday, Rebecca and I saw Macy Gray perform.

But the rest was all work, all of the time. I handled almost the entire liability case, which involved whole bunches of engineering experts on both sides: accident reconstruction, automotive design, stability testing, and injury biomechanics. At the end of the trial Ford's four attorneys congratulated me on carrying a very heavy load. And, indeed, we did a fine job. Our biggest tactical error was alleging too many different defects in the Explorer—a top heavy, narrow design that allowed rollovers; a weak roof that crushed on the driver's side to fatally injure the young mom; and a bad seatbelt in the back that allowed a baby girl to fly from the rolling car. To top it off we sued the manufacturer of the booster seat as well. We were right about all of it, but it removed the jury's focus from the root of it all—the unstable, top-heavy design of the Ford.

The jury deliberated five full days. As the youngest attorney on our team I was left behind to await the verdict. Ford's primary lawyer and I were friendly enough but avoided each other like the plague for the first several days. He told me later he thought we had won.

We hadn't.

At the start of the case one of the local Ford attorneys cast our fate in stone by doing a masterful job of jury selection—or juror dese-lection. We had a good jury pool, but this man sensed something. He kept asking one potential juror, over and over, if he could be fair. Finally the juror said no. "I think Ford is responsible for that woman's death!" the juror said, and was immediately excused by the judge. But before that juror had left the box, we heard sniffles from another juror. Could she be fair? "No! I hate Ford for killing that woman and her baby." And then a third juror raised a hand and the horror repeated itself. Three likely plaintiff votes, properly excused from the jury because they admitted they came into the case with a closed mind.

And four weeks later, after five days of jury deliberation, we were called in for a verdict.

Five days of deliberation would normally be a good sign for people in our line of work. It usually means that the jury has decided on fault and is talking about how much to award in damages.

Not this time.

When the jury returns it's just me, my client, and the youngest attorney for Ford. The jury doesn't look at me, but I see that the Ford attorney is smiling. She has seen something—perhaps a friendly nod as the jury came in.

"Have you reached a verdict?"

"We have, your honor."

I will always remember how useless I felt standing next to my mother and watching her whither with grief when the doctor told us Stevo had passed. Now I am next to my client, a young man who lost his wife and daughter to an unstable vehicle, when the jury says that Ford was not at fault for the deaths. I put a hand on his shoulder. He crumples wordlessly.

One of the jurors starts sobbing.

That night I invite the paralegals to my house. After two years of trial prep, and two big trials, I had plans to get drunk no matter what the result was.

I achieve my goal.

We file an appeal that seems nearly hopeless—so hopeless that I am sent to San Francisco to argue it at the Ninth Circuit Court of Appeals. I have never argued an appeal. I have never been in a courthouse so opulent or so intimidating. Although I have faced some brilliant judges, I have never faced three at a time, two of whom interrupt with difficult questions.

But somehow we win. The decision comes through on the day Rebecca and I are married, a year and a half after the trial. Ford's primary attorney on the case—the one who wished me a happy Valentine's Day—reaches me by phone to give me the news, paraphrasing a line from a movie that I am unfamiliar with—"sometimes you get the bear, and sometimes the bear gets you." I thank him and tell him he's caught me on my wedding day. It is a welcome gift. Ford settles the case for a reasonable amount under the circumstances. More remarkably, my partner Paul Stritmatter convinces an insurance company to throw in a sum that seems nearly impossible. We are able to resolve the case for our client despite the trial loss.

A week or so later, on a walk through Seattle's Ballard neighborhood, I tell Rebecca I am ready to quit my partnership and do something completely different. I have one of best jobs an attorney could ask for—partner at one of the best plaintiff law firms in Washington. I'm surrounded by top tier attorneys who bring in great cases. They respect my work and give me an entirely free hand on the liability aspects of the cases. We wear the white hats. We're the good guys.

But I don't like the business of law. I like my cases, but not the meetings and other business aspects.

"Do you mind if I quit?" I ask Rebecca. "Would it be crazy?"

"Not at all" she tells me.

Her support means the world to me. A few days later I send a letter of resignation to my partners, but do it in a very strange way, giving more than a year's notice. Fifteen years later I will return the favor. Rebecca will tell me she wants to quit her job to start a theater company that will provide opportunities for professional growth to women and non-binary people. I will tell her to go for it.

It's what I told my therapist: We like each other, and love each other, and support each other, despite each other's quirks. Especially mine.

When Rebecca and I were first talking, I tried to discourage her. "I'm older than you and have two kids. You don't have any," I told her. It seemed pretty forward to say that so early in a potential relationship, but it was true. I now recognize blunt, autistic honesty poking through. It didn't slow down the growth of our relationship.

Rebecca had recently separated. She had a nice apartment but was hunting for a place to buy. After touring a condo with her, I said she ought to think about moving in with me, Jade, and Gemma. She did.

From a parenting perspective it was probably a mistake. Once, driving with Jade before I met Rebecca, I asked Jade what she'd think if I dated someone. Jade said she'd kill the person. As it turned out, they nearly killed each other. Our "blended family" was a rocky affair for a time, but Rebecca hung in there and became a stable force in the lives of both Jade and Gemma.

The glue was ultimately baby Rafferty, born five weeks early during the summer of 2004. The call from Rebecca came while I was driving a bunch of Jade's friends home from a movie. Jade and Gemma went to their mom's house, and I went to the hospital. Twelve hours later we were a real family. Something about Rafferty—tiny, bald, pasty white, but with just a hint jaundiced gold—captured the girls' attention and hearts and kept them until he grew up to be the tallest in our little family. As I write this he's working his first real job and getting ready to move to college.

Rebecca, on the other hand, is getting ready for opening night of her theater company's first big production. It should have happened two years ago, but Covid intervened to cancel the first live show. Covid is still intervening. The whole production could fall like a house of cards if any member of the team gets sick. Cross your fingers.

What I appreciate most is that Rebecca has supported me no matter what, and no matter how weird or antisocial I might seem to others. She first secured her position in my life by surprising me with a signed photograph of Chuck. That was in 2003. I don't even remember talking about Chuck Berry in those days, but I obviously did, and obviously with enough intensity and repetition to cause her to make an e-bay purchase and have it delivered in time for my birthday five months after we met. She was my wing person at dozens of work related cocktail parties and retreats.

And she bought me a $25 ticket to go see Chuck at a St. Louis bar and restaurant called Blueberry Hill.

I do remember talking to her about Blueberry Hill. I'd heard rumors, read short accounts, knew it was a small place where the elder Chuck Berry truly liked to perform. I didn't want the sun to go down on me, or on Chuck, or on the Blueberry Hill shows, before I attended one, but things kept getting in the way. Then along comes Rebecca, and cuts past all of that. She bought me the ticket and gave it to me on Christmas morning as we ate cinnamon rolls, drank coffee, and filled the living room with wrapping paper. And somehow, in the next few weeks, I wrangled a free ticket out of Delta Airlines, and a cheap motel, and learned online how to ride Metrolink, and how to walk, frozen, from Metrolink to the King Henry the Eighth Motel and then to Blueberry Hill. (Autistic people prepare for their journeys with lots of research!) That visit was life changing. It resulted in me posting an anonymous online review that caught the attention of Chuck's son, and then a blog, and finally a manuscript about my odd, autistic fascination with Chuck. Rebecca let me go back to St. Louis several more times and even joined me there twice.

She lets me stay home from parties. She absorbs my bluntest comments. She lets me buy guitars I don't need or deserve. She lets me recover my energy through endless games of solitaire and endless noodling on the guitars. She lets me enjoy my long walks, and—oh to be younger again—long runs, alone. She's currently letting me plan a seven week trip to Italy alone until she can get there to join me. And when she occasionally rails against the ways of men and I point out that I am a man she tells me, "But you are different."

I am. I am, was, and always shall be.

And happy to have Rebecca in my life.

38

Lessons From My Own Life

Nowadays an autistic child has a good chance of being identified in primary school or soon after, and the best of schools might find ways to accommodate an autistic child's learning style. In my day that didn't happen. You didn't get identified, at any rate. So, like most autistic people born in the 1950s, I carried on and lived my life as best I could.

As I've said, I was also very lucky. I was born into a loving if dysfunctional family that smothered me with equal amounts of trauma, drama, love, encouragement, and acceptance.

I went to two Catholic schools that were terrible, but I survived on the fringes. Thanks to my parents' status at the school, I was even allowed to graduate after cutting class for a month in the weeks before graduation.

After a typically repressive 1960s Catholic education, I found a high school that accepted me and allowed me to thrive.

In college I had less luck, except for the short parade of beautiful, funny, smart young women who each took me one step closer to a more normal life. I learned something from each of them. Then I went to Africa and found a culture that didn't see me as any weirder than other foreigners, and taught me new social skills. Like every other foreigner who wanted to know the culture I had to learn a new set of social rules from scratch. I found a wife and began passing for normal, if only marginally.

At work back in the States I found a boss who recognized and valued my unique strengths. He made accommodations that helped me thrive in the workplace, and he didn't worry about my social skills, my dress, or my participation in office business meetings.

I found a woman who likes and loves me exactly how I am, (most of the time,) and a family of adult children and a granddaughter who do the same.

I have been lucky. I have also been smart. I simplified my work life. I gave myself plenty of free time. I let myself be me.

I can see how life could have turned out differently for me—could have gone south at any moment.

Imagine if I had a family who called me weird, or worse yet, stupid? Many of the autistic people I've encountered suffered through exactly that as kids.

Imagine if my primary school had flunked or expelled me for cutting class and sent me back for another miserable trudge through eighth grade? If my parents hadn't been founders of the school that probably would have happened.

Imagine if I had been sent to that Catholic boys high school. I've known my entire life that would have turned out poorly.

Imagine if, at the high school I did attend, I had been bullied or shamed for being different.

Imagine if I presented just differently enough that none of those beautiful young women had tried to cajole me into joining real life? How much further behind would I be socially without each of them taking me a few steps forward?

Imagine if I hadn't gone to Africa and found acceptance? Imagine that my loneliest years, in the late 1970s, had just kept getting progressively lonelier? If I had stayed put it seems almost certain that would have happened.

What if I never had a boss like Paul Whelan, who recognized and appreciated my gifts of intelligence, ingenuity, persistence, and creativity? There are plenty of bosses out there who would not have given me the opportunities he gave me.

What if I'd focused on riches instead of a rich life? What if I'd worked myself to the bone without regard for my own sanity?

What if I hadn't found Rebecca, or never had my children and granddaughter?

It is easy to imagine myself broken and alone almost anywhere along this trajectory. It could have been really bad for me. Instead, I found myself in situations where I could grow and thrive—at least from my point of view. And more recently I lucked into a "diagnosis" that clarifies every aspect of my life and has allowed me to grow even more.

I don't know what lessons can be drawn from my experience. The primary lesson might be that luck, both good and bad, plays a huge role in any life. But so do other people.

I hope every family with a quirky kid celebrates the quirks and creativity of their neurodivergent child and loves and accepts them for exactly who they are. I hope those families search out schools where that child can be accepted and thrive. (You never know when you will need a rosary repaired.)

I hope those same families take time to help a socially awkward child learn how greet people, make friends, and handle fledgling romances. Some kids might need a little extra help and guidance in that department. But I hope that assistance is offered with love, and understanding, and firm reassurance that the autistic or neurodivergent child does not have to change who he or she is to find love or friendship—that they can do it on their own terms.

I hope that neurotypical office managers, human resource professionals, and professionals who do hiring, learn to accommodate the "odd" or "quirky" applicants and staff members who do good work but might not thrive at the office parties, or who might do best with working conditions that are a little different from their neurotypical peers. There are books on this stuff, but the most important thing is simply to recognize that people who are different from you are still people, each with unique strengths and challenges, who often come with extraordinary talents. Get to know them. Get to know their strengths, and give them a real chance. Act like Pam at the undergraduate library. Act like Paul and help them fashion a job unique to their talents. Enjoy having them in your life and your workplace.

When I look back at my life I can count dozens of neurotypical people who ultimately wrote me off. I could watch it happen. I never spoke rudely to these people. I always greeted them with a word or a smile. Our encounters were professional and polite. But what seems clear is that, by being me, I didn't quite live up to their expectations. I stayed at the edge of their gatherings. I didn't gush with small talk. I didn't smile with the alacrity they expected. And ultimately, I paid the price of being left outside the center of their worlds. But, of course, they paid that price, too. They missed out on someone valuable and good, and yes, different.

And yet, those differences in how I see and experience the world are exactly what make me valuable and worth having around.

Not long ago I met up with a friend I hadn't seen in decades. I showed him and his family around town. I noticed how the family treasured the offbeat knowledge of their teenaged son and brother. When he brought a particular arcane fact to the table, his whole family laughed and his sister exclaimed, "I love how you know so many weird things!"

I have no idea if the kid is a fellow autistic, but I know that whatever his neurology, he is in an environment where he will thrive, and his family enjoys every bit of his difference.

I wish all of us could learn to offer that same acceptance and love to people who are different. They make us richer. And I hope that all neurotypical people will take time to learn more about neurodiversity and make an effort to accept neurodivergent people into their lives with new understanding. When that happens, everyone will win.

39

American History and Practical Math

It's 2012. Rebecca spends the spring and summer training for her first marathon. I spend the spring training for my third marathon and spend the summer limping. But I will eventually run a third one. So will she. Every day she carries in huge baskets of zucchini, green beans, tomatoes, peppers, onions, garlic, raspberries, strawberries, lettuce, arugula, potatoes, cucumbers, peas, and greens from our tiny garden. She keeps becoming more and more skilled at it. Rebecca saved our lives, and mine in particular. She accepted challenges few would willingly have dealt with. The thing people sometimes soothingly and misleadingly call a "blended family" can be a wild mad mouse circus ride with dramatic ups and downs—Mr. Toad's Wild Ride. We all ride it together. In 2012 we still hit exciting patches, but more and more we're in that smooth part at the end, on calm, inviting waters—our reward for hanging in there. On the way Rebecca has accompanied me to see Macy Gray, B. B. King, Billy Preston, Pinetop Perkins and Willie "Big Eyes" Smith, Sonny Rollins, Dr. John, Hubert Sumlin, Taj Mahal, and Mavis Staples.

And finally, in this winter of 2012, Chuck Berry.

Rebecca has never seen him—never even watched "the Chuck Berry movie" with me. She puts up with him the way she might put up with a far off, cranky, but well-loved uncle I talk too much about. But she has procured me another ticket to Blueberry Hill, and this time she gets one for herself, too. There are two birthday shows. Rebecca can't attend both, but she lets me go on ahead, and arranges to join me for the second. A year later she will join me for a third.

The first show is at Blueberry Hill. I meet up there with Doug and Blueberry Hill stalwarts Judy and Karen. I met all three online doing my Chuck Berry blog. Judy and Karen have seen more Chuck Berry shows at Blueberry Hill than anyone and have earned permanent seating in the front row. This night, they let us join them there. I've never met Doug, but we will take a chance and spend a few nights driving down to Memphis together. He is as infected by Chuck Berry as I am. I don't think there's any chance he is autistic, just a fan.

Chuck, who is celebrating his eighty-eighth birthday, is wild that night, hopping and dancing all over the stage. He almost falls once, so a few seconds later he walks to the very edge of the stage and stands on one eighty-eight-year-old foot while dangling the other over the audience just to prove he can. He looks tired and has trouble with the lyrics but summons energy from someplace deep within and puts on a spotty but wonderful show.

The next day Doug and I make our mad dash to Memphis in my rental car, talking for hours on end, visiting all the studios, eating fried chicken and ribs. We visit Sun Studios, where Howlin' Wolf recorded "Riding in the Moonlight," and stumble into a personal tour of Royal Studios from Boo Mitchell, son of the great producer Willie Mitchell, and a producer of note himself. We visit the Lorraine Motel, and later peer over the wall outside of Graceland. We talk about work, family, and Chuck. (Doug's wife good-naturedly scolds us on speaker phone. "There are only five people in the world who even care, and two of you are in that car!") I have a hard time making new friends, but Doug is an old friend right from the start. (This will happen again with Carmelo in Italy.)

We get back to St. Louis in time for me to pick up Rebecca at the airport. The next day we all cross the Mississippi River to a casino built from an old river boat. Chuck's piano player, Bob Lohr, has arranged passes that will get us backstage and allow us to see the sound check.

There are three dressing rooms. I am in the hallway outside the one Chuck's band is using when I turn and see a familiar figure in black in the other room. Doug is near me, and I motion to him. He looks quickly, then turns back to me with big eyes. I look again to see the dressing room door shut slowly and quietly.

When it is time for the sound check we go to the main hall where Bob Lohr has found us seats in front of the sound board. I don't want to lose them, so Rebecca and I stay put while Doug goes backstage again.

I have brought a framed copy of a photograph of Chuck Berry as a child. Peter K. of Sweden sent it to me and it is my favorite—a photograph of twelve-year-old Chuck using a telescope. I love that we had the same hobbies and interests as children—telescopes, cameras, and dark rooms. (I doubt, however, that he ever repaired rosaries.) Together, Peter K. and I have figured out that young Chuck is using his telescope to observe the sun. All the shadows are directly behind him. There's a filter on the front lens of the telescope. Peter K. has gone even farther and identified two eclipses in St. Louis around that time. In other words, Chuck is doing serious astronomical observing at the age of 12. I figure I might not get a chance to give the picture to Chuck in person, so I ask Doug to pass it on to Chuck's son, Charles. "Ask him to give this to his dad," I say.

The show that night is a good one. Bob Lohr says the casino has good sound. Chuck can hear himself, so his guitar playing is sharp.

When it's over our "all access" passes get us backstage again.

I am a bit disappointed to see the framed photograph still sitting on a chair in Charles' dressing room. Doug must see my disappointment. He tells me, "Peter, Charles said you should give that to him yourself."

"I'll introduce you," says Charles, nodding.

When Chuck Berry passes through the hallway on his way home, Charles stops him.

"Dad, my friend from Seattle has something for you."

When I'd met him at The Pageant a year and a half earlier I was struck by the human stature of the man. That night after the show at The Pageant, Chuck Berry had seemed exhausted, elderly, quiet, and a bit frail. I remember the white hairs that curled out from beneath his admiral's cap. We had a wonderful chat—Chuck told me about selling fruit downstairs near the theater when he was 14—but I was so excited I woke up the next morning remembering very little of it.

This time he is tall, regal, in charge, and in a bit of a hurry. He is dressed entirely in black in full rock and roll mode with a leather jacket and dark aviator shades. He is now every bit the Father of Rock and Roll.

"Seattle friend!" he says, turning to bump forearms and grasp my hand.

This time I am in control of my emotions. I tell myself I will see and remember everything. *He is different, and I am different, too. I will remember this.*

I give him the picture of himself, as a child, with his telescope.

He holds it with both hands, slowly lowering his head but raising the picture, focusing through dark glasses on a long lost memory. He shakes his head and utters something like "Oh-wee!"

"Where'd you get this?" he asks me. My brain falters again. I forget momentarily that it was sent to me by Peter K. I tell him that I don't know—that it's out there on the internet. And then, suddenly, Chuck Berry is on the move.

"I've got to show this to *Patrick*!" he says, or at least I think that's the name. He looks back at me and points. "And *you* are going to be there when I do it!"

He walks quickly down the hall to show the picture to several friends near the door. There is a woman who appears to be in charge, and a younger man I assume is Patrick. The manager of the casino is also there, beaming. Chuck shows them the photograph but doesn't let go. The general consensus among Chuck Berry's friends is that he was probably using the telescope to peer through some girl's window. Chuck ignores that. And since I know the truth I ask if he remembers once observing an eclipse of the sun. Chuck is lost inside the picture and for a few seconds doesn't respond. When he finally speaks, it is about something more important than planetary and stellar allignment.

"Look at those *shoes*!" he says, laughing, pointing to the long, two-toned leather "brogans." Except for being very long for a twelve-year-old, they are not that different from shoes I have seen him wear on stage as an adult.

Then Chuck Berry turns to Rebecca, who is talking to Charles, and the three work together on some American history and practical math. "What's 1926 plus 11?" the author of "School Days" asks Rebecca. They seem like old friends for a moment. Rebecca and Charles respond simultaneously, "1937." I've given Chuck a pen and a second copy of the photograph, hoping that he'll sign it for me. He puts the date "1937" on the top of my copy—close enough to the year 1938, then signs it with a smiley face.

It's magical. Chuck Berry is visibly moved by the gift that Peter K. found and that I have had the honor of giving him. A few days later Charles tells me in an e-mail that Chuck took the picture home and showed it to his wife. That makes me happy.

They still have that Silvertone!

Before he leaves Chuck Berry raises his aviator shades and looks me straight in the eye for just an instant. He is just inches away.

"You *look* like Seattle," he says, ambiguously, but with finality.

I hope it means he has been following my blog, which features a small, thumbprint picture of my face, partially and purposefully hidden and obscured by Rafferty's, and says where I'm from. I've been told he might.

And then he's gone.

It is not the last time I will see him in the flesh, but it is the last time I will meet him. The first time was in 1971. I was 15 years old. Chuck Berry was sitting next to the stage between sets. I was a skinny, long haired boy, just reaching my full height. I reached out my hand. Chuck Berry took it and gave an appraising look at a new generation of fans. I yelled over the noise of the crowd, "You're my idol."

Over the decades I had several more brief contacts with the man. In 1974 in Monterey, California I passed him a note making a request that he play a newer song called "Got It and Gone." It made him laugh. He didn't play it—a sensible choice because I was probably one of ten people in the audience who knew it. In Seattle, decades later, he spoke to me during a rendition of "Wee Wee Hours." (At that show the raspy-voiced, eight-year-old Gemma was on my shoulders at the foot of the stage. During the relative quiet of "My Ding-a-Ling" she yelled, "He's singing about his penis!" for Chuck and everyone within twenty feet to hear.) At a couple of St. Louis shows I was able to bring him small gifts and speak to him for just a moment. Once I was taken backstage to spend five or six minutes talking to him.

A year from now we will go back, and Chuck will be much older than he is today. I will have a final bit of contact by shouting out a request for the song "No Money Down." He will look down and agree to sing it but will not find the words to his own song. His lovely daughter, Ingrid, will sing it instead.

But tonight, he is in full form, and I am thrilled that our small gift has made him as happy, for a moment, as he has made me for a lifetime.

40

Autistic Life in the Twenty-First Century

My final years as a lawyer have been rewarding. After quitting the law partnership I have worked on fewer cases, on purpose. I make just as much money, or more, but the most important thing, to me, is that I have more time for other things. I knew that a reduced caseload would allow me to do my work with more focus, but it has also given me the time my spirit needs to wander, to think, to recover, and to return to old loves. I bought a good telescope and relearned the night sky. I found all but one or two of the Messier objects—those faint whispers of ancient, deep-space light that I love. I ran marathons and half marathons. I put together various musical groups to play blues, soul, and a bit of country. I got on stage for the first time with a guitar and then got on stage a hundred more times after that. With Rebecca's help I went to Saint Louis several times to see and say goodbye to Chuck Berry—or, at least, his physical presence. I did a blog about him, and found time to turn that blog into a book manuscript—a manuscript that I now see as a case study in undiagnosed autism.

For several years I continued to work occasionally with Paul Whelan, but eventually he stopped calling for reasons beyond his control. (Let's call it neurotypical interference.) I missed working with him and his assistant, Kristen, and I know they missed working with me, but in some ways it was good for me to gain new independence as an attorney; I learned I could lead the charge myself.

In 2018, after a brief but hard decline, Paul fell gravely ill. I got the call while on a trip to New Orleans with Rafferty. Paul's wife Kathryn and his friend Larry Baron held a phone up to Paul's ear so that I could say goodbye. That final, one-sided phone call to Paul presaged future, similarly difficult visits. In the next two years I would travel twice to a Vancouver, Washington hospital to say goodbye to both Jesse Magana and Larry Tompkins.

Three people who instinctively understood me, gone in the course of a few years.

In the years since I stopped working full time I have traveled with my family to Mexico three different times, to London twice, to Paris several times, to Italy, Wales, and to Ireland. We have also made various trips in the United States, including a wonderful road trip to the southwest. My therapist says this special interest in travel is unusual for an autistic person, but we are all different, and I love to break routine as much as I love the gentle routines of my everyday life. I love new sights and sounds—especially when they're different enough to give me a jolt. Besides, I can carry on my favorite routines from anywhere: I can take time to read the same papers online and drink loads of morning coffee from anywhere in the world, and wherever I am I can walk and talk to myself.

When I'm not traveling I work, or I walk, or I read, or I learn to identify birds, or I play music.

My legal work has become increasingly efficient. Forty years of experience have given me instincts that surprise even me. I trust myself implicitly. I figure out cases quickly, and in a matter of hours I can turn an undifferentiated mass of PDFs or photocopies into a coherent theory of liability.

In older middle age or early old age I have become an expert litigant in entirely new subject areas: rodent fires, mobility scooters, concrete barriers, and road design. For a brief period rat nests built in the engine compartments of brand new cars took up a tremendous amount of my time and thought. We were forced to figure out from scratch what the auto company you love already knew from the experience of its customers. *Mon ami, you did not know?* They didn't tell you that rats climb into the engine compartment to escape the fall chill under the warm glow of a cooling engine? They didn't tell you the rats build nests with twigs and leaves on the fantastically convenient flammable plastic shielding the company has chosen to place beneath the engine for streamlining purposes? Well, then I will tell you what happens. Rats or mice climb into the car to escape the fall chill. They build the nest in a matter of hours. You start the car. The rodents jump ship. Heat from the car's motor and exhaust system dries the leaves and twigs over the course of a few hours or days, then ignites them and starts a fire. Rubber hoses melt. Gas spills from lines under the hood. If you are young, spry, and lucky, you spot the smoke and flames emitting from under the hood of your car and jump ship, like the rats. All is well that ends with a call to your insurance company.

But our case involved an elderly German grandma with a sense of order. She couldn't leave a car to burn on a neighborhood road, so when she spotted the smoke she pulled over and parked on the sloping shoulder. Maybe in her panic she got a bit too far off road. When she stopped her car was on uneven terrain, dipping to the right. The angle of rest and the force of gravity meant that this tiny seventy-six year old woman couldn't push the door open. Besides, by then flames were climbing from beneath the driver's door. She leaned right, hoping to scramble out that side. Smoke from burning plastic and rubber filled the car. We can hope that, overcome by smoke, she drifted into unconsciousness. People saw the fire and called 911.

Her body was found with the key still in her hand.

We filed the case after the company refused to discuss an early settlement proposal designed to help the woman's two grandchildren. Filing was a long shot, but we were annoyed. We were not expecting to find much evidence. Instead, we found a dozen or so similar incidents in the company's files. We interviewed survivors of those fires, who told us about the smell of burning leaves and their stark terror as their cars erupted in flames.

I told our team we needed to find an expert on the nesting habits of rats and mice. I invented the word "rodentologist" and we all laughed at our new word. Then Matt found a rodentologist at a famous university in Indiana! Good job, Matt! When we settled the case, our rodent expert sent me a card that said "Cong-Rats!"

After that I became an expert in mobility scooters. So did Ann. And then, after those two cases, we took on two road design cases in rapid succession. Each time we were able to turn reluctant document dumps into litigation gold and we were able to help our clients.

But it's time to move on. I see my legal work becoming more and more of a part time thing, or fading completely into memory. I have done it forty years, and it takes time and energy I could put to use traveling, or painting, or writing, or learning the names of birds and trees, or using my telescopes, or learning languages, or reading, or cooking, or playing music. Worse, the lawyers on the other side are getting meaner and meaner—mean enough to make the evilest man alive seem like a gentleman in comparison, which in many ways he was.

I've begun to see that even though I enjoy doing all sorts of things, I can rarely focus on more than a few of them in a given period of time. A few days of intensive work sorting through documents leaves me nearly incapacitated. I don't go to bed to recuperate, but I get quiet: I walk or play solitaire, or do something similarly mindless to recover and process. That's autistic life for you.

Little by little I am coming to terms with the parts of my past that hurt so much. One fine Christmas day, six years before my diagnosis, the young woman from Florence, she of the incomprehensible wink and smile, answered my friend request on Facebook. When her name appeared on my screen my heart leapt. Although I didn't yet know that I'm autistic, I knew that I had learned a lot in the intervening decades and now had communication skills I didn't have back in the mid-1970s when we shared a few evenings of youthful romance. We communicated shyly at first, by text, and it took a few months before things got rolling; but one evening I found myself laughing through tears during a rapid fire text exchange that confirmed the connection I felt back then was real. From time to time we talk on the phone. The first call lasted for hours. I realized then I had to ask Rebecca's permission to continue this conversation. Rebecca granted it happily. So we keep chatting. Most of it is silly stuff about horoscopes, work, or "butter coffee," but not all of it is silly. We talk about raising our children. We talk about the loss of our parents.

Once, during a call, she asks if I have seen a certain movie. I tell her no. She says it reminded her of Florence and of me. When we get off the phone, I look it up and realize that I do know the film, and that I had enjoyed it. It's about two young people who meet on a train and spend that night walking, talking, and falling for each other on the beautiful streets of Vienna. As they walk past floodlit monuments, or the river, it might as well be Florence. Funny that I never saw that. The two go their separate ways the next morning. When I understand this woman thought of me and our time together when she saw this movie I am profoundly moved. Movies about young love often hurt. They remind me what I missed or squandered, though perhaps through no real fault of my own. Now I learn that one of my early, failed romances—one in which I had regretted my own inaction for a lifetime—could stand on its own. Indeed, with a bit of poetic license, it was the stuff of a popular Hollywood movie.

In the years after we reconnect, we text back and forth enough to fill the pages of *War and Peace* and spill over into *Anna Karenina,* and we supplement our texts with occasional long phone calls. I joke at times that it's an imaginary friendship, like the one I had with Chuck, but it is real for me, too, and allows me to make something of a friendship I let slip away as a befuddled, undiagnosed autistic young man. I'm grateful for it.

My therapist and I are seeing less and less of each other. I won't know for a year or two whether I've licked the clingy depressions, but I can say with confidence that she gave me a unified theory of me and helped me solve the important mystery of why my life as a young man was so different. For that I will always be grateful. Since she is acting as consultant on things autistic in this manuscript, we still talk from time to time. When our sessions stop, I will look back on them fondly and with appreciation. And though I have to say this with a couple of sharp knocks on the table, I think the clingy depressions are in the past.

As the months have passed, I've told more and more people about my diagnosis or identification. Family members have all been happy for me and some have shared their own suspicions about themselves. Friends and acquaintances have sometimes had more shaded reactions. "Well, you're certainly high functioning!" Or, "It must, in some sense, be a relief." Part of why I have written this book is to let them and the world know that it is more than a relief—my new identification has brought me actual joy. I can revel in my accomplishments and understand my past for the first time. I look forward to a future in which I know and appreciate exactly who I am—and more importantly, who I was, and why. Because that was the hard part—knowing I'd been a good person, funny, interesting, smart, but had failed terribly at important things like love and friendship. Now I know that I was a fish out of water who nonetheless survived, and even thrived. I'm proud of that.

Even before my diagnosis I had begun to allow myself to be more freely autistic, reversing the trajectory of those decades where I had "learned to operate my hard to operate personality." Over several decades I had learned to engage more successfully with the neurotypical world, which allowed me to *join* in to some extent even where I didn't *fit* in. But at a certain point, around age sixty, I began just being me, come what may. If a person or group resisted my efforts to join them, I either left them or ignored them, knowing it was their loss and not mine. I spent more and more time alone, or with family, or walking, lost in my faintly vocalized thoughts.

With my identification as an autistic individual I have gone even harder in that direction. I have always understood *who* I am. Now I understand *why* I am that person, and I feel less inclined than ever to fit myself into uncomfortable positions and situations. Life is too short, and the world is too big, complex, and beautiful.

I am also taking baby steps in the direction of other autistic and neurodivergent people. Perhaps I will someday find a community, other than family, that I both fit and can happily join.

In 2017, the world lost Chuck Berry. My friend from Florence saw the news before me and was the first to commiserate. Rebecca took me out for drinks and good Mexican food. I wore my black Chuck Berry t-shirt. A few months later Chuck's last studio album came out, and a few years after that, an album of songs recorded live at Blueberry Hill. (My name's on it—misspelled, as usual—along with a photo I took of his daughter.) More recently I found my name (misspelled again!) in the pages of a new biography of the man. I will miss being in his presence on those rare but important occasions, but his best music will live forever, and that last studio album is an inspiration to anyone who wants to carry their creativity into old age. I know that I do. More gratitude there.

Recently I bought a beautiful eight inch reflector telescope built in 1969. I am only the third owner. As a thirteen-year-old in 1969, I used to gaze in wonder at this sort of telescope in the back pages of *Sky & Telescope* magazine. Now, fifty-three years later, I own one. The man who sold it to me took more than an hour talking to me about it before he let it go. He showed me how to disassemble it to fit it into my car. As we talked, we each gazed into the distance.

It made me wish that autistic people had a secret handshake.

The same thing happened with the man who repairs my amplifiers. When I picked up my Fender tweed amp a few months ago he told me more than I could ever understand about the rectifiers and switches and electronics as the two of us happily avoided eye contact.

The amp sounded great afterwards.

What happens next is unclear but exciting. My immediate plans are simple.

I will finish work on what could well be my last case.

I will finish this book and learn how to put it into publication. If it has any success, I may reach back and publish my first one—the one about Chuck and me. (If you've read this far you've read several chapters from that manuscript. I thank the author for granting me permission to use them.) Or I may write another book altogether. Only time will tell.

I might invest in acrylic paints and canvases. Every decade I have made a painting or two. It started in Florence. I've often thought of doing small paintings of Chuck Berry's better songs. I can already see Nadine's shoe being lifted into a Yellow Cab, and Johnny's mother waving. Or maybe I'll find completely new and original subjects.

Perhaps I'll spend more time playing music. My latest group, a "collective," is growing larger and stronger by the week, but I'm still not good at belonging to any group. We'll see what happens. I hope I can manage to hang in there. But surprise: a really good autistic singer songwriter just sent me wonderful feedback on some songs of my own that I shared with him. Someday I will find the time to record good versions of my "greatest hits." I might even play all the instruments.

And this fall I will go to Italy. My trip will be more abbreviated than I would like, but it will be long and spectacular anyway. I have not been on an airplane since well before the start of Covid. I haven't missed airplanes, but I have missed the places they can take me.

For decades I have dreamed of living abroad again long enough to become roughly fluent in the native language, but life, and then Covid, kept intervening. I like living abroad. I like being a stranger in a strange land. That's who and what I usually am, anyway. I love the sensation of being in a place where everything I see is new and unfamiliar to me. It's different now, in the age of globalization, when there's good pizza in Seattle and West Coast IPA in Arezzo, but it's still good. I especially love being in places where everyday life takes place in what can only be described as art, whether in the form of a magnificent gothic cathedral you pass or enter on a daily basis, or a wooden table piled artistically with cigarets, matches, nail polish, and canned mackerel. And I enjoy struggling to communicate in languages that aren't mine (also what I do everyday) and I would like to get better at it. I speak a simple, African schoolboy version of French, with a limited vocabulary, rolling R's, and without slang. I would like to learn more about the way the French speak it in France. I speak a bit of Italian and would like to make my Italian serviceable enough to talk about life, work, climate change, and politics—the elements of my own sort of small talk. I once learned enough Spanish to stumble by in Mexico City, Madrid, Toledo, and Barcelona. I would like to relearn that bit, and improve on it, if I can. I'd like to speak well enough to speak up with the tens of thousands of Spanish speaking people who work in my town and in my neighborhood.

But for now, it's Italy. Rebecca's commitment to her theater company makes it impossible for her to join me for most of my trip, so I've opted for an abbreviated version of the "year" abroad, with more weeks, months or years to come in the future, should the universe be willing. I will study Italian in Rome and Florence and then hit the road in Northern Italy until Rebecca can join me for a few weeks. Perhaps I will be able to show her what I've learned.

I am ready and raring to go. Wish me luck, and that I find people in Italy willing to talk to an awkward, unsmiling, autistic American guy with bad grammar and a small vocabulary. I think I might.

But in the not-unlikely event that I don't make a slew of new friends in Italy, I will go walking. I will walk through sections of Rome I have never visited, including the surrounding hills, and parks, and the less touristy neighborhoods. I will walk through my own memories on the streets of Florence, and by the Arno. I will walk down narrow curving streets into sunlit piazzas in Bologna, Verona, Bergamo, Milano, Parma, and Arezzo. I'll drive through Toscana with Gianni, watching uneasily as his gesturing hands leave the steering wheel. I'll hole up with Covid in Bologna, cared for by

Lucia, but tortured by knowing that Italy is right outside my door. When I finally test negative I will get a sandwich made with a *rosetta* bread roll and an inch or more of *mortadella*. I will be drenched by rain in Verona, but saved by the kindness of a bar manager who will give me a lost umbrella. I will climb to the *Città Alta* in Bergamo, and in Milano I will have Michelangelo's Rondanini Pietà to myself for as long as I can stand it. I'll watch people squeeze in the door of a little Milanese hamburger place, KD House, as Carmelo and his band rock the joint, and the bartender revs up the crowd with a cardboard applause sign. I'll have a beautiful flat in Parma with marble floors and a bed to die in. I'll eat a half inch pile of *finocchiona* inside a slab of *focaccia* on a street corner in Arezzo, with a glass of good red wine. I will visit 100 churches and actually pray. I'll light candles for Birdy. I will sample Italian IPAs in Rome and Florence. I'll try a sour beer in Arezzo. I'll watch the sunrise over Tuscan farm land and hilltop castles from the window of a fast red train. I'll see fog enveloping abandoned farm houses near Montepulciano. I'll meet Rebecca in Trastevere. Together we'll walk on ancient cobblestones, past ancient monuments, along ancient brown rivers, across Roman bridges. We'll be happy in Testaccio and sample Roman dishes like *cacio e pepe* and *polpettone*. Together we'll visit Rome, Orvieto, Florence, and Siena.

And until she arrives, I'll walk, and talk to myself, as I always do, but now mostly in cracked Italian, (an expression I steal from the poetry of Richard Hugo,) creating new scripts for everything from the purchase of a bottle of interesting wine to gaining purchase on a whole new life, with new and different horizons, with no exploding trucks anywhere but in memory. But perhaps one night, with Jupiter and a half moon vying for my attention above some crenelated tower or ancient dome, I will hear, ever-so-faintly from a juke box across the piazza, what is, was, and always shall be—the familiar double notes and bending strings of a Gibson guitar over a rippling piano, delivering me to and from the days of old yet again, and I'll smile inside, a complete person, a stranger in a strange and beautiful world, happy, free, and ready for more.

1. Morton Reff, The Chuck Berry International Directory, Volume 2, (York, Music Mentor Publishing, 2008) 566.

2. Id.

3. Asperger/Autism Network staff, 'Asperger Profiles: The Big Picture – Strengths', AANE Asperger/Autism Network, https://www.aane.org/asperger-profile-strengths, (Accessed 2022 and 2023).

4. American Psychiatric Association's Diagnostic and Statistical Manual, Fifth Edition, or DSM-5,

5. Chuck Berry, Chuck Berry The Autobiography, (New York, Harmony Books, 1987) 138.

6. Philip Wylie, Wenn B. Lawson, and Luke Beardon, The Nine Degrees of Autism: A Developmental Model for the Allignment and Reconciliation of Hidden Neurological Conditions (London/New York, Routledge Taylor & Francis Group, 2016) 74.

7. The Nine Degrees of Autism, p. 72.

8. John Elder Robinson, look me in the eye: my life with asperger's (New York, Broadway Books, 2007-2008) 167.

9. J. Patrick Wright, On a Clear Day You Can See General Motors, (Grosse Pointe, Wright Enterprises, 1979) 128.

10. Herman Melville, Moby-Dick

11. Wright, On a Clear Day, at p. 117.

Acknowledgments

I first, of course, thank Rebecca, Jade, Gemma, Rafferty, and Leila, for putting up with me both in life and through this new journey. They have heard more about Chuck than they ever wanted to, counted trucks, watched for nailed concrete barriers, and helped me recognize autistic traits they had observed for years. I love you all, and thank you for the love you give me. Same to my brothers and sisters, each of whom taught me about life, music, and so much more. Special thanks to Stevo for Chuck, and to my parents Reba and Steve for life, love, and acceptance. Paul Whelan, thanks for knowing me, and helping me, even though you probably didn't know I was autistic. Big thanks also to early readers Rebecca, Ann, Paul, Dorothy, Alice, Marcia, Fred, Larry, Laura, Clarsa, Rivka, Veronica, and Beth, whose reactions helped me shape a better book and, hopefully, tell a better story. Special thanks to Jenna Anderson O'Neil and Kirk Hostetter for their work on the cover. Bryan Tomosovich, thank you for your editorial wisdom. Huge thanks to my two therapists, and especially the exact right one, who gave me new understanding of my own life. And finally, thank you to the hundreds of autistic and neurodivergent people on the internet whose comments and stories helped me to understand my own life so much more fully.

Oh, and Chuck—thank you, too, for everything.

Milton Keynes UK
Ingram Content Group UK Ltd.
UKHW020826110823
426718UK00015B/607

9 798218 156985